D0073258

Religious Belief and the Will

The Problems of Philosophy:
Their Past and Present

General Editor: Ted Honderich
Professor of Philosophy
University College
London

Each book in this series is to bring into clear view and to
deal with a great, persistent or significant problem of
philosophy. The first part of each book presents the
history of the problem. The second part, of an analytical
kind, develops and defends the author's preferred
solution.

Religious Belief and the Will

Louis P. Pojman

Routledge & Kegan Paul
London and New York

In Memory of
Everett Quinton Pojman
(1944–1984)

First published in 1986
by Routledge & Kegan Paul plc

11 New Fetter Lane, London EC4P 4EE

Published in the USA by
Routledge & Kegan Paul Inc.
in association with Methuen Inc.
29 West 35th Street, New York, NY 10001

Set in Times
by Inforum Ltd, 1 Guildhall Walk, Portsmouth
and printed in Great Britain
by Billing & Sons Ltd, Worcester

Library of Congress Cataloging in Publication Data

Pojman, Louis P.
Religious belief and the will.
Bibliography: p.
Includes Index.
1. Belief and doubt–History. 2. Faith–History
of doctrines. 3. Will–History. I. Title
BD215.P65 1986 200'.1 85-18457

British Library CIP data also available

ISBN 0–7102–0399–3

Contents

Contents

Introduction

Can we ever obtain beliefs by direct acts of the will? If it will help us to be happier persons, should we get ourselves to believe propositions which the evidence alone does not warrant? What is so important about believing propositions in the first place? Why have religious creeds made propositional belief a necessary condition for salvation? Is this a reasonable requirement? Might it not be the case that other propositional attitudes are equally adequate for religious commitment? Can one be rational and still use the will to believe what the evidence alone does not warrant? How is faith, which is usually recognized as having a volitional element, related to belief, which is propositional? Are faith and belief generically related or are they distinct attitudes? These are the sort of questions that I shall examine in this book. I am concerned with a constellation of problems related to believing and willing, and although my analysis is of general interest to epistemology and ethics, my main concern is that of religious faith and belief.

Let me illustrate the central problem with the use of an analogy. Imagine three different scenes.

(1) You are sitting on a fence and notice some luscious apples several feet to your right and are inclined to reach for them, but, as you are deliberating whether to get off the fence, you notice some even more delicious looking pears a little distance on your left side. You decide to fetch some of the pears and so get off the fence.

(2) You are on the same fence and someone comes and suddenly pulls you off the fence.

(3) You are on the fence and your lover pulls you down from the fence and into her arms.

Suppose we compare the act of entertaining a proposition to sitting on a fence, contemplating its possibility, evaluating evidence and argument in its favor, but not yet believing. Now which of these three situations is more like believing? Is believing a sort of seeing and doing? seeing the evidence in favor of the proposition and voluntarily coming off the fence? Or is it more like being pulled off the fence by the way the evidence strikes you – either gladly or reluctantly? A volitionalist is one who takes the first model as representative of the crucial instances of belief formation. Believing a proposition is sometimes voluntary, and, he usually adds, the really important beliefs in life, which are not well supported by reason, are acquired by acts of the will. The nonvolitionalist, on the other hand, takes (2) and (3) as analogous to the event of obtaining a belief. Believing is never an action, something that is decided directly by the will or a fiat of the will. It is not something we do but something that happens to us, though sometimes we experience emotional concurrence with the belief state.

In this work I shall use the term 'volit' to signify 'directly obtaining a belief by willing to have it', believing by the fiat of the will. Actually, there are five different positions on the direct relation of the will to belief acquisition, each of which has adherents in the history of philosophy and theology. Examples are given in parentheses.

(1) It is logically impossible to volit (Bernard Williams and Richard Swinburne).

(2) It is psychologically impossible (though not logically impossible) to volit (Spinoza and Hume).

(3) It is logically and psychologically possible to volit sometimes (Augustine, Aquinas, W.K. Clifford, William James and Roderick Chisholm).

(4) It is logically and psychologically possible to volit over every proper candidate for belief (Descartes, Kierkegaard and Tolstoy).

(5) It is logically impossible for us to believe without voliting (Descartes and Kierkegaard).

While virtually everyone admits the will's indirect influence on belief formation, philosophers such as Pascal, James and Jack Meiland prescribe *indirect volitionalism*, viz., getting oneself into a context where propositions not supported by impartial judgment will become beliefs. Philosophers like Locke, Hume and Clifford oppose such a move.

The history of Western thought is replete with instances where the will's relation to belief is salient. The creeds make it a necessary condition for salvation. During the Inquisition heretics were ordered to renounce their unorthodox beliefs, implying thereby that they had control over their beliefs. On the other side, John Locke in his plea for tolerance of beliefs uses the thesis that one cannot help the beliefs one has to support the cause of pluralism. Since people cannot help the beliefs they have, it is imperative that we withold censure or punishment from belief-states. Our language sparkles with volitional idioms, such as 'I have decided to believe you', 'Please, try to believe me', and 'I can't believe some of the things that I should.'

I have chosen to approach the subject of faith and reason from the view-point of volitional activity (i.e., that related to the will), because I believe that the will is central to religious commitment, and because by understanding the relationship between the attitude of belief and the activity of willing, one may be able to get fresh insight into a classical problem. As far as I know, this is the first full-length treatise on religious belief that approaches it from the vantage point of volitional activity. It seems to me that many works on religion and theology misconstrue that relationship. In this work I attempt to rethink that relationship.

In the first part of this book I trace a constellation of problems connected with belief, faith and the will through the history of Western thought, beginning with an analysis of the concept of belief in the New Testament and in Plato's philosophy. Next, I treat the first sustained philosophical analysis of faith in the work of St. Augustine, an analysis which has been neglected in the history of philosophy and sets the stage for the thinking of St. Thomas Aquinas on the subject. A brief comparison is made between St. Thomas and the reformers, Luther and Calvin. I examine Pascal's Wager as a prime example of indirect prescriptive volitionalism, and then move on to Descartes, the first self-conscious radical *volitionalist* (one who thinks that we can obtain beliefs by a fiat of the will), offering Spinoza's criticism as the first response to Descartes's position. I treat the empiricists, Locke and Hume, who were both concerned with normative relations between the will and belief, and go on to Kant and Kierkegaard, both of whom saw a place of volitional activities in belief acquisition. After analyzing three Roman Catholic philosophers who espouse a strong volitional position, I turn to the contemporary debate, dealing with the British and American debates on the nature of belief, the ethics of belief, and the relation between the will and belief acquisition, focusing especially on the work of H.H. Price, Roderick Chisholm, and Bernard Williams. I end the expository part of this work with an analysis of the contemporary debate over faith and reason, examining Wittgensteinian fideism, the rationalism of Richard Swinburne and Alvin Plantinga's reformed religious epistemology.

Because of space constraints I have had to be highly selective in this part of the work. Rather than try to cover every major philosopher on the subject, I have chosen to concentrate on thirty or so, giving a fuller analysis to them than would have been possible had I spread the expository net as wide as the subject deserves. I have omitted Aristotle, Leibniz, and Berkeley because the problems studied here are not given prominence in their work. I have had to omit many important modern philosophers for the same reason, though in some cases I have had to omit philosophers who have something important to say on the issue, but who, I judged to be of lesser importance (or duplicative) than the ones chosen. Doubtless, my choice is subject to honest disagreement.

In the second part of this work I take up the ideas set forth in the first part and offer my own analysis, pointing to a solution of some of the major questions. My aim is to show the right and wrong use of the will in relation to belief and faith. First, in Chapter XIII, I analyze the concept of belief and set it in relation to the will. I spend a great deal of time working out as precisely as I can an answer to such questions as: Can one acquire beliefs directly upon willing to have them? What would have to be the case for us to be sure that we acquired a belief by fiat of the will? And do we have direct, partial control over some belief acquisitions? I offer two arguments against various types of volitionalism, but admit that certain other types may have some merit.

In Chapter XIV, I concentrate on the matter of the ethics of belief. To what extent are we responsible for the beliefs we obtain? Are there times when we *ought* to deceive ourselves and obtain beliefs that the evidence alone does not warrant? Is believing a moral activity or only a prudential one, as H.H. Price and others have contended? I sketch out various possibilities for an ethic of belief.

In Chapter XV 'Rationality and Religious Belief', I turn my attention to the matter of rational religious belief, deeming this an aspect of the ethics of belief which I have outlined in the previous chapter. I suggest that our notion of rationality needs to be expanded to include non-rule governed, intuitive judgments, much in the spirit of John Henry Newman. With a 'soft-rationalist' view of evidence, I proceed to set forth a program of what a rationalist justification of religious belief might look like. I address some major objections against such a perspective and offer my views as the basis for future exploration.

In Chapter XVI 'Faith, Doubt and Hope', I work out an alternative approach to religious faith, wherein belief is seen as overvalued. One may have faith without belief, and one may live in hope of God instead of in belief that he exists. Since traditional Christianity makes propositional belief a necessary condition for salvation, doubters must be regarded deficient, condemned, or lacking the one thing essential. I examine the assumptions on which such a theory rests, asking what is so important about believing, anyway? I suggest that believing may have been valued out of all proportion to its worth and that doubt may have impressive virtues of its own which should attract our admiration – especially for the religious person. I suggest that there are other propositional attitudes just as valid for religious commitment as belief and argue that a morally good Supreme Being must respect those having such attitudes as much as if they actually believed in his existence. I offer the concept of hope as a candidate for such an alternative to believing and develop a concept of profound hope which is eminently suitable for modern, rationally circumspect religious people. If the proofs for God's existence fail to convince, and if the ethics of belief proscribe pragmatic but nonvolitional belief acquisitions, then many religious people will have to learn to be content with hoping in God. An experimental faith may be less robust than absolute conviction or setting God in the foundations of one's noetic structure, but it may have attractions of its own. The hoper in God may have to alter the liturgy and form of worship, but he or she may bring new insights to the religious experience – or rather the hope may cause us to rediscover what the mystics have known all along, that in the dark night of the soul, in the absence of God, one waits on God, worships, and is faithful to one's vision.

In the first part of the work I have had to exercise great care in the selection of writers to analyze. Much of my research had to be distilled into a few pages, and some worthy authors had to be left out altogether. I have had to use only a few technical terms in this work. These are: 'doxastic', which comes from the Greek 'doxa', meaning 'appearance or belief' or 'having to do with beliefs'; 'volitional', meaning 'having to do with the will' and 'volit', which I use to mean 'to obtain a belief (directly or indirectly) upon willing to have it'; and 'noetic structure', which means 'the set of one's beliefs and certain relations existing between them'. Other than these few terms, the layman should be able to work through this book with minimal difficulty, for my intention is to have written a work that both sheds new light on an important philosophical problem, so that scholars might profit from it, and yet may be useful to the novice and student in coming to grips with the philosophical dimension inherent in religious and ideological beliefs and commitments. While the work is primarily one in the area of religious epistemology, it should have bearing on beliefs in general and other ideological commitments more specifically.

This work arose from two experiences in my life. As a child, I found myself doubting religious statements and being told that there was something disloyal or apostate about such attitudes. I often found it impossible to make leaps of faith into orthodoxy, as I was supposed to. As I grew up, went to college and theological seminary, and became a Protestant minister, the doubts increased amidst deep religious feelings. After a tour of guilt trips over doxastic states, I gradually learned what Luther meant when he advocated that we 'sin bravely' and began to enjoy my doubt. So much did I enjoy the questions more than the answers that I decided to become a philosopher. As a philosopher I became engaged with the problem of how much control we have over our beliefs and doubts.

The second experience that led to working out these ideas was studying the work of Soren Kierkegaard, the Danish Christian existentialist. Kierkegaard, as the reader will see, was a consummate volitionalist, apparently believing that every belief was a product of the will in some way. It was trying to come to grips with his thought in graduate school that convinced me that there was something wrong with, at least, some types of volitionalism. My first foray on this subject was a section in my Oxford D. Phil. dissertation, which was recently published as *The Logic of Subjectivity* (University of Alabama Press, 1984).

This book was started while I was at the University of Notre Dame in 1978 and 1979, where I benefited from the acute criticisms of members of the Philosophy Department, especially Gary Gutting and Neil Delaney. Earlier drafts of two sections of this work were delivered as papers at the American Philosophical Association, where Wayne Davis and Stephen Barker offered cogent criticisms. Robert Audi, Alvin Plantinga and John Donnelly have been very helpful in reading over different parts of this work. My graduate seminars at the University of Texas at Dallas from 1979 to 1984 provided a pleasant context for developing many of the ideas contained in this work. My students, Karen Schmersahl and Tim Atkins, and Karen Namorato were very helpful in going over the final draft of this work.

My wife, Trudy, and children, Ruth and Paul, were graciously and humorously supportive during the extended periods of my research. Finally, this work is dedicated to my close friend and brother, Everett, who died while this work was being written.

Acknowledgements

The following published articles have been used in this work with the permission of the publisher: 'Believing and Willing' in the *Canadian Journal of Philosophy* (March, 1985), 'Faith without Belief' in *Faith and Philosophy* (April, 1986), and 'Rationality and Religious Belief' in *Religious Studies* vol. 15 (1979).

PART ONE

Belief and Will in the History of Western Thought

CHAPTER I

Belief and Faith in the Bible and the Early Christian Movement

'Faith' and 'belief' are, to a large extent, religious words and have their origin within the context of that culture which formed the basis of Judaism and Christianity. It is, therefore, appropriate, at the onset of our study, that we take a brief look at how the words which we translate as 'faith'/'belief' are used in the original documents of the Judeo-Christian tradition. In this chapter we shall highlight the major uses of these concepts in the Bible and in the early Church fathers, giving special attention to the relation between the will and belief/faith.

In the Old Testament the word that comes closest to our concept of belief is *he'min* which may be roughly defined as 'saying Amen to something with all the consequences for the subject and the object'.[1] Arthur Weiser, in his close study, tells us that the Hebrew root *'mn* is a name for a family of concepts or a name for a set which includes acknowledgement of God, trust in him, hope in him, fearing him, as well as obedience to him. 'The structure of the Jewish concept of faith . . . exhibits the leading motifs of the Old Testament throughout; faith is trusting, just as much as believing; it is loyalty and obedience just as much as hoping and expecting. Because these motifs have an underlying connection, it often cannot be discerned which of them is predominant.'[2] While it is the religious use that predominates in the Old Testament, there are profane uses of *he'min*, e.g., Jacob's disbelief in testimony (Gen. 45:26) and Moses' statement that his people will not believe him, but only a sign (Ex. 4:1,8), and other straightforward references to the attitude of trusting (Micah 7:5 and Job 15:15). However the primary meaning has to do with its special role in the relationship to God (Ex. 14:31; Num. 14:11; Deut. 1:32; Ps. 106:24). *he'min* means 'to take God as God with complete seriousness'.[3] It is to trust him

3

utterly and obey him unquestioningly. In a sense, the relationship of trusting obedience to God (*Yahweh*) pervades Israel's life-blood, identifying her and distinguishing her from her neighbors.

There is the correlative notion that in such a cleaving or holding fast to what is wholly reliable, the agent himself becomes reliable, steadfast. Just as tenacious loyalty and steadfastness are attributed to the object of faith, so in holding steadfastly and loyally to that object, the subject himself becomes the mirror image of that object – at least in relation to the virtues of loyalty and steadfastness (Deut. 28:64–7; Ps. 1; Is. 26:3f). In the New Testament the Greek word *pistis* is found to mean 'to rely on some object' (John 4:50; Acts 27:25), to trust or to give credence to (Mark 13:25; John 4:21), and always has a dative or accusative construction. Rudolf Bultmann shows that the basic meaning of the word is 'trusting obedience', as was the case with *he'min* in the Old Testament.[4] There is a negative use of *pistis, apistia* ('faithlessness', Rom. 3:3; Heb. 3:12,19), which signifies disobedience. In Hebrews 11, the classic chapter on faith in the New Testament, *pistis* refers to the obedience (or faithfulness) of the heroes of Israel, but it also refers to propositional belief in God's existence (Heb. 11:6). The term is used in a propositional sense in Rom. 10:9, John 20:31; I Cor. 15:11; and I Thes 4:4.

Bultmann makes a case that there is a specifically Christian sense of *pistis* which is indicated in the formula *pistis eis*. 'Here *pistis* is understood as the acceptance of the Christian *kerygma* [the early creed of the Church] and consequently of the saving faith which recognizes and appropriates God's work of salvation brought about by Christ.'[5]

Faith is not the final eschatological state as *gnosis* (knowledge) is with the Gnostic sects. It is not an escape from the temporary nature of historical existence, but it embodies the eschatological existence of this life on earth. It stands besides hope as mutually sustaining concepts and develops into knowledge, impressing the truth upon the believer's heart in a way that excludes all doubt. 'Only when human existence comes to an end as an earthly human one will the faith which knows or the knowledge which believes be replaced by sight which will then no longer be directed to the glory of the Son veiled in flesh, but will behold this glory directly.'[6]

There is a volitional aspect attached to faith in the Gospels, where faith is seen as a virtue, something that is to be cultivated and which empowers people to do great deeds. Jesus reprimands his disciples because of their unbelief and says, 'If you have faith as a grain of mustard seed, ye shall say unto this mountain, Remove hence to yonder place; and it shall remove; and nothing shall be impossible to you' (Matt. 17:20f) and 'If thou canst believe, all things are possible to him that believeth' (Mark 9:23; cf. Matt. 14:31; 21:21).

Jesus holds his disciples responsible for their beliefs, reprimands them for doubting, and speaks of the ability to believe as if it were optional. It is unclear whether he is saying, 'You all have good evidence for the things that I am asking you to believe' (as he does on the Emmaus Road in Luke 24 or to John the Baptist's disciples in Luke 7:20f) or whether he is saying, 'You can get yourself to believe by willing to do so.'

Paul in Romans makes the strong equation of doubt with sin: 'And he that doubteth is damned if he eat, because he eateth not of faith; for whatsoever is not of faith is sin' (Rom. 14:23): a text which Kierkegaard later takes to show that belief must be within our direct control. While *pistis* usually has a connative emphasis in the New Testament, Paul sometimes uses the term propositionally as in Rom. 10:9,10: 'That if thou shalt confess with thy mouth the Lord Jesus and shalt believe in thine heart that God hath raised him from the dead, thou shalt be saved. For with the heart man believeth unto righteousness and with the mouth confession is made unto salvation.'

This verse and many others (e.g. John 3:16; Acts 16:31; Gal. 3:6) shows the close link between believing and salvation in the New Testament. Those who believe are justified and shall be saved. Although faith is not a sufficient condition for salvation (for even the devils believe but do not trust and obey, James 1:22), it is a necessary condition, for without it, one cannot please God (Heb. 11:6).

Just as there is a tension between grace and free will in the New Testament, so there seems to be a tension between the volitional and event-like aspects of belief. On the one hand, God must enable us to believe. Faith is a gift. 'By grace are you saved by faith; and that not of yourselves: it is a gift of God' (Eph. 2:8). On the other hand, we can affect our salvation. 'Work out your own salvation with fear and trembling, for it is God who works in you' (Phil. 2:12). Whosoever will may come.

To summarize: in the New Testament faith involves trustful

obedience to God, shown in actions, such as confessing Christ before magistrates and in public. Faith, in another sense, involves propositional belief regarding God's existence, the person of Christ, and his resurrection. Although it is not a sufficient condition for salvation, it is necessary for salvation, for without faith it is impossible to please God. Faith is a general virtue and empowers one to do great deeds. It is both a virtue and a gift from God.

Recently Wilfred Cantwell Smith in his book *Belief and History* has challenged the thesis that the New Testament contains our notion of propositional belief.[7] Our concept, which sees belief as attached to propositions, which, in turn, are either true or false, is largely a product of the Enlightenment, though close to what the Ancients and Medievalists called 'opinion', an attitude of uncertainty and lacking all the affective traits of loyalty, commitment, and inner surety. Smith argues that modern philosophy of religion is guilty of the myopia of failing to understand other cultures, wherein words that seem the same as ours really have nuances of their own. 'Just as the Hebrew world-view cannot stomach idolatry, so our science system is anti-mystical, and our logical systems anti-metaphor. More basic: all our systems, religious and secular, are anti-alternative systems. Modern logic has perpetrated the unsubtlety that every meaningful statement is either true or false' (p. 27).

In the New Testament *pistis* and its near relatives are used some 603 times. The King James Version of the New Testament uses the term 'faith' for this word 233 times and uses 'belief' only once. The verb 'believe' (translating the Greek *pisteuo*) is used 321 times; 43% of the time with no object; 41% of the time with a personal object; 12% of the time with a thing as an object and only 12% of the time with a propositional object. The propositional aspect of faith in the New Testament, Smith argues, is minimal, the emphasis always lying in the confessional, experiential aspect of the term.

Smith suggests that we divide up belief-related statements into three types:

1 Recognition statements: S recognizes that A is B.
2 Opinion statements: S is of the opinion that A is B.
3 Imagination statements: S imagines that A is B.

In the first case, the wording suggests that S is right; in the last that he is wrong and in 2. no stand is taken. In the Bible 'believe'

6

typically is used as 1., as a recognition of the truth, not as 2., which is closer to our notion.

The verb 'believe' in modern English usually means to hold an opinion, whether it be right or wrong, but, avers Smith, 'no serious theological thinker has ever held, and the Bible nowhere suggests, that it is important to hold the opinion that God exists, whether that opinion be right or wrong. Belief, in the modern meaning of the word, has no place in the history of Christian thought. *The concept is not in the Bible*' (p. 78). Here Smith quotes W.H.P. Hatch, 'Nowhere in the discourses of Jesus does the substantive [*pistis*] denote conviction or belief . . . It is trust rather than belief with which we are concerned in the life and teaching of Jesus', as supporting his general thesis that faith in the New Testament is not propositional. For Jesus and St. Paul it is not an intellectual assent (which our concept implies) but a vital, personal engagement (p. 72).

In order to make his point Smith takes the two passages that are most often cited as propositional: James 2:19 ('Thou believest that there is one God; thou does well: the devils also believe, and tremble.') and Heb. 11:6 ('Without faith it is impossible to please him: for he that cometh to God must believe that he is, and that he is a rewarder of them that diligently seek him.') and analyzes them, pointing out that even in these passages the existential element of commitment and obedience emerge as central. In the passage about the devils' believing, Smith points out that 'believe' here is really the state of 'recognition', closer to knowledge, and that what they lack is trust and commitment to replace their defiance and 'trembling'. Again, in Hebrews 11, the context makes clear that the writer supposes that the individual has experienced God and that the 'believe' here is the believe of recognition, which involves trust and commitment.

Faith, insofar as its intellectual component is concerned, is recognition, insight, the capacity to discern . . . commitment. There is involved the self-engagement of giving oneself to what one sees as worthwhile; the active adhesion to the truth that one has perceived. It is a sub-hypothesis of mine that if one comes to understand what [the New Testament writers] meant when they talked this way, how they felt, what they saw, what they purposed, how they ordered their personalities, then one will begin to understand what faith is, and begin also then to realize that belief has essentially relatively little to do with it – or anyway, less to do with it than we used to think: not only those persons' believing, but one's own not believing (pp. 80, 86).

Smith's argument, though a little strained, is plausible. While, it is facile to equate the modern notion of 'belief' with the ancient 'opinion', there are significant overlappings and while a propositional core is presupposed in the biblical notion of belief, it is just that, *presupposed* and not the center of focus. The biblical view of faith is a sort of 'knowing', a recognition, wherein the believer commits himself or herself to the one encountered in deep personal experience. The relationship involves both the intellect in giving assent and the will in holding fast to the object of faith. The exact nature of the intellect and the will's roles are left for posterity to interpret in a myriad of ways.

Faith and Will in the Early Church Fathers

In the early Church there was a debate as to the relative merits of faith and knowledge, some of the fathers, such as Tertullian and Irenaeus, arguing that there was only one acceptable relation to the Christian religion, faith, and others, such as Justin Martyr, Clement of Alexandria and Origen, arguing that there were two acceptable relations: faith and a superior knowledge. Tertullian poured contempt on those timid believers who sought solace in the works of philosophy or tried to use philosophy to reach Christian conclusions. Drawing on Paul's warning to the Colossians ('Beware lest any man spoil you through philosophy and vain deceit'), he excoriates the thought of a rapproachment between Christianity and the wise pagans.

What indeed has Athens to do with Jerusalem? What concord is there between the Academy and the Church? . . . Our instruction comes from the 'Porch of Solomon' who has himself taught that the Lord should be sought in simplicity of heart. Away with all attempts to produce a mottled Christianity of Stoic, Platonic and dialectical compositions (*The Prescription Against Heretics* (henceforth 'PAH'), 8, 10).

8

Christianity is not a philosophy but something altogether different. 'So then, where is there a likeness between the Christian and the philosopher? . . . between the disciple of Greece and of heaven?' (*Apology* 46). 'We want no curious disputation after possessing Christ Jesus, no inquisition after enjoying the Gospel. When we believe, we desire nothing beyond it to believe.' (PAH 7). The disassociation from philosophy and all its reasoning couldn't be more radical. 'The Son of God was crucified; I am unashamed of it because men must needs be ashamed of it. And the Son of God died; it is by all means to be believed, because it is absurd. And he was buried and rose again; the fact is certain because it is impossible.'

In direct contrast to Tertullian's version of Christianity is Origen's system in which Christianity becomes a superior philosophy, drawing upon and surpassing the Stoics and Neo-platonists. Only because the multitude lacks the time and effort to study philosophy is faith an acceptable condition for eternal salvation. The true disciple is a philosopher who reasons his way to righteousness.

Clement of Alexandria and Origen both speak of a double conversion, one by faith for the masses and one of knowledge (*gnosis*) for the elite.[8] These Alexandrian Christians seem more concerned with speculation and cosmology than salvation. They provide a sharp contrast with the anti-rationalists in the Church.

A strong volitionalist position clearly appears for the first time in Clement of Alexandria, Origen's teacher, who defines faith as a strong assumption or a 'vehement assumption' and as such is under our direct control. Our assenting to it or not depends upon our will. Wolfson thinks that this notion was taken from the Stoics, who also defined assent as a free act, meaning by it that we were not coerced from without, though still determined by inner laws (since they were determinists).[9] Clement who like all the early Christians believed in free will thought that the concept applied not only to our actions but to our theoretical judgments.

For the early Church fathers it was important to have right beliefs. Origen refuses to pray with heretics, preferring to pray alone until he found himself condemned as one. The significance of right belief in the early Church probably had something to do with self-identity. This was a struggling movement, beset on every hand by controversy, persecution, and the need to present a clear witness to the world. Actions, rituals, and customs depend on a significant amount of agreement. Note that the change of the date of Easter caused enormous upheaval in the Church and those who failed to go along with the ruling faction were condemned as heretics.[10] What may seem like small differences to disinterested parties were viewed as making all the difference in the world. One's salvation was attached to recognizing the truth. From our perspective it looks as though the early Christians were overly zealous in condemning those with whom they disagreed and anathematizing the opposition. Right belief was seen as essential to salvation. Wilfred Cantwell Smith, in his argument that the early Christians did not have our notion of belief, points out that the Apostles Creed and the Nicene Creed both omit any propositional statements, but even if one failed to see the propositional element in them, one could not fail to see it in other creeds. Right belief is a necessary condition for salvation, and the heterorthodox are anathematized.

> Whosoever desires to be saved must above all things hold the Catholic faith (*fidem*). Unless a man keeps it in its entirety inviolate, he will assuredly perish eternally . . . Now this is the Catholic faith, that we worship one God in Trinity and Trinity in unity without either confusing the persons or dividing the substance. . . . So he who desires to be saved should think thus of the Trinity.
> It is necessary, however, to eternal salvation that he should also faithfully believe in the Incarnation of our Lord Jesus Christ. Now the right faith (*fides recta*) is that we should believe and confess that our Lord Jesus Christ, the Son of God, is equally both God and man. . . . This is the Catholic faith. Unless a man believes it faithfully and steadfastly, he will not be able to be saved (*Athanasian Creed*).

Whatever plausibility Smith's thesis has with regard to the writers of the New Testament largely disappears when applied to the early Church. While the notion of belief here may not exactly coincide with ours, it does contain an explicit propositional element that cannot be swept aside.

The early Church fathers saw that agreement in belief was needed in the community to unite Christians against the intellectual and political enemies which surrounded the Church. They saw that common beliefs led to a common front. They worked hard to arrive at the best formulations, believing that a Providential hand was guiding them. It seemed obvious to them that those who had heard the Gospel had control over their belief states. Failure to believe in Christ as well as failure to believe correctly was tantamount to sin. We find something like this idea embedded in the writings of Clement of Alexandria, Irenaeus, Origen, Athanasius and Augustine.

Clement wrote, 'But faith, which the Greeks disparage, deeming it futile and barbarous, is a voluntary anticipation, the assent of piety . . . the subject of things hoped for, the evidence of things not seen . . . for hereby the elders obtained a good report. But without faith it is impossible to please God (Heb. 11)' (*Stromata* p. 349). It involves voluntary assent, for to obey someone is to believe that authority (p. 350).

Irenaeus gives a clear recognition to a volitional aspect in believing. Humans are not only free to do but also to believe as they will, so that we may properly command others to believe what is true as well as to do what is right. 'And not only in works but also in faith God has kept the will of man free and subject to man's control, saying "according to thy faith be it unto thee", thus showing that man's faith is his own because his will is his own' (*Against Heresy* 4:37,5). And Origen writes:

> If a man only believes that he must entrust himself to God and do everything in order to please him, he will be transformed. But even if it be exceedingly difficult to effect a change in some persons, the cause must be held to lie in their own will, which is reluctant to accept the belief that God over all things is a just judge of all the deeds done during life (*Contra Celsum* p. 491).

When Athanasius rails against Arius in his *Oration* and accuses him of blasphemy for distorting the tradition, it is as if he is accusing Arius of willfully deceiving himself or blaspheming God. Volitional motifs arise from belief-oriented epistemologies. It makes little sense in knowledge oriented salvation-systems to speak of obtaining knowledge by willing to know that such and such is the case. The statement 'I willed to know that there is a God' makes little sense – unless interpreted as wanting to have the sort of evidence that would count as knowledge. The early Church had a Platonic notion of knowledge as distinct from belief, involving 'sight', a vision of the truth. The experience of deep knowing was procured for the Christian Neo-platonists through a combination of reason, dialectics and perhaps recollection, and culminated in a vision, a 'seeing',

11

such as is described in Plato's allegory of the cave. This is illustrated in Origen when he speaks of two conversions, one for the masses by faith and one for the knowers by knowledge.

Before we continue with out look at the notion of belief/faith in Augustine and Aquinas we must turn to Plato to see how he treats the concept.

CHAPTER II

Plato on Knowledge and Belief

The classic characterization of the fundamental epistemological categories is found in the work of Plato (427–347 B.C.). In his work we find the first sustained discussion of 'knowledge', 'belief', 'statement', and a number of related concepts. While there are serious problems in harmonizing various accounts as they appear in different books, some features stand out as dominant and as having been especially important in forming and informing the major schools of Western Philosophy. In this study we do not have to decide the difficult question of what positions Plato himself really espoused in order to characterize the main theories set forth in his works. We may take the positions as interesting in their own right and important for the casual role they play in the history of epistemology. We shall examine two strands of the Platonic tradition. The first, which may be called the Idealist Theory of Knowledge, is found in such works as the *Meno*, *Phaedo*, *Phaedrus*, and especially, the *Republic*, and centers around the idea that knowledge is the apprehension of the forms. The second strand of theory, which may be called the True Belief Theory of Knowledge, is found in the *Theaetetus*, *Timaeus*, and *Sophist*, and centers around the ideas that knowledge is a type of true belief and that belief is a conclusion of a process of internal, intrapersonal dialogue. Both ideas have been of the utmost significance in epistemology and will appear throughout this work as influencing succeeding views.

The Idealist Theory of Knowledge. In the *Meno* Plato distinguishes the philosopher from the sophist by showing that the former leads people through dialectics (a series of questions that progressively lead to precise analysis and definition) to knowledge, while the latter leads people through rhetoric only to believe (97a–98c). Right belief (*ortho doxa*, from which we get the term 'orthodoxy') is nothing to be despised, for it will guide us as well as genuine knowledge. A guide who has a true belief about the road to Larissa would take us there as successfully as one who knows the way. While, for practical purposes right belief is as valid as knowledge, it has one serious liability. This would not be a drawback if you could ensure that one always retained one's right belief, but we can't. Beliefs are like the fabled statues of Daedalus, which can walk off like runaway slaves and so need to be fastened down. The statues are of great value as works of art, but they are of little value if these are loose. 'This is an illustration of the nature of true opinions: while they abide with us they are beautiful and fruitful, but they run away out of the human soul, and do not remain long, and therefore they are not of much value until they are fastened by the tie of the cause' and are thus transformed into knowledge. 'And this is why knowledge is more honorable and excellent than true opinion, because fastened by a chain.'

The way back to knowledge is through a process of recollection. In this same dialogue, *Meno*, Socrates proves that an untaught slave has innate knowledge of mathematics. All that is necessary, it is argued, for one to know, is for a suitable guide, a teacher, to bring out the best in us, to question and guide us like a mid-wife inducing labor, until at last we give birth to knowledge. The teacher has no truths of his own to impart, but helps us to recover knowledge which we must have learned in a previous existence. There is no better explanation of why the untutored slave can do geometry or that we can recognize the universal in particulars (e.g., see that all these imperfect triangles imperfectly point to the reality of a perfect triangle from which they derive their triangularity).

Knowledge, then, is comprehension of universals, which are called by Plato 'forms' (*eidos*, ideas). Every significant word (noun, adjective, and verb) and thing partakes of and derives its identity from a form or forms. The forms are single, common to all objects and abstract terms, perfect as the particulars or exemplars are not, independent of any particulars yet their cause, having objective existence (they are the truly real, while particulars are only apparently so). While independent of the human mind, they are intelligible and can be known by the mind alone and not by sense experience. The forms are divine, eternal, simple, indissoluble, unchanging, self-subsisting reality, existing outside space and time. Salvation of the soul is found in recapturing a vision of the forms, especially the form of the Good, the highest form. In the *Phaedrus* (247c) Plato writes of salvation consisting in the growth of spiritual wings which takes place through mystic contemplation of the forms.

> But of the place beyond heaven no one of our poets has yet sung nor will ever sing in a manner worthy. It is as follows, for one must dare to speak the truth, especially when talking of the true: in that place truly existent reality dwells colorless, shapeless, and intangible. As the object of true knowledge it is perceived only by that capacity for wisdom which is the pilot of the soul. The thought of the gods, matured by pure knowledge and wisdom, and that of every soul concerned to receive what is akin to it, seeing Being at last, rejoices, is nurtured by the contemplation of the true and is happy until it is brought back by the revolving circle to the same place. While thus going round it beholds justice itself, moderation itself and knowledge – not the knowledge that comes to be or that exists in another thing of those we call real, but that which is truly knowledge in that which truly is. And feasting on the contemplation of the other things that likewise truly are, diving back into the inner heaven, the soul goes homeward (Grube tr.).

It is in the *Republic* (books V–VII) that Plato compares belief and knowledge. Whereas, in the *Meno* knowledge was just the filling out or fastening down of a belief, in the *Republic* the two concepts are seen as distinct, and that in two ways.[1] (1) They are two separate mental states and (2) they involve two separate classes of objects, the forms on the one hand, and the many particulars on the other, and these classes correspond to the two states of mind.

(1) Let us first turn to the distinction between belief-states and knowledge-states. In *Republic* 477c Plato defines various faculties of the mind (*dunameis*, powers or capacities). Each faculty or power is concerned with different sets of objects (e.g., the power of seeing with visual objects, the power of hearing with sounds). He argues that knowledge and belief must also be powers. Knowledge is a state of mind in which the person cannot be mistaken, for to say that someone knows something is to say that he cannot be wrong. Hence, knowledge always is of what is true and so it must be that knowledge is infallible. If you know something, you do not merely know it, but you must *know that* you know it. Furthermore, knowledge can only be gained through a dialectical process of recollection.

15

In believing, on the other hand, we may often be wrong. Beliefs can be produced by persuasion (so the Sophists can induce beliefs in us), and are shifting and unstable. They ebb and flow and they bring no self-evident sense of infallibility with them. Whereas knowledge partakes of being itself and ignorance of non-being, belief is somewhere in between, partaking of both being and non-being (478e). Belief is more obscure than knowledge, but more revealing than ignorance, a middle power.

(2) While it could be argued that throughout the *Republic*, as well as in the other dialogues, there is a sense in which true belief is only distinguished from knowledge by being less clear than it (e.g., the Guardians clearly perceive what the Auxiliaries only dimly sense), Plato wants to say that there is a fundamental or qualitative difference in the way each is related to its object, so that they really have different objects which they apprehend. In knowing, Plato is saying, I am directly acquainted with the object known, while in believing I am, at least, once removed from it. In knowing I am in direct contact with the form, while in believing I am related to a particular, which has its reality in the form, but which is not the really real. The lover of belief (the philodoxer) loves beautiful objects, but the lover of wisdom and knowledge (the philosopher) loves the Beautiful itself. As such, the person content with mere beliefs is as far removed from the light of reality that the philosopher enjoys as a dreamer is from a state of wakefulness.

> As for the man who believes in beautiful things, but does not believe in beauty itself nor is able to follow if one lead him to the understanding of it – do you think his life is real or a dream? Consider: is not to dream just this, whether a man be asleep or awake, to mistake the image for the reality? (476c, Grube tr.).

The Attempt to Define Knowledge in Terms of True Belief. In his later writings Plato offers a second account of belief and knowledge, which though incomplete, seems to indicate that he was not altogether satisfied with the account given in the *Republic*. Whether the main strands of the two accounts can somehow be reconciled is beyond the scope of this essay,[2] but the second account suggests the possibility of defining knowledge in terms of belief or, at least, shows that the mental state of belief is not to be disparaged, as seems the case in the *Republic*. While this second account is briefly described in the *Timaeus* and *Sophist*, it is in the *Theaetetus* that it receives its fullest treatment. Although Plato does not accept either of the two formulations defining knowledge in terms of true belief, the possibility of such a definition is never denied.

First, Socrates considers Theaetetus' suggestion that knowledge is simply true belief or true judgment (*doxa, to doxazein*, 187b–200c). Immediately, the question arises, how is false belief possible? For either we know something, or we do not know it, but in neither case we can not be mistaken. However, false belief, if it exists, is thinking what is not, and therefore thinking of nothing, not thinking at all. To explain how it is possible to have false beliefs Socrates offers an analogy that has influenced epistemology until this very day. He suggests that within each of us there is something like a wax block capable of receiving impressions from various objects. The constituency of the wax varies from person to person, in some being muddier, in some purer, in some harder, in others softer, and in some of just the right consistency. Whenever we wish to remember something, we hold this wax under the perceptions and 'imprint them on it as we might stamp the impression of a seal-ring. Whatever is so imprinted we remember and know so long as the image remains; whatever is rubbed out or has not succeeded in leaving an impression we have forgotten and do not know' (191d). Mistakes arise only when I know both objects, say Theodorus and Theaetetus, and so have the impressions made by past perception of both still remaining in the waxen block, but in seeing either one (or both) I attempt to fit the new impression of one into the old imprint of the other, like the man who tries to put his foot into the wrong shoe. It turns out that false belief is always a misinterpretation of the present sensation, while true belief is always the right interpretation of a present sensation.

Unfortunately, this cannot be the whole explanation of false belief, for there are other types of error besides that of misinterpretation of present sensation. We often do abstract thinking incorrectly (e.g., add 7 + 5 and erroneously get 11). The wax figure analogy does not account for this type of error. So Socrates resorts to another metaphor to account for these kinds of cases.

> Now consider whether knowledge is a thing you can possess in that way without having it about you, like a man who has caught some wild birds – pigeons or what not – and keeps them in an aviary he has made for them at home. In a sense, of course, we

might say he 'has' them all the time inasmuch as he possesses them, mightn't we?. . . But in another sense he 'has' none of them (197c).

The mind is like an aviary. When we are infants the aviary is empty (a tabula rasa), but each new item of knowledge adds a wild bird to our cage. Actual knowing (over against dispositional knowing) is like putting our hand into the cage and grasping a bird. But sometimes we pull out the wrong bird. This is what happens in false belief. We really know, but we cannot get hold of our knowledge. False belief is simply the wrong use of knowledge (197d–199c). But the metaphor seems inadequate, for it does not really explain how it is possible to *know* and yet fail to recognize what one knows? Furthermore, there is no way to decide whether you believe falsely or truly. Instead, there would be no cases where true belief would not be knowledge, but we know that there are. In a law court the jurors can be rightly persuaded of the defendant's guilt in cases where we are sure they do not have knowledge. Knowledge demands something more in terms of certainty, some definite psychological criterion that is self-authenticating.

Theaetetus now amends his definition to include a reason or account (*logos*, 201d–210d). Knowledge is true belief together with an account. However, it turns out that every attempt to give an account of the term 'account' here fails. The suggestion of Socrates' 'dream', that knowledge is an account of a complex 'syllable' in terms of its simple but unknown elements, fails because there is no way to show that the whole is not the sum of its parts. If we do not know what the simpler elements are, neither do we know what the composite is. The attempt to give an account in terms of the characteristic marks of the object by which it differs from other things is rejected because it turns out, on inspection, that we must already *know* the differentia in order to apply them, but it is exactly knowledge that is in question. The dialogue ends with the question of a definition of knowledge unresolved. Socrates does not think that the exercise was in vain. Although our pregnancy turned out to produce mere wind-eggs, we understand our subject better than before and future endeavors may have a better chance of succeeding as a result of today's failures (210b).

In the dialogue we have two items that must not go unnoticed. The first is Plato's characterization of belief as internal thinking to a conclusion, and the second is the non-volitional character of belief. In 189e Socrates describes thinking as a

> discourse that the mind carries on with itself about any subject it is considering. . . . [It] is simply talking to itself, asking questions and answering them, and saying Yes or No. When it reaches a decision – which may come slowly or in a sudden rush – when doubt is over and the two voices affirm the same thing, then we call that its 'judgment'.

In the *Sophist* (262e–264b) this theme is repeated. A thought is a statement in the mind, and, as such, true or false. It is the mind's inner silent talking to itself, whereas the vocal stream issuing from the mouth is called the 'statement'. But the mind asserts or denies these statements in its inner dialogue. A belief is the outcome of a thought. Belief-acquisitions are internal 'yesings', assentings, which we can consciously experience.

Finally, we should note, though not make more of the fact than it merits, that Plato's account is non-volitional. There is not the slightest hint of the volitions entering into the believing process. The typical metaphors for a belief state are the impression in wax, the accidently pulling out the wrong bird, and the blurred vision. Beliefs are things that 'occur in our minds' (*Sophist*, 263d), not something we choose. No one would choose a false belief if one could help it, for the truth is united with the highest form, the Good, which we all really desire. False belief is somehow a failure to pay adequate attention to the relevant evidence or a failure to pursue the truth with whole-hearted devotion, whereas what is desired, knowledge, is the result of seeing, which comes from an obedient pursuit of the truth. The Will comes in only at the point of willingness or unwillingness to pursue the truth (through dialectics or whatever), not in actual believing.

These themes of knowledge being a special, self-authenticating mental state, infallible, with a different object than belief or, at least, a far clearer vision than belief, and of belief being an internal assenting resulting from the internal dialogue in the soul, repeat themselves within the history of epistemology and will be seen in various philosophers and theologians throughout this work. What else is noteworthy is that there is no conscious notion of faith or will involved in belief states. Knowledge is the desideratum, even for salvation, not faith or belief, so that it makes no sense to speak of willing to believe or leaps of faith. These activities, which go virtually unmentioned, would be characterized as irrational and, hence, as evil. It is an altogether different tradition than that which makes faith a virtue and affirms justification by faith.

CHAPTER III

Augustine on Faith

Moreover, when the mind has been imbued with the first elements of that faith which worketh by love, it endeavors to purity of life to attain unto sight, where the pure and perfect in heart know that unspeakable beauty, the full vision of which is supreme happiness. Here surely is an answer to your question as to what is the starting point, and what the goal: we begin in faith and are made perfect by sight. This is the sum of the whole body of doctrine (*Enchiridion*, ch.v).

We saw in the early Church fathers a strong quest for certainty regarding matters of religious belief. Gnostics claimed to offer more than mere faith and chided Christians for their credulity. Why settle for mere believing when you can have knowledge (*gnosis*)? As we have noted, the more Platonic Christian philosophers, for example, Clement of Alexandria and Origen, accommodated Christianity to the Gnostic challenge by saying that Christianity too offered knowledge for the philosophers who had time and leisure to pursue reason to its telos. They preached the doctrine of double conversions, the first by faith and a second for the elite unto knowledge. They sometimes referred to this second state as involving the possession of 'secret knowledge'.[1] For Origen it was impossible to be truly devout without philosophizing. Faith saves, but we reach perfection through knowledge which comes through philosophical speculation.[2] These Gnostic-Christians were more interested in cosmological questions than in questions of salvation which marked the mainstream of the Christian tradition and community.

On the other hand, there were those who rejected the happy marriage of Platonism and Christianity, rejecting the idea of gnosis as heresy. Such was the position of Irenaeus (130–200) and

21

Tertullian (160–220), the latter stating the classic anti-rational credo: 'Where is any likeness between the Christian and the Philosopher?, between the disciple of Greece and of heaven? Away with all projects for a "Stoic", a "Platonic" Christianity. After Jesus Christ we desire no subtle theories, no acute inquiries after the Gospel.' Christianity is to be 'believed because it is absurd'. Christ 'was buried and rose again; the fact is certain because it is impossible' (*De Praescriptiam* VII).

In the early work of Augustine of Hippo (354–430) something like the Neo-platonic two conversions doctrine is prominent. We begin with faith, but some of us can go on to knowledge of the truth in this life.[3] Later, however, he retracts this, stating instead that the beatific vision, knowledge of the truth, comes only in eternity.[4] But the formula remains the same in both cases. We begin with faith and are made perfect with sight. His motto throughout was a mistranslated verse from the *Septuagint*, Isaiah 7:9, 'Unless you believe, you shall not understand.'[5] From the very beginning of his authorship authority is emphasized as a necessary condition for salvation, and it is exactly in this authority that faith must be placed in order for an eventual ascent to knowledge and salvation to take place. Like Clement of Alexandria and Origen before him what separates Augustine from the Gnostics and the Manicheans is the significant place of simple faith in the New Testament. Christianity could never be faithful to its tradition and at the same time be an elitist philosophy of gnosis. St. Paul writes:

> Where is the wise? where is the scribe? where is the disputer of this world? Hath not God made foolish the wisdom of this world? For after that in the wisdom of God the world by wisdom knew not God, it pleased God by the foolishness of preaching to save them that believe (I Corinthians 1:20,21).

Although Paul in the same paragraph makes place for a special wisdom ('Howbeit we speak wisdom among them that are perfect: yet not the wisdom of this world, nor of the princes of this world, that come to naught: but we speak the wisdom of God in a mystery, even the hidden wisdom, which God ordained before the world unto our glory.' I Corinthians 2:6,7), the accent is laid on the primacy of faith. No amount of allegorizing of the text could remove this feature of the New Testament. The just shall live, not by works or knowledge, but by faith.[6]

Luther wrote that except for his concept of prevenient grace (i.e., grace which enables one to have saving faith), which came into prominence towards the end of his life, there was nothing interesting in Augustine's notion of faith. 'See then how great darkness is in the books of the Fathers about faith! Augustine writes nothing special about faith, except when he disputes against the Pelagians. They woke Augustine up and made him a man.'[7] This probably says more about Luther's own interests than it does about Augustine. Indeed, it seems to me that Augustine spends more time with the concept of faith than anyone before him and has some very interesting things to say. What I shall do is analyze Augustine's notion of faith as it appears in three separate places. First, we shall look at his defense of the attitude of faith in his short work *Concerning Faith of Things Not Seen* (399). Then we shall examine his important tract *On the Usefulness of Belief* (391), and after that his famous work *On the Trinity* (417–428).

In *Concerning Faith of Things Not Seen* Augustine considers the arguments of those who reject Christianity on the grounds that it is not empirically verifiable. Augustine points out that there are many things which we believe that are not verifiable, which cannot be perceived. For example, you cannot see your friend's good will; yet you still believe in your heart that he has good will towards you. 'Thy friend's face thou discernest by thy own body, thy friend's faith thou discernest by thine own mind' (ch.2). The skeptic objects that the analogy doesn't hold, for there is more to friendship than blind faith in another's good will, for true friendship has been tested in adversity.

Augustine responds by pointing out that often we enjoy friendship without adversity and that purposefully choosing adversity to test friendship can be an unfriendly act. But more importantly, even when we do risk danger on the assumption that our friend will help us if necessary, the very risk itself presupposes faith which had not yet been proved. That is, our faith in the good will of our friend usually goes well beyond any available empirical evidence. While it is not without evidence altogether, it often is stronger than what may be warranted. It is, furthermore, only by risking in faith that we come to know with certainty our friend's loyalty.

If we were to follow the skeptic's counsel, we would have to restrict a spouse's unproven love in the beloved because love itself cannot be seen, nor will children be permitted to trust their parents because trust is not observable. Furthermore, history and all testimony would be precluded from being believed. Indeed, we would all be the poorer without faith. Society cannot exist without belief that goes beyond proof.

Augustine applies this to religious faith:

> Since therefore, if we believe not those things which we cannot see, human society itself, . . . will not stand; how much more is faith to be applied to divine things, although they be not seen; failing the application of which, it is not the friendship of some men or other, but the very chiefest bond of piety that is violated, so as for the chiefest misery to follow (*Concerning Faith of Things Not Seen*, ch. 4, 338).

Granted, one should not believe just anything. There is a difference between faith and credulity, and this difference is recognized by the Christian Church. For there is a difference between believing in Christianity and believing other religions, for unlike other religions, Christianity already has an enormous amount of evidence in its favor for faith to latch onto, so that we can say that we ought to believe that Christ is the Saviour of the world. Here Augustine cites passages from the Old Testament which he shows to have been fulfilled in Jesus Christ. There is ample evidence for Christianity. The Church is now seen as the middle term between the prophecies of the past and the promise of the future kingdom.

Responding to a crude form of the verificationist principle, Augustine has shown that a skeptical position is unreasonable, that most of the goods we enjoy in social existence come to us through trust in other people, in their friendship, integrity, testimony and judgment. We have good grounds for trusting our friends, but not visible evidence of the kind which the rigid empiricist would demand. Likewise, with religious faith, we cannot have perceptual evidence, but we have abundant evidence of past fulfillment to give us confidence that the future will also confirm the beliefs we have and the trust we place in the Catholic Church. Augustine's position is far removed from the desperate fideism of Tertullian. He might well agree with Hume's dictum that we ought to tailor the strength of our belief to the strength of the evidence, for he has no doubt whatsoever that the evidence for Christianity is abundant.

Concerning Faith of Things Not Seen offers a brilliant analysis of the necessity of faith in ordinary life. It represents the first sustained argument for the validity of faith in both ordinary and religious life. The arguments reappear centuries later in Butler's *Analogy*, without mention of Augustine. Nevertheless, we have only a general argument for the need for faith in life in this tract. A more extensive analysis of the role of faith in the Christian Church is offered by Augustine in his work, *On the Usefulness of Belief*, a work written to his dear friend, Honoratus, a Manichean, in order to persuade him to consider the Catholic faith.

Augustine begins the work by facing head on a charge that must have often given intelligent Christians pause, viz., the charge of the Manicheans and Gnostics, that Christianity is inferior to other religions because it fails to give certain knowledge and calls on prospective adherents to believe without reason. 'This is the chief charge they bring against the Catholic Church, that it bids those who come to it to believe, while they themselves impose no yoke of belief, but glory in opening the fount of knowledge' (ch. 21). But, answers Augustine, the false religions are not able to fulfill their promises, and the adherent only 'sucks in the poison of deceivers'. True religion cannot be approached without 'the weighty command of authority'. Things must first be believed before one can achieve understanding of them, provided one conducts oneself well and proves oneself a worthy seeker.

Augustine gives an abbreviated form of the argument for trust in friends, urging that we must likewise trust credible authorities for a good life. He imagines his auditor objecting that it would still be better if we could provide proofs, knowledge of the truth, instead of mere belief. Perhaps it would, Augustine agrees, but it is a difficult matter for one to know God by reason. 'Do you think that all men are fitted to grasp the reasons by which the human mind is drawn to the knowledge of God? Or are a good many so fitted, or only a few?' he asks. Only a few, of course. If this is the case, would it not be unfair of God to deny the benefits of religion to the many who cannot understand reason? Why should we suppose God only favors the intellectual elite? Because of this, it is positively harmful for the elite to begin with reason, even if they could, for it would serve as a bad example for the many, bringing confusion. Sometimes the sure indirect, slower path is to be preferred to the direct, dangerous path. There is nothing more pathetic than the intellectual who has used his finite reason to believe falsely that he has knowledge of the truth.

Next Augustine analyzes various types of attitudes towards religion. There are two types of praiseworthy people: (1) those who have found the truth, the blessed (later in the *Retractions*, I, xiv, he modifies this, saying that this cannot occur in this life but only in eternity); and (2) those who seek it rightly and earnestly. There are three kinds of people to be blamed; (3) the opinionated – who think that they know what they do not know; (4) the self-consciously ignorant, who believe that they know nothing but fail to seek knowledge and (5) the wayward seekers – those who know that they are ignorant of the truth, seek for the truth, but not in the right way.

Some further distinctions are then made. There are three types of persons in relation to mental activities: (a) the knowing who are always faultless; (b) the believing who are sometimes faultless; and (c) the opining who are never faultless. Sometimes we are not responsible for our false beliefs, for example, historical beliefs which have passed down to us (he cites the proposition 'most wicked conspirators were put to death by the virtuous Cicero'). Augustine elaborates on this point in *On the Trinity* (bk XV) where he says that we are allowed to speculate and doubt where there is no clear injunction given by a suitable authority. Believing is culpable if one believes anything unworthy of God or too readily of man. But opining is always culpable and that for two reasons: (i) because we could often learn to know what we only opine and (ii) because it shows an innate temerity, bad character in not coming to a conviction or belief. Continuing with the analysis of these three states of mind towards propositions, Augustine says that we owe our knowledge to reason, our beliefs to authority and our opinions to error. 'Knowledge always implies belief, and so does opinion. But belief does not always imply knowledge and opinion never does' (ch. 25).

It is not clear what is meant by 'opinion', for it does not seem to be our idea of weak belief but is rather faulty, false belief, so that we will never be able to say what our opinions are, only what other people's are. His use has a Platonic ring to it. Opinions are somehow attached to the shadows of existence rather than the universal forms.

Augustine now applies all this to the five classes of attitudes towards religious belief mentioned above: (1) the truly blessed believe the very truth (they know the truth); (2) the studious believe upon authority; (3) the opinionated believe with a faulty credulity and are in error; (4) the self-consciously ignorant who do not seek the truth do not believe anything in this regard and (5) those who seek the truth in the wrong way believe nothing of significance either. Augustine's point is that except for the very few who are the blessed, the best the rest of us can do is believe on good authority. The matter is too serious to be dilettante about, as is the case in (3), (4), and (5). Hence, the Catholic position is reasonable. 'We may know that in believing what we do not yet understand, we escape the charge of being rashly opinionated.' In believing on authority, one is both rational, humble, and seeking the truth in the best way available.

But why is it necessary to believe anyway? Why isn't ignorance or skepticism permissible with regard to so difficult a matter as religion? Here Augustine argues that the highest virtue, recognized by all philosophers, is to be wise, but wisdom entails knowledge of God and man; but we cannot obtain such knowledge unless we at least 'believe that God is and that he brings help to human minds'. He never doubts that a divine being exists and believes that a version of the ontological argument can prove this (*De Libero Arbitrio* XV), though one need not know the proof in order to believe. We already have innate ideas (*intelligibili*) given at birth by the Logos, which assure us of metaphysical truth. In the *Soliloquies* he tells us that if we would only look inwards, we would find ineffable truth. Unlike the Protestant Reformers, Augustine never claims that reason has been directly corrupted by the Fall, though it has been indirectly because of the will's control over it. Reason would be sufficient to lead us to God were it not for the perversion of our wills. It is because of our perverse wills that we are in danger of egregious self-deception in using unaided reason to find the truth. Hence, we need to have faith in a reliable witness, which is the authority of the Catholic Church.

The relationship of the will to knowledge is developed a little further in ch. 33 of *On the Usefulness of Belief*. We must set our hearts on God in order to know that he exists. No one can obtain the supreme good unless he perfectly loves it. 'He cannot [love it] as long as he fears bodily evils and fortuitous circumstances. By being born miraculously and by doing miracles he procures our love and by dying and rising again he drove away our fears.'

We must turn our love from temporal things unto things eternal. It is the Church which urges us to do this and which guides us in this difficult task. In this authority we have the means of raising our minds above their earthly habitation. Through it we find our conversion from love of this world to the true love of God. 'It is authority alone which urges fools to hasten to wisdom.' So long as we cannot know pure truth it is misery no doubt to be deceived by authority, but it is certainly greater misery not to be moved by it. 'If there is no God who providentially looks after the world, there is no need to worry about religion, but all the best minds urge us to seek and to serve God', for the outward beauty of the universe assures us that there must be some fountain of true beauty and hence that there is hope that God himself has constituted some authority which we may rely on as a sure ladder upon which to rise to God. The authority of the Church has two media of appeal to our faith, miracles and the moral integrity of the masses of believers. The miracles, essentially wonders, are given to draw attention to the marvelous. To the question, why don't miracles happen today? Augustine responds that they can only be temporary events, for they are merely extraordinary experiences. If they happened continually, they would lose their extraordinary aspect and become as commonplace as the rising and setting of the sun. The moral courage and integrity of believers who live in love and die in hope bear strong testimony to the reliability of the Church.

These thoughts, which are repeated in *Faith and the Creed* (393), show that Augustine thought belief was propositional (though the word was not available to him) and that it was tied to earnestly seeking truth. The pattern seen in several works is something like this:

1 Reason, because of our evil wills, is unable to bring us to the truth, so we need some reasonable and reliable authority to believe in.
2 The Church is that reasonable and reliable authority, evidenced by the fulfilled prophecy, miracles, and morality of the masses of Christians.
3 Faith in the authority inspires devotion, which in turn leads to works of righteousness.
4 Righteousness cleanses the heart, enabling it to see (know) God.
5 Therefore, since only the pure in heart may see (know) God, the only way to blessedness is through faith in the authority of the Church.

It is true that in the Anti-Pelagian writings and elsewhere Augustine states that grace is necessary to infuse love within our hearts to bring us to faith, but there is little reference to prevenient grace in these more philosophical writings.

Contra Wilfred Cantwell Smith there is a strong propositional element in Augustine's notion of faith/belief. Augustine defines the concept (*credo*) as 'thinking with assent' (*On Predestination*, ch. 2) and fights against heresy as hard as any of the Church fathers. He makes it clear (e.g., *Commentary on the Gospel of John* 83.3) that trust is also necessary for saving faith.

It is in his most complex work *On the Trinity*, that the notion of doctrinal belief, a form of propositional belief, is given most attention. Here we are repeatedly told of the salvific necessity of believing that God is Father, Son and Holy Spirit, that God became a man in Jesus Christ, that he died for our sins, that he rose from the dead, that God has certain properties (e.g. incorporèity). We are told that the common faith of the Church involves believing the same doctrines. All believers share a common set of beliefs.

Nevertheless, emotional and volitional attitudes ought always to be tied to the Creed. Interestingly enough, however, they are not emphasized in relation to belief as much as they are to knowledge. That is, love (Augustine's prime non-cognitive state) is primarily related to knowledge, not to faith. What is known, truly known, is, finally, what is loved. True enough, because of our perverse will, we must begin by evincing our love by having faith in the Church, turning from earthly love to love of the divine. But he asks 'Who loves what he does not know? We cannot love God before knowing him. And what is it to know God except to behold him and steadfastly perceive him with the mind?' But we must have a pure heart before we can see him (Matt. 5:8). How, then can we love him? Here faith comes in as an intermediary, temporary disposition. 'Except he is loved by faith, it will not be possible for the heart to be cleansed, in order that it may be apt and meet to see him' (VIII. 4.6).

Essentially, love is a type of desire; every inquiry is a mode of love, seeking an object, knowledge. We can call this form of desire 'will' (*voluntas*) since everyone who seeks wills (*vult*) to find; and 'if that is sought which belongs to knowledge, everyone who seeks wills to know' (IX. 12.18, p. 133). The implication of this is that unless we love the object of knowledge, we will not come to know that object, so that knowledge is dependent on love as deep desire.

Augustine illustrates this with regard to knowing that our soul is incorporeal. When we truly love our souls in themselves we can see that they are independent of the body, but because most of us love corporeality along with our souls, we confuse matter with our essence and come to believe in the corporeality of the soul (X.8.11, p.140).

Elsewhere, in the *City of God* this idea of pure, passionate love as the necessary and sufficient condition for ultimate blessedness is linked to Socrates:

> Socrates realized that his predecessors had been seeking the origin of all things, but he believed that these first and highest causes could be found only in the will of the single and supreme Divinity and, therefore, could be comprehended only by a mind purified from passion. Hence his conclusion, that he must apply himself to the acquisition of virtue, so that his mind, freed from the weight of early desires, might, by its own natural vigor, lift itself up to eternal realities and, with purified intelligence, contemplate the very nature of that immaterial and immutable light in which the causes of all created nature abidingly dwell (*City of God* VIII.3).[8]

Socrates' only flaw, if it can be called such, is that he used his 'own natural vigor' to lift himself to a state of blessedness and knowledge. He is to be applauded for the herculean effort. All he lacked was faith in the authority of the Church whose time had not yet come.

Knowledge is dependent upon right love rather than right love being dependent on knowledge. Faith, then, is the intermediary state, a thankful humility which lovingly believes and obeys the authority of the Church in order to come eventually to blessedness wherein is the contemplation (supreme knowledge) of God.

Whereas for Aristotle the will is dependent on reason, the practical on the theoretical intellect, with Augustine the intellect is dependent on the will or practical reason. For Augustine both belief and knowledge have a volitional aspect. The will is involved in the search for truth in two ways. First, it is by willing to possess the right object-relation that happiness in the truth can be achieved. We must will to possess our souls in relation to the eternal rather than to possess our souls in relation to the temporal and corporeal if we are to ascend the ladder to the truth. Secondly, we can will to believe the Church. Augustine says that it is a reasonable belief, but we can stubbornly resist it as well as voluntarily embrace its doctrines. Sometimes in discussing the will regarding faith in authority, he means trusting it, but more often the attitude is one of positive belief that the Church is the legitimate authority for all belief and morals.[9] But, finally, all believing involves an act of will. 'The speculative intellect or reason is the subject of faith, because the mind is moved to assent to the things of faith by the command of the will, for no one believes except by willing.'[10] Anticipating Descartes and Kierkegaard, he affirms that all believing is volitional. Our beliefs are the conclusions of our resolutions.

In Augustine we have the synthesis of biblical motifs with Neo-platonic thought. The volitional aspects of faith, including a deep need for trust are biblical, but the quest for knowledge, the goal of faith, are Platonic. He brings these polar ideas together and, in so doing, offers the first sustained analysis of the concept of faith, how it functions in ordinary life as a virtue and how it becomes a sacred virtue in Christianity, preparing us for the *summum bonum*. 'Unless ye believe, ye shall not understand.'

CHAPTER IV

Aquinas on Faith

During the Middle Ages Augustine's interpretation of the Christian faith was taken as the point of departure for further discussion. But as there were often different emphases in different parts of Augustine's works, successive theologians latched on to one emphasis rather than the other, as they saw fit. As we have noticed, there is both a propositional and an affective/connative aspect in Augustine's concept of faith, the former generally predominating. The aspect generally emphasized during the Middle Ages was the affective motif. Faith is seen primarily as a commitment to God as the Truth. It involves an inner certitude about transcendent reality. In fine, the aspect of propositional assent found in Augustine is underemphasized and the lesser aspect of inward certainty now becomes dominant. It is Hugh of St. Victor (d. 1142) more than anyone else who defines the faith's formula: 'Faith is a form of certitude of mind concerning things not present, which stands as greater than opinion, but less than science' (*De Fide*, 2). Certainty becomes the central property of faith. Victor's formula is the eventual victor in the battle with its more thoroughly propositional counterpart set forth by Hugo's contemporary, Peter Abelard (d. 1142), who sees belief more in terms of *existimationem*, a supposing. St. Bernard and others rejected Abelard's definition as a trivialization of faith, reducing it to opinion. It is in Thomas Aquinas (1224–1274) that we find something of a return to the Augustinian synthesis between the affective aspect and the cognitive aspect. Using Aristotelian categories, he divides the subject into formal and material components. Formally, faith's object is the first truth, God, not a proposition; but materially, faith is propositional, for what we believe always involves predicating some concept of some other concept. Faith is both affective, involving the

32

will, and cognitive, involving thought.

Aquinas's discussion of faith is found primarily in *Summa Theologiae* (abbreviated 'ST' hereafter) 2a2ae and *De Veritate* (abbreviated 'DV' hereafter) Question 14.[1] The context of the discussion is that of the theological virtues: faith, hope and charity. A virtue is 'a good habit (or disposition) of the mind, by which we live righteously, of which no one can make bad use' (ST 1a2ae, 55,4). Like the pagan virtues, the theological virtues are dispositions, have a voluntary aspect to them, can be had in varying degrees, and are interconnected (although faith and hope can exist without charity, charity cannot exist without faith and hope). They differ from natural virtues in that they derive, not from natural endowments, but grace; they are not means between extremes; and they must be learned through revelation, and they not only come from God but are aspects of God's nature in us. 'That which exists in God as his own substance, comes to exist as an accidental quality in the soul of the one who becomes a sharer in God's own good' (1a2ae.110.2). On the other hand, faith is meritorious, something that we can do and which earns divine favor.

Faith is the first of the theological virtues. Whereas hope and charity are the dispositions of trust and fellowship with God, faith is the cognitive virtue. As a virtue, faith has a voluntary dimension, consisting in two acts. The first is the inner act of faith, *assent*, which voluntarily and inwardly affirms those propositions about God set forth in the creeds.[2] The second is the outward act of faith, *confession*, through which we directly express our affirmation. The twofold dimensionality of faith is a self-conscious attempt to reflect Paul's statement in Romans 10:9, 10: 'If thou shalt confess with thy mouth the Lord Jesus, and shalt believe in thine heart that God hath raised him from the dead, thou shalt be saved. For with the heart man believeth unto righteousness; and with the mouth confession is made unto salvation.'

Faith (*fides*) is a cognitive state which lies midway between opinion and scientific knowledge (*scientia*, knowledge deduced from self-evident premises). It rests upon divine truth, God himself, who is its prime mover. Its assent is under the loving prompting of the will. Faith as a knowing is before all else an acceptance of God's word, a holding fast to him, a surrender of self to him and a response made possible only by the same effective divine love that wills the blessed destiny that faith begins.

Although it is the basic virtue upon which the other theological virtues are constructed, it is not the final state of salvation. As a type of knowledge it is still an 'imperfect operation of the intellect, having regard to what is on the side of the intellect, though the greatest perfection is discovered on the side of the object. For the intellect does not grasp the object to which it gives assent in the act of believing. Therefore, neither does man's ultimate felicity lie in this kind of knowledge of God' (*Contra Gentiles* III, ch. 40). Faith is more like hearing than seeing, a trusting in the authoritative testimony of another, but the ultimate beatific vision will be full knowledge of God. When clear vision comes, faith will vanish (2a2ae4.4).

Nevertheless, faith has a sort of self-authenticating aura about it. Since its formal object is God himself, faith is a sure grasping of the source of all truth, the Truth itself. In this regard it is like scientific knowledge. It is both certain and true. But it is more like knowledge by acquaintance than propositional knowledge. On the other hand, its material object is propositional. Yet it cannot be false, for if it were, it would not really be faith! The pagans who are theists but not Christians really do not have faith but only pseudo-faith, for, citing Aristotle, he who does not completely know an object does not know it at all (2a2ae2.2). One knows that one has true faith, rather than pseudo-faith, because of the inner witness of the Holy Spirit.

Thomas follows Augustine in defining faith (*credere*), as 'thinking with assent' (DV 14.1). There are two ways in which the mind may assent to a proposition: (1) by coercion, as for example when it immediately intuits first principles such as the law of non-contradiction or when it reasons scientifically from first principles to conclusions as in deductive arguments and (2) voluntarily, wherein the mind assents of its own free will.

Faith, as an assenting to propositions, is midway between scientific knowledge, which is coercive, and opinion, which lacks conviction. Aquinas distinguishes four intellectual states that lack the objective certainty of scientific knowledge but have a volitional dimension: (1) doubt – when the subject is not clearly inclined either to affirming or denying; (2) suspicion – where the evidence inclines one in one direction but only weakly; (3) opinion – where the assent is given to a proposition but with concomitant fear that the opposite may be true; and, finally, (4) belief (*credere*) – which is different from these other acts of assenting in that it represents 'firm adherence to one side rather than the other' with none of the hesitation characteristic of the others types of assent. All involve the will in assenting in spite of non-coercive evidence, but faith alone produces the firmness of conviction which is characteristic of scientific knowledge.

As an incomplete cognitive state, faith is nevertheless, superior to all other knowledge except the vision of God. Measured from the perspective of the formal object faith is second in terms of certainty, but measured from the point of view of its material object, i.e., measured against its propositional warrant, it is below scientific knowledge. The classifications look like this:

In terms of material certainty	*In terms of formal certainty*
1 Vision of God	1 Vision of God
2 Intuition of First Principles	2 Faith
3 Scientific knowledge (reasoning from first principles to conclusions)	3 Intuition of First Principles
4 Faith	4 Scientific knowledge
5 Opinion	5 Opinion
6 Suspicion	6 Suspicion
7 Doubt	7 Doubt

Faith is less certain (materially) because of the imperfection in it, but more certain (formally) because it rests on divine authority. What gives faith its inner certainty? The will, as prompted by God. Although faith resides in the intellect, it is the willingness of commitment that makes faith a virtue and, as such, meritorious.

We are, in the first instance, motivated to believe for self-interested reasons. Although grace enables us to believe when the intellect has not been fully persuaded, the will must overcome natural timidity and temptations to doubt and believe for the sake of eternal life. 'We are moved to believe what God says because we are promised eternal life as a reward if we believe. And this reward moves the will to assent to what is said, although the intellect is not moved by anything which it understands.'[3]

After deliberation, the believer's mind 'settles upon the one side of a question not in virtue of his reason but in virtue of his will. Therefore assent is understood in the definition as an act of mind in so far as the mind is brought to its decision by the will' (2a2ae,2.1).

It is God who commands the will to believe, who enables it to believe, and who moves it to believe; but it is the individual who finally decides whether or not to obey God and believe. How does the individual know that it is God who is at work and not someone or something else? The witness of the Spirit is self-authenticating.

Ultimately, faith rests on *authority*. All believing, versus scientific knowledge, rests on someone else's authority, but what is important is that the chain of authority is unbroken, so that we can be confident that the content of our faith has been accurately communicated. Aquinas believes that the grounds for trusting the Catholic Church as the bearer of the truth are weighty. Putting various strands of the argument together, we end up with the following outline of Thomas's position:

1 Scientific knowledge based on conclusions derived deductively from absolutely certain premises is a more perfect form of intellectual activity than believing on testimony.

2 But sometimes we are not equipped or don't have time to do the difficult, scientific reasoning, so we must accept the authority of the true scientist.

3 God and spiritual beings are super-scientists, the highest authorities.

4 There is solid evidence that the creeds of the Church are based on a chain of testimony going back to God.

5 But the evidence cannot be seen or proven but only believed (no deductive proof or immediate intuition is available). Our intellects are not coerced in believing as they are in scientific knowledge.

6 So it is the will which causes our belief in these matters and that creates the absolute certainty which we experience in faith.

7 But because the will is moved by God through grace we can be sure that we are on firm ground in believing the creeds, since they have the guarantee of God as their truth.

Problems with Aquinas's formulations have been noted by scholars such as John Hick, Timothy Potts, and Terence Penelhum.[4] First, it seems to denude faith of any phenomenological properties by defining it as already possessing the truth. Anyone who seems to have the same attitude towards a different doctrine than ours is, *per definitionem*, not in faith. While our task here is not to render an extensive critical analysis of these points of contention, the focus of this work directs us to mention Penelhum's criticism of Thomas's volitionalism. After confessing that he finds it hard to understand how one could choose to believe wholeheartedly a proposition for which one does not consider the evidence one has to be conclusive, Penelhum suggests that the problem can be met by saying that grace is needed for the will to command the intellect to believe. We could perhaps save Thomas by suggesting that he only means that we must want God to enable us to believe. Penelhum writes:

> The difficulty prompts me to suggest again that Aquinas, and a great many other thinkers who follow him, are mistaken in holding that the voluntariness, and hence the merit, of faith depends upon the inconclusiveness of the grounds for it. Perhaps acceptance can be given voluntarily even though the grounds are conclusive. If this seems absurd, let us reflect first that there are two ways in which one can accept what is proved to one: one can be reluctant to accept it, . . . or one can be glad to accept it. Perhaps the man of faith has merit because he is glad to accept the truths of faith when the devil is not. The natural objection to this is that whether it is glad or whether it is reluctant, such acceptance is not to one's credit either way, because it is not free. But this may be to locate freedom in the wrong place, to be too dominated by the picture of free action as action explicitly commanded ('The Analysis of Faith in St. Thomas Aquinas', p. 152f).

Penelhum's criticism has been attacked by Michael McLean in his defense of Aquinas. He gives as an illustration the case of a teacher who is not sure on the evidence whether he has mastered a subject or not, but who knows that if he believes that he has mastered the subject, he will more than likely do a good job teaching it. So he simply believes the proposition and begins his lecture confident of my mastery of the material. 'Many similar examples could be adduced (particularly from the lore of famous locker room speeches and Dale Carnegie courses).'[5] Whether McLean has successfully defused Penelhum's criticism, I will let the reader decide. We shall return to the subject in the second part of this work.

It remains only to make a brief comparison between Aquinas and the Reformers and point out the necessity of the propositional element of belief which was made a necessary condition for salvation throughout the Middle Ages and Reformation. In Martin Luther (1483–1546) we find a greater emphasis on the aspect of trust than in Aquinas or any of the medievalists. The Christian obviously believes the Gospel, but, what is more important, he commits himself to the Gospel. 'A quick and living faith is not only the common belief of the articles of our faith, but it is also a true trust and confidence of the mercy of God through our Lord Jesus Christ, and a steadfast hope of good things to be received at God's hands.'[6] With his view that original sin corrupts the intellect as well as the will, Luther rejects rationalist natural theology. He stressed the subjective aspect of faith as no one since Tertullian. Faith is now seen not only as a necessary condition for salvation, but a sufficient condition. Good works are irrelevant regarding justification and there is no place for the notion of supererogation. Grace is alone sufficient and faith is its manifestation. Luther in his denial of freedom of the will, also seems to have denied that believing is effected by a fiat of the will.

In John Calvin (1509–1564) something like the Thomistic balance between the heart and the head reasserts itself. In his *Institutes of the Christian Religion* Calvin defines faith as 'a firm and certain knowledge of God's benevolence towards us, founded upon the truth of the freely given promise in Christ, both revealed to our minds and sealed upon our hearts through the Holy Spirit' (III.2.7).

In their studies of Calvin's notion of faith both Paul Helm and Kenneth Konyndyk agree that Calvin's position is remarkably close to Aquinas's.[7] Konyndyk argues that there is found no significant animosity to natural theology in Calvin, as there is in Luther and the later Calvinists. Helm shows that although Calvin calls faith 'a firm and certain knowledge of God's benevolence towards us', the difference between Aquinas and himself is mostly terminological. They both distinguish this concept from knowledge in the sense of sense-experience, and both distinguish it from opinion. Faith is 'so far above sense that man's mind has to go beyond and rise above itself in order to attain it. Even where the mind has attained, it does not comprehend what it feels.'[8] Both agree that we have some natural knowledge of God's existence, but that this knowledge is insufficient for salvation. Furthermore, both agree 'that it is impossible to know the essence of God and that therefore God is to be known only by his effects. . . . God is incomprehensible' (Helm, p.

103). Both Helm and Konyndyk agree that Aquinas's theory of faith is worked out in far more detail and subtlety than Calvin's.

Calvin seems more self-conscious about the self-authenticating nature of faith than Aquinas. He compares being convinced of the truth of divine revelation to someone who, having the sensation of sweetness or bitterness, is convinced of its sweetness or bitterness.

> As to their question – How can we be assured this has sprung from God unless we have recourse to the decree of the church? – it is as if someone asked: Whence will we learn to distinguish light from darkness, white from black, sweet from bitter? Indeed Scripture exhibits fully as clear evidence of its own truth as white and black things do of their colour, or sweet and bitter things do of their taste (*Institutes* I.7.2).

To have faith is to be beyond doubt about one's relationship to God. This comes about through the work of the Holy Spirit which overcomes our natural inclination to vanity which militates against the truth.

> But our mind has such an inclination to vanity that it can never cleave fast to the truth of God; and it has such a dullness that it is always blind to the light of God's truth. Accordingly, without the illumination of the Holy Spirit, the Word can do nothing. From this, also, it is clear that faith is much higher than human understanding. And it will not be enough for the mind to be illuminated by the Spirit of God unless the heart is also strengthened and supported by his power (*Institutes* III. 2. 33).

It does little good to argue with believers, not because there is no evidence for God's reality, but because the unbeliever is in sin and cannot appreciate the force of the evidence. As Karl Barth says, faith can only preach to unbelief, not reason. There is, with regard to the interpretation of the evidence, an incommensurability between the believer and unbeliever's positions which can only be bridged by a conversion brought about by the work of the Holy Spirit.

Although the connative aspect was often stressed more heavily than the cognitive, there was in all shades of Protestant and Catholic orthodox, a strict requirement for definite propositional beliefs without which salvation was not possible. This is reflected in the Lutheran confessions, such as the *Confession of Augsburg* (1530), (people are justified when 'they believe that they are received into grace and that their sins are remitted on account of Christ . . . God imputes this faith for righteousness in his own sight'), as well as in the Catholic councils, such as the *Tridentine Profession of Faith* (1564). The latter proclaims:

> I, with steadfast faith believe and profess each and all the things contained in the Symbol of faith, which the holy Roman Church uses, namely [the Nicene Creed] . . . I hold unswervingly that there is a purgatory . . . that the relics [of the saints] are to be venerated and invoked . . . I affirm the power of indulgences . . . I accept and profess without doubting, the traditions, definitions and declarations of the sacred Canons and Oecumenical Councils and especially those of the holy Council of Trent; and at the same time I condemn, reject and anathematize all things contrary thereto, and all heresies condemned, rejected and anathematized by the Church. This [is] the true Catholic Faith (without which no one can be in a state of salvation).

Heretics were punished by both Catholics and Protestants, as though right belief was somehow under our control. Often they were offered the opportunity to renounce their beliefs. These beliefs were not confined to theological utterances but extended to the realm of science as well. Galileo was condemned and forced to 'voluntarily' renounce his belief that the sun is the center of the universe.

CHAPTER V

The Rationalists on Belief and Will: Descartes and Spinoza

In the work of René Descartes (1596–1650) we find the most self-consciously volitional position in the history of Western Philosophy, equalled only by Kierkegaard two hundred years later. For Descartes no distinction is made between 'belief' and 'opinion' as with the Scholastics, nor is there really any significant place for belief in much of his work. In the *Meditations* 'belief' seems to be a product of weakness. What Descartes seeks is certainty, knowledge which is infallible, a science with secure foundations upon which all other knowledge can be built. Other than that there is no place for judgment whatsoever. He seeks to demonstrate the truth of certain propositions so that 'there will no longer be any one who dares to doubt the existence of God and the real distinction between the human soul and the body' (p.7). There is permitted only knowledge and agnosticism, withholding of judgment or treating all that is probable as though it were false. 'For however probable may be the conjecture which inclines me to a particular judgment, the mere recognition that they are only conjectures and not certain and indubitable reasons is enough to give me grounds for making the contrary judgment' (p. 57, cf. *Rules* II).[1]

We have the first instance of Descartes' view that we can choose our beliefs in the First Meditation where he speaks of his 'serious and unimpeded effort to destroy generally all my former opinions' (p.17). In order to do this, however, we must do non-volitional reasoning which shows that there are grounds for distrusting all our beliefs; 'for reason already convinces me that I should abstain from the belief in things which are not entirely certain and indubitable no less carefully than from the belief in those which appear to me to be manifestly false'. There is a problem here right from the start, for Descartes' discussion seems ambiguous. He doesn't distinguish

41

between disbelieving a proposition and withholding judgment on a proposition, for we don't merely 'abstain from believing' what we judge to be false but we disbelieve it, believing its contrary. For Descartes' project to make sense, he must mean by 'doubt' withholding judgment.

Foremost in his mind as a candidate for doubt is the set of all empirical proposition. They must certainly be rejected as unreliable. 'Everything which I have thus far accepted as entirely true and assured has been acquired from the senses or by means of the senses. But I have learned by experience that these senses sometimes mislead me, and it is prudent never to trust wholly those things which have once deceived us' (p. 18).

The argument seems to be as follows:

1 A K-kind of thing sometimes deceives one.
2 What sometimes deceives one ought never to be believed.
3 Therefore, one (prudentially) ought never believe a K-kind of thing.

There seems no good reason for accepting premise 2. It may be prudent to trust fallible testimony at times in order to reach our goals. Be that as it may, an even more interesting problem in the passage is the reason cited for doubting: 'but I have learned by experience that these senses sometimes mislead me'. Descartes fails to note the incoherence in this statement, for it is only by trusting experience (viz., my memory reports) that I have evidence that experience has sometimes deceived me. On Descartes' principles we ought not accept even the reports of experience when they show that experience has sometimes deceived us! Descartes must accept a more radical skepticism, the 'pyrrhonic' type, and simply state that with regard to empirical judgments there is nothing certain, not even the proposition that there is nothing that is certain.

There is a problem, which has been debated in the literature, as to whether Descartes really doubted any of this or whether he only pretended to doubt, but, given his views on the power of the will, it would follow that he believed that he really did come to doubt all empirical judgments. In the *Principles* he makes this quite clear.

Finally, it is so evident that we are possessed of a free will that can give or withhold its assent, that this may be counted as one of the first and most ordinary notions that are found innately in us. We had before a very clear proof of this, for at the same time as we tried to doubt all things and even suppose that He who created us employed his unlimited powers in deceiving us in every way, we perceived in ourselves a liberty such that we were able to abstain from believing what was not perfectly certain and indubitable. But that of which we could not doubt at such a time is as self-evident and clear as anything we can ever know (xxxix).

It is in the Fourth Meditation that Descartes discusses the power of the will as the decisive principle in coming to believe. He has already proved that the thinking self exists, that the mind is more certain than the body, and that God exists. His criterion of knowledge is whatever is both clear and distinct, that is, apparent to the mind and separate from all else. This cannot be doubted even if one would like to, so long as one is thinking attentively about the matters. But all else is subject to the will.

The concern here is to explain whence comes false belief, and Descartes poses the discussion within the context of the problem of evil. Error in belief, he states, is a weakness, an imperfection. But God could not be directly responsible for such a state, for that would make him into a deceiver. But this very assertion is tantamount to blasphemy, for deception is itself a weakness, an imperfection, and God contains no imperfections. So God cannot be responsible for our false beliefs. Hence, by elimination, we must be the cause for our false judgments. False belief arises when we misuse God's gift of a special ability.

Then, I know by my own experience that I have some ability to judge, or to distinguish the true from the false, an ability which I have no doubt received from God just as I have received all the other qualities which are part of me and which I possess. Furthermore, since, it is impossible that God wishes to deceive me, it is also certain that he has not given me an ability of such a sort that I could ever go wrong when I use it properly (*Meditations* IV p. 51).

The special ability to judge is my free will which operates in choosing to assent or deny or withhold judgment in matters which are not clear and distinct. Error is a sin of the mind which arises when I misuse my freedom and assent to propositions which are not

43

absolutely certain. I need not ever be deceived or believe falsely, if I would only learn the habit of refraining from non-coercive assenting. 'When I orient myself completely upon him, I discover in myself no cause of error or falsity. But when a little later, I think of myself, experience convinces me that I am nevertheless subject to innumerable errors' (p. 52).

The aetiology of false belief is a combination of a limited understanding and an unlimited free will. In understanding I entertain the idea of things, neither assenting, nor denying them. There is no error in the understanding, but it is limited. Because the understanding is limited to accepting or knowing only what impresses it as clear and distinct, there is needed another faculty to decide on all other matters. Herein dwells the will's power which, in some ways, is infinite. It cannot will not to believe what is clear and distinct, but it can invent or assent to an infinite number of propositions.

> Whence, then, do my errors arise? Only from the fact that the will is much more ample and far-reaching than the understanding so that I do not restrain it within the same limits but extend it even to those things which I do not understand. Being by nature indifferent about such matters, it very easily is turned aside from the true and the good and chooses the false and the evil. And thus it happens that I make mistakes and that I sin (*Meditations* IV p. 56).

While God could have created me without the ability to make false judgments, as he could have created me without the ability to sin in general, he must have known that it is better to be free and have the possibility for sin and error than not to be free. Ultimately, we must leave this matter to the inscrutable ways of God.

In the *Meditations* volitionalism is seen as the conclusion of an argument from God's goodness and our free will, viz., error must come from our free will for it would be intolerable to suppose that God is directly responsible for it. However, in the *Principles* the notion of doxastic responsibility is not seen as a product of inference but, rather, as a clear and distinct intuition. 'It is so evident that we are possessed of a free will that can give or withhold its assent, that this may be counted as one of the first and most ordinary notions that are found innately in us' (xxxix). Furthermore, since knowing states are phenomenologically distinct from belief states, we can always know when we know and when we are merely believing.

If this is an accurate interpretation of Descartes' thoughts on belief as a volitional exercise, involving an assent which is a direct result of our free wills, it must be the case that we never ought to *believe* anything. There are only two mental states open to the virtuous person: *knowledge* of whatever is coercively impressed on the mind in the way of clear and distinct ideas and *agnosticism* or doubt about all else, for even probability is of no use, for however probable a proposition may be which 'inclines me to a particular judgment, the mere recognition that they are only conjectures and not certain and indubitable reasons is enough to give me grounds for making the contrary judgment' (p. 57).

The reasoning seems strained. Surely, we want to say, there is a great difference between the inherent credibility of propositions, so that even though memory beliefs may not be clear and distinct they warrant greater acceptance than the testimony of a mad man or such baseless propositions as 'no other people besides me sleep' or 'Australia doesn't exist.' But on Descartes' logic these propositions are of equal credibility in spite of some inherent tendency of the former to 'incline us' to belief.

In letters written a few years later to Father Mesland and Princess Elizabeth of Sweden Descartes recognizes this problem and modifies his view, admitting that sometimes we are justified in believing falsely – though it is still a moral error.

> The moral error that occurs when we justifiably believe some thing false because a reputable man has said so, etc., involves no privation, so long as we use our assurance only as a guide to our actions in life, in a matter as regards which it is morally impossible to know better; thus properly speaking, it is not an error at all. But it would be an error if we were assured of it as we are of a truth of physics; for the testimony of a reputable man is then not sufficient (Letter to Father Mesland, May 2, 1644).[2]
>
> Although we cannot have demonstrative certainty about every thing, we must nevertheless take sides, and embrace, as regards all ordinary affairs, the opinion that seems most probable, in order never to be irresolute when it is a matter of action. For it is just our irresolution that causes us sorrow and remorse (Letter to Princess Elizabeth, September 15, 1645; A&G, p. 282).

45

These latter quotations seem to undermine Descartes' argument that false belief is a sin for which we are fully responsible and that it were better that we refrained from judgment where the judgment is not coercive. He could give that thought up, and with it his doxastic theodicy, without giving up his central idea of volitionalism, that belief is under the direct control of our wills. But, then, the argument for volitionalism in the *Meditations* fails, though his intuitive appeal in the *Principles* could still work.

But there is a problem with the intuitive approach. It is this: if all our beliefs are the result of acts of will in assenting to propositions, must we assent afresh each time we recall a proposition previously believed? Am I really free to give up my memory beliefs or the thought that the world is round? And what about dispositional beliefs? In the *Discourse on Method* (Part III, HR, p. 95) Descartes admits that we may be ignorant of our beliefs. But how could we be ignorant of a belief if it was a necessary condition that it be consciously assented to? Again, in the *Principles* he writes of the infusion of false beliefs in childhood when we were not fully aware of reason:

It is here that the first and principal of our errors is to be found. For in the first years of life the mind was so closely allied to body that it applied itself to nothing but those thoughts alone by which it was aware of the things which affected the body; nor were these as yet referred to anything existing outside itself, but the fact was merely that pain was felt when the body received some good, or else if the body was so slightly affected that no great good nor evil was experienced, such sensations were encountered as we call tastes, smells, sounds, heat, cold, light, colours, etc., which in truth represent nothing to us outside of our mind, but which vary in accordance with the diversities of the parts and modes in which the body is affected. . . . And as all other things were only considered in as far as they served for the use of the body in which it was immersed, the mind judged that there was more or less reality in each body, according as the impressions made on body were more or less strong. Hence came the belief that there was much more substance or corporeal reality in rocks or metals than in air or water, because the sensations of hardness and weight were much more strongly felt. . . . And we have in this way been imbued with a thousand other such prejudices from infancy, which in later youth we quite forgot we had accepted without sufficient examination, admitting them as though they were of perfect truth and certainty, and as if they had been known by means of our senses or implanted in us by nature (*Principles* lxxi).

It would seem that the tendency in children to assent prematurely is one aspect of original sin, passed down through generations.

However, there is one great exception to Descartes' mandate against assenting to non-coercive propositions. That is in the area of religious authority. With regard to the mysteries of the faith, e.g., the doctrines of the incarnation and the Trinity, we are to assent willingly even though our intellects do not understand, let alone know, the truth of these propositions.

Thus if God reveals to us or to others certain things concerning himself which surpass the range of our natural power of intelligence, such as the mysteries of the incarnation and the Trinity, we shall have no difficulty in believing them, although we may not clearly understand them. For we should not think it strange that in the immensity of his nature, as also in the objects of his creation, there are many things beyond the range of our comprehension (*Principles* xxv).

Descartes does not address the question of how we are to know that it is, indeed, God who has revealed these things, showing instead his own willingness to subordinate his philosophy to authority.

But, to return to our main concern, even if some beliefs do occur as we receive impressions or testimony from reliable authority which we are not free to doubt, Descartes could still be correct if he qualified his theory to state that we are *sometimes* free to choose to believe or doubt propositions. Just as the libertarian need not state that every act is a free choice, but only some, so likewise, the volitionalist only has to maintain that some beliefs are chosen freely. Perhaps, this is the best stance for the volitionalist to take, for it escapes some of the most severe problems noted above. We have some control over our belief acquisitions which is direct and which entails that we are morally responsible for many of the beliefs we have.

It was Benedict Spinoza (1632–1677) who first challenged Descartes' volitionalism. At the end of Part II of the *Ethics* he contends that the faculties of the will and the intellect which play such an important role in Descartes' work are fictions, that the will is not more extensive than the understanding, and that we are not free to believe whatever we wish (*Ethics* II, 48, 49). As E.M. Curley has shown, Spinoza's arguments are not clear, but they seem to proceed from a general assumption that is deterministic.[3] We are not free to believe what we will because we are not free to do anything in the libertarian sense of the term. The mind is determined to willing whatever it does by a cause which is itself caused by other causes, and so on *ad infinitum*. Curley shows that Spinoza views the will and the intellect as universals, related to particulars as 'stoneness' is to particular stones. In his system universals do not have real existence, hence these faculties are mere abstractions, convenient ways of speaking about particulars.

Spinoza further criticizes Descartes' contention that because the will is more extensive than the understanding, it can decide whether or not to suspend judgment. Spinoza points out that if understanding includes perception, the will is not more extensive than the understanding, for our immediate perceptions are infallible. Furthermore, while we may withhold judgment over given propositions, it is not by our will that this is done.

> When we say that anyone suspends his judgment, we merely mean that he sees, that he does not perceive the matter in question adequately. Suspension of judgment is, therefore, strictly speaking, a perception, and not free will. In order to illustrate the point, let us suppose a boy imagining a horse, and perceiving nothing else. Inasmuch as this imagination involves the existence of the horse, and the boy does not perceive anything which would exclude the existence of the horse, he will necessarily regard the horse as present: he will not be able to doubt of its existence, although he be not certain thereof. We have daily experience of such a state of things in dreams; and I do not suppose that there is anyone, who would maintain that, while he is dreaming, he has the free power of suspending his judgment concerning the things in his dream, and bringing it about that he should not dream those things, which he dreams that he sees; yet it happens, notwithstanding, that even in dreams we suspend our judgment, namely, when we dream that we are dreaming. . . . I deny, that a man does not, in the act of

perception, make any affirmation. For what is the perception of a winged horse, save affirming that a horse has wings? If the mind could perceive nothing else but the winged horse, it would regard the same as present to itself (*Ethics* II, 49, tr. Elwes, p. 124f).

I cannot suspend judgment on what I perceive, whether in reality or in imagination, unless I have some further reason for doubting. If the mind perceives the existence of horse, it necessarily affirms its existence and if it perceives that the perception is only within a dream, it necessarily denies the existence of the horse. Curley unpacks the logic implicit in Spinoza's argument thusly.

> Doubt is inherently a second-order activity. I cannot doubt whether *p* unless it already seems to me in some measure that *p*. I cannot 'suspend judgment' unless there is in some sense a judgment to suspend. But equally, I cannot doubt whether *p* unless I already have some existing tendency to believe *not-p*, unless it already seems to me in some measure that *p* is false. These conflicting tendencies are necessary conditions for doubt, and insofar as it is something mental, not the abstention from a public pronouncement – it is not an action I take as a consequence of finding the arguments pro and con are pretty evenly balanced. It is simply the state itself of finding them to be so ('Descartes, Spinoza, and the Ethics of Belief', p. 175).

Whether Spinoza's brief arguments adequately refute Descartes' direct volitionalism is a matter that must be left for the reader to decide. What is of interest for us is that Spinoza is the first self-consciously non-volitionalist in the history of Western philosophy, neatly juxtaposing his thought in opposition to Descartes' volitionalism in virtually every way. Together they seem to epitomize two virtually irreconcilable mind sets in philosophy: the strong libertarian who includes within the ambiance of freedom the freedom to assent and the determinist who denies freedom of the will in the strong sense of the term, let alone freedom to believe what we will. Of course, one can be a libertarian and deny doxastic volitionalism and one can be a determinist and admit that in a non-libertarian sense we can choose our beliefs. But there has been a natural tendency to link the two types of freedom and determinism.

CHAPTER VI

Pascal's Wager: A Case of Indirect Volitionalism

While most of our discussions have centered on direct volitionalism, the thesis that we can obtain beliefs directly upon willing to believe a proposition, the first mention of the indirect functions of the will is found in the miscellaneous writings of the contemporary of Descartes and Spinoza, Blaise Pascal (1623–1650). A brilliant mathematician and scientist, the discoverer of the probability calculus, Pascal applied his notion of probability to the matter of eternity and belief in God. In this argument he does a cost-benefit analysis, concluding that it is in our best interest to get ourselves to believe that God exists.

In an early entry in the *Pensees* Pascal makes his first reference in the history of philosophy to the will's indirect role in belief formation.

> The will is one of the chief factors in belief, not that it creates belief, but because things are true or false according to the aspect in which we look at them. The will, which prefers one aspect to another, turns away the mind from considering the qualities of all that it does not like to see; and thus the mind, moving in accord with the will, stops to consider the aspect which it likes, and so judges by what it sees (*Pensees*, p. 30, Entry #99).

Pascal is denying direct volitionalism, but stating that the way we look at the world will influence what we see. We only, or at least quite often, perceive what we are looking for, and we fail to see what we do not want to see. If we want to see the faults of the Church, they are there to be seen, and we will no doubt see them, but we will also in the process be prevented by our intentions from seeing its virtues.

Turning to his Wager argument, Pascal tells us that while we can never know God's essence, we have just enough evidence to whet our appetites for the chase, though not enough for any objective certainty. God is hidden, and we in our guilt and darkness see very dimly the possibility of his existence (#194). However, the realization that death stands over us as an infallible curse and the possibility of eternity, should concern us absolutely. 'Let us imagine a number of men in chains, and all condemned to death, where some are killed each day in the sight of others, and those who remain see their own fate in that of their fellows, and wait their turn, looking at each other sorrowfully and without hope' (#199). This is our state, which ought to drive everyone of us to feel discontent with his lot and to pursue the matter of immorality and the existence of God. Those who fail to perceive the seriousness of the situation are fools in the most profound sense of the term. Their carelessness over these matters 'astonishes and shocks me; it is to me monstrous' (#194). While we can not know whether there is an eternity or a God, we have practical reasons for getting to believe that they do. A cost-benefit analysis from self-interest dictates a course of action for us.

> 'God is, or He is not'. But to which side shall we incline?
> Reason can decide nothing here. There is an infinite chaos
> which separates us. A game is being played at the extremity of
> this infinite distance where heads or tails will turn up. What will
> you wager? (Entry # 233)

Reason would tell us that since there is insufficient evidence for either disjunct, we ought to withhold judgment. The rationalist claims that 'the true course is not to wager at all'. But he is mistaken.

> You must wager. It is not optional. You are embarked. Which
> will you choose then? Let us see. Since you must choose, let us
> see which interests you least. You have two things to lose, the
> true and the good; and two things to stake, your reason and
> your will, your knowledge and your happiness; and your nature
> has two things to shun, error and misery. Your reason is no
> more shocked in choosing one rather than the other, since you
> must of necessity choose. This is one point settled. But your
> happiness? Let us weigh the gain and the loss in wagering that
> God is. Let us estimate these two chances. If you gain, you gain

51

all; if you lose, you lose nothing. Wager, then, without hesitation that He is. . . . It is all divided; whether the infinite is and there is not an infinity of chances of loss against that of gain, there is no time to hesitate, you must give all. And thus, when one is forced to play, he must renounce reason to preserve his life, rather than risk it for infinite gain, [which is] as likely to happen as the loss of nothingness (Entry #233, p. 66f).

Note that the argument, the precursor to and pattern for William James's pragmatic argument in 'The Will to Believe', is leveled at those for whom the proposition that 'God exists' is a live option. Reason cannot decide since the evidence seems equal. But, for these people, the option is also forced. Not to choose is to choose against the possibility of infinite gain and in favor of infinite loss. The calculus of relative gains and losses goes something like this:

	God exists	*God does not exist*
I believe	(A) infinite gain with minimal finite loss	(B) overall finite loss in terms of sacrifice
I do not believe	(C) infinite loss with finite gain	(D) overall finite gain

There is some sacrifice of earthly pleasures involved in belief in God, but by multiplying the various combinations, we find that there is an incommensurability between A and C, on the one hand, and B and D on the other. For no matter how enormous the finite gain, the mere possibility of infinity will always be an infinitely greater quantity. So the only relevant combinations are A and C, and it turns out that A is infinitely to be preferred. Hence, the only rational decision is to believe that God exists. No other option makes sense.

But Pascal considers the person for whom the evidence is not so balanced, who finds it impossible to believe, and who complains that he is forced against his will to believe without being able to do so. 'My hands are tied and my mouth closed; I am forced to wager, and am not free. I am not released, and am so made that I cannot believe. What, then, would you have me do?' Pascal replies:

True. But at least learn your inability to believe, since reason brings you to this, and yet you cannot believe. Endeavor then to convince yourself, not by increase of proofs of God, but by the abatement of your passions. You would like to attain faith, and do not know the way; . . . Learn of those who have been bound like you, and who now stake all their possessions. These are people who know the way which you would follow, and who are cured of an ill of which you would be cured. Follow the way by which they began; by acting as if they believed, taking the holy water, having masses said, etc. Even this will naturally make you believe, and deaden your acuteness (ibid.).

Why not look at the evidence for God's existence? It is useless, because the arguments are not sufficient to convince the mind (either because they are inconclusive or because our passions prevent us from seeing their force). What we need is not more reason but a doctor and medicine to 'cure of an ill'. Holy water, masses, prayer and the warm embrace of the Church will put you in the proper frame of mind in order to bring about faith. It will come naturally. So, if you cannot get yourself to believe directly where the evidence is relevantly equal in your mind, get yourself into the proper context where faith is likely to be cultivated.

The Wager argument will be repeated with some changes by William James, but Pascal's version is logically purer. By playing the gambling game it will always turn out that it is rational to choose the option that has the possibility of infinite value – whether or not it is a live option (as James's version insists). If it's not a live option, get into the context or use whatever means necessary to make it one!

The main weakness of the Wager argument is that there is an infinite number of possible options which promise infinite reward for acceptance and infinite punishment for rejection. There are many religions whose credentials may be meagre but whose claims are possibly true. How do I choose between them? Could not someone come up with a Satanic religion which offered infinite bliss to anyone who worshipped the devil and acted devilishly?

Furthermore, note that Pascal makes belief that God exists the necessary and sufficient condition for eternal felicity. By this token the devils would be saved but not the noble atheist or moral agnostic. But not even orthodox Christianity, the religion that Pascal thought he was proclaiming, makes such a claim that propositional belief is sufficient for salvation. Theism is only a necessary, but not a sufficient condition for salvation in orthodox Christianity.

He nowhere considers the possibility of an ethics of belief that might set moral limits to our endeavors to get ourselves to believe what the evidence alone does not warrant.

Be that as it may, the interesting thing about Pascal for our purposes is that he is the first recorded instance of a strong indirect volitional position. Accepting the idea that a belief is not something that we can obtain simply by willing it, he offers a pragmatic argument for manipulating one's belief forming mechanisms through getting into a suitable context.

CHAPTER VII

The Empiricists' Notion of Belief: Locke and Hume

Locke on Belief

When we turn from Descartes' *Meditations* to Locke's *Essay Concerning Human Understanding*, we move from a tradition which is skeptical about empirical perceptions to one which sets it firmly within the bounds of knowledge. While both philosophers agree that clear and distinct ideas are the foundation of knowledge, they differ on the scope of what we can know. There is a difference, too, on the epistemological status of belief. For Descartes in his major writings there is no legitimate place at all for belief. Clear and distinct ideas (knowledge) are forced upon our noetic structure, but we are always free and obligated to withhold assent from any other propositions. For Locke belief according to probable evidence is acceptable and necessary. We are to proportion the degree with which we assent to a proposition to the objective probability of the proposition, all things considered. But it is just at this point of appreciating the need for rationality in believing that Locke runs into problems. On the one hand, he sees that belief has the same structure as knowledge, being irresistible; but, on the other hand, he wants to assert a normative aspect to belief. Obtaining a belief is an act that can be performed both when it ought and when it ought not to be performed. These two concerns lead him into certain apparent consistencies which have been pointed out by those who have written on the subject.[1]

Locke agrees with Descartes that we cannot choose to know or not to know what presents itself to us as clear and distinct. Intuitive truths, the basis of all other knowledge, are perceived by the mind at first sight by bare intuition. 'This part of knowledge is irresistible, and like bright sunshine, forces itself immediately to be perceived as soon as ever the mind turns its view that way; and leaves no hesitation, doubt, or examination, but the mind is presently filled with the clear light of it' (Bk IV2). Using the experience of sight as the paradigm of knowledge, Locke argues that knowledge is unintentional and event-like. 'What a man sees, he cannot but see; and what he perceives, he cannot but know that he perceives' (IV 13).

The only difference between belief (or 'assent', 'judgment', and 'opinion' which are all roughly synonymous for Locke) and knowledge is that analogous to the difference between sight in the bright noon sunlight and sight during twilight (IV 14.3). As we must live by probabilities in much of life, such judgments are entirely warranted.

Locke's definition of belief reflects this realization of the validity of being guided by probabilities. Believing is 'the admitting or receiving [of] any proposition for true, upon argument or proofs that are found to persuade us to receive it as true, without certain knowledge that it is so' (IV 15.3). It is a positive attitude toward a proposition in terms of accepting propositions at the end of a deliberative process. We may note in passing that this definition is narrow, leaving out as it does spontaneous belief acquisitions which are not the result of deliberative processes.

It is precisely here, in discussing the matter of believing on the grounds of probability and seeking to mark off a normative element, that Locke seems to introduce a volitional aspect into the picture. There is an ethics of believing, so that we ought to proportion the strength of our belief to the total available evidence.

> The mind, if it will proceed rationally, ought to examine all the grounds of probability, and see how they make more or less for or against any proposition, before it assents to or dissents from it; and upon a due balancing the whole, rejects or receives it with a more or less firm assent proportionably to the preponderancy of the greater grounds of probability on one side or the other (IV 15.5).

Again in chapter 19 in criticizing religious fanatics and 'enthusiasts', Locke speaks of our duty to regulate our beliefs. We have an obligation to seek the truth which the enthusiast violates. There is one unmistakable mark of the truth-seeker: that of not entertaining any proposition with greater assurance than the proofs it is built upon will warrant.

Whoever goes beyond this measure of assent, it is plain receives not truth in the love of it, loves not truth for truth's sake, but for some other bye-end. For the evidence that any proposition is true . . . lying only in the proofs a man has of it, whatsoever degrees of assent he affords it beyond the degrees of that evidence, it is plain all that surplusage of assurance is owing to some other affection, and not to the love of truth; it being impossible that the love of truth should carry my assent above the evidence there is to me . . . (IV 19.1).

The language of obligation implies that we can choose our beliefs. While some beliefs are thrust upon us and we have no choice, not every belief is like this. 'In propositions, where though proofs in view are of most moment, yet there are sufficient grounds to suspect that there is either fallacy in words, or certain proofs as considerable to be produced on the contrary side, there *assent, suspense, or dissent, are often voluntary actions*' (IV 20.15 italics mine).

Locke is addressing these words to the phenomenon of different people arriving at different conclusions given the same evidence. How is it that people can agree on the evidence and yet arrive at different beliefs? For there is nothing more common 'than contrariety of opinions; nothing more obvious than that one man wholly disbelieves what another only doubts of, and a third steadfastly believes and firmly adheres to' (IV 20.1). It does sound as though Locke believes that we can voluntarily believe or withhold belief in these cases, as such scholars as Curley, Kinnamann, and Passmore have been led to conclude.[2] However, on balance, I think that the fault is simply Locke's misleading rhetoric. In his zeal to promote rationality he rashly speaks as though doxastic states were directly in our power. When more guarded, he modifies this to mean, not that we can obtain beliefs directly upon willing to have them, but that our actions and desires can indirectly affect the process.

This point becomes clear at the very end of the book IV of *Concerning Human Understanding* (chs 12–16). Shortly after admitting that the passions can affect our minds in forming irrational beliefs, Locke turns to the typical way of forming beliefs. Where the evidence is clear and there is no strong evidence to the contrary 'a man who has weighed [the evidence] can scarce refuse his assent to the side on which the greater probability appears'. In less clear cases it is in a man's power to suspend his assent and perhaps favor what suits his inclination, and so 'stop from further search'. But this does not imply that we can acquire beliefs directly by willing to have them, but only that we may put off having a belief while in the process of obtaining one. We have a veto power over proposed propositions. This is made clear in chapter 16 where Locke writes:

> As knowledge is no more arbitrary than perception, so, I think, assent is no more in our power than knowledge. When the agreement of any two ideas appears to our minds, whether immediately or by the assistance of reason, I can no more refuse to perceive, no more avoid knowing it, than I can avoid seeing those objects which I turn my eyes to, and look on daylight; and what, upon full examination, I find most probable, I cannot deny my assent to. But though we cannot hinder our knowledge where the agreement is once perceived; nor our assent, where the probability manifestly appears upon due consideration of all the measures of it; yet *we can hinder both knowledge and assent by stopping our enquiry* and not employing our faculties in the search of any truth.

If this passage is accorded the weight that Locke seems to give it, it should serve as a qualifier to his looser talk regarding the ethics of belief. What distinguishes the truth-seeker from the less serious person is not that the truth-seeker voluntarily chooses to assent to a proposition because there is evidence in favor of the proposition and the enthusiast does not. Rather, what separates the two is that the former loves the truth so much that he is willing to pursue the inquiry to its end whereas the latter does not. It is the intention to pursue the truth, not a direct intention to believe a particular proposition that makes the difference.

We may conclude, then, that while there is some apparent inconsistency in Locke's treatment of the matter, especially in conjunction with his theory of an ethics of belief, in the end, he recognizes the similarity in the structure of knowing and believing. While the former has a distinctness and certainty attached to it that the latter does not, both are representational in character, having to do with evidence impressing itself upon us. Neither is a volitional activity directly, though both are indirectly.[3]

Locke applies his notion of involuntary belief formation to the socio-political issue of tolerance. In his *Letter of Toleration* he argues that we have no right to punish or persecute people for their beliefs, since people are not directly responsible for their beliefs because believing is not within the scope of our will. Where we are not free to do otherwise, blame is inappropriate and punishment becomes unjust.

Finally, we must say a word about Locke's belief in the reasonableness of theism. Locke believes that it is entirely reasonable to believe the truth of Christianity based on his notion of probability and proportioning our belief to 'preponderancy of the greater grounds of probability on one side or the other'. But, contra Locke, it is doubtful whether the notion of objective probability applies here, for one would have to take into consideration the total evidence of the universe in order to fix a probability index for the existence of God.[4]

Typically, in probability calculus we have a fixed number of data, which we judge within closed parameters. The standard example is the vase with 100 marbles in it: 10 white and 90 non-white. The probability of the statement 'the next ball will be white' being true is 1/10. If we had 100 worlds and 60 of them were created by a God, we could apply a probability calculus to the situation and believe that there was a 60% chance that this world was created by God. But, as Peirce notes, universes are not as plentiful as blackberries.[5]

Hume's Theory of Belief

Hume is the first philosopher to take the concept of belief seriously in its own right, to recognize the difficulty inherent in analyzing it, and to offer a detailed description of it. It is significant that his section on belief in his *Treatise of Human Nature* (henceforth 'T') was the only one of which he expressed serious dissatisfaction and attempted to amend in the 'Appendix' to that work.[6] Yet, in the end, he has to admit that he has not altogether succeeded in articulating what others before him had not even noticed to be a problem.

> This operation of the mind, which forms the belief of any
> matter of fact, seems hitherto to have been one of the greatest
> mysteries of philosophy: tho' no one has so much as suspected
> it, that there was any difficulty in explaining it. For my part I
> must own, that I find a considerable difficulty in the case; and

> that even when I think I understand the subject perfectly, I am
> at a loss for terms to express my meaning. . . . I confess, that
> 'tis impossible to explain perfectly this feeling or manner of
> conception (T p. 628).

The concept is of special importance for Hume because it re-
places the state of knowledge as the central epistemological state in
human experience. In Part IV Section I of the *Treatise* Hume shows
that if we were strictly rational creatures we would doubt every
proposition by subjecting it to infinite scrutiny. But while such
pyrrhonic skepticism is theoretically possible, it is practically
impossible. 'Nature will always maintain her rights, and prevail in
the end over any abstract reasoning whatsoever' (*Enquiry* p. 41).
There is no danger that the valid arguments for skepticism will
overthrow the experience of believing.

Whereas those before him, Plato, Aquinas, Descartes and
Locke, had seen belief mainly in terms of its inferior status to
knowledge and had concentrated on deliberative beliefs, Hume
focuses for the first time on the psychology of believing, showing
that it is more like a sensation than a cogitation. We are believing
animals who from childhood are inclined to believe whatever
testimony reports. We have 'a remarkable propensity to believe
whatever is reported . . . however contrary to daily experience and
observation' (T p.113).

What, he asks, is believing and 'wherein consists the difference
betwixt believing and disbelieving any proposition'? Believing is
either wholly possessing ideas or it is essentially a feeling. But if it
were simply a combination of ideas, we could obtain beliefs at will
simply by adding the idea of existence to our other ideas (e.g., we
could come to believe that God exists simply by adding the idea of
existence to the idea of God). Ideas are subject to the imagination
and there is nothing so free as the imagination. But it is obvious that
we cannot produce beliefs simply by willing to have them. Hence,
believing is not simply possessing ideas. So, it must be a feeling (T
pp. 94, 123f).

'Wherein consists the difference betwixt incredulity and belief?'
It must lie not in the content of what is believed but in the manner
of apprehension. It is obvious, according to Hume, that the only
thing which distinguishes believing from incredulity or not believing is an additional force and vivacity attached to the idea. 'An

opinion, therefore, or belief may be most accurately defin'd, A LIVELY IDEA RELATED TO OR ASSOCIATED WITH A PRESENT IMPRESSION' (T p. 96).

He defends this view by appealing to our common experience in reading fiction. Two people read the same work, but one takes it as history and the other as a romance. They will read it differently. The former will have a lively conception of all the incidents. 'He enters deeper into the concerns of the persons: represents to himself their actions, and characters, and friendships, and enmities; He even goes so far as to form a notion of their features, and air, and person', while the other gives 'no credit to the testimony of the author, has a more faint and languid conception of all these particulars' (T p. 97f). The illustration probably says more about Hume's own bias towards history and against literature than it does about our common experience in believing.

Hume recognizes the unsatisfactoriness of his definition and struggles to amend it in the 'Appendix'.

> Belief is nothing but an idea, that is different from a fiction, not in the nature, or the order of its parts, but in the *manner* of its being conceiv'd. But when I wou'd explain this *manner*, I scarce find any word that fully answers the case, but am oblig'd to have recourse to every one's feeling, in order to give him a perfect notion of this operation of the mind. An idea assented to *feels* different from a fictitious idea, that the fancy alone presents to us: And this different feeling I endeavor to explain by calling it a superior *force*, or *vivacity*, or *solidity*, or *firmness* or *steadiness*. This variety of terms, which may seem so unphilosophical, is intended only to express that act of the mind, which renders realities more present to us than fictions, causes them to weigh more in the thought, and gives them a superior influence on the passions and imaginations. Provided we agree about the thing, 'tis needless to dispute about the terms (T p. 629).

This statement is significant, for it actually alters the definition of belief from being a mere feeling of vivacity into one involving dispositions and actions. A belief gives ideas more force and influence; 'makes them appear of greater importance; infixes them in the mind; and renders them the governing principles of all our actions'. Hume does not develop this insight, so that for the most part he is wedded to an occurrentist model. All believing is a conscious occurrence.

How are beliefs caused? How do they arise in the mind? Not primarily by reasoning, but by experience of constant conjunction of objects. If a person of the strongest rationality were brought suddenly into the world, he would not, at first, by any reasoning, be able to reach the idea of cause and effect; 'since the particular powers, by which all natural operations are performed, never appear to the senses; nor is it reasonable to conclude, merely because one event, in one instance, precedes another, that therefore the one is the cause, the other the effect' (E p. 42).

The power in the mind which forces conclusions upon us is *custom* or *habit* which operates through the experience of constant conjunction of two objects (e.g., heat and flame, snow and cold, weight and solidity). We are determined by custom alone to expect the one from the appearance of the other.

> All belief of matter of fact or real existence is derived merely from some object, present to the memory or senses, and a customary conjunction between that and some other object. . . . This belief is the necessary result of placing the mind in such circumstances. It is an operation of the soul, when we are so situated, as unavoidable as to feel the passion of love, when we receive benefits; or hatred, when we meet with injuries. All these operations are a species of natural instincts, which no reasoning or process of the thought and understanding is able either to produce or to prevent (E p. 46f).

What actually happens in an act of believing is that the observed constant conjunction of events creates a 'union in the imagination' between two types of things, whereby the principle of transmission of vivacity and force causes the one to partake of the present force of the other. 'I wou'd willingly establish it as a general maxim in the science of human nature, *that when any impression becomes present to us, it not only transports the mind to such ideas as are related to it, but likewise communicates to them a share of its force and vivacity*' (T p. 98).

We may sum up Hume's essential theory on belief with four propositions:

1 Beliefs are not simply ideas in the mind, for then we could

produce beliefs at will simply by manipulating our imagination directly, adding the idea of existence to another idea and so producing a belief, which is impossible.

2 Beliefs are sentiments in the mind, depicted by vivacity and forcefulness attached to ideas and thus separating them from what we regard as fiction. Like other feelings (e.g., gratitude, anger, and pleasure) they are unbidden, spontaneous, and indefinable, but we all understand them upon reflection.

3 Beliefs are caused by experiencing things in constant conjunction, whereby the feeling of vivacity and force of one becomes transmitted onto the other.

4 Beliefs, as spontaneous occurrences of vivid ideas in the mind, are passive occurrences, completely involuntary, beyond the pale of the will to effect. It makes no more sense to say that I choose to believe that p than to say I choose to feel anger or pain when someone punches me in the gut.

Hume has been rightly criticized by Price, Stroud, Passmore and others for having given us too narrow a conception of belief. Force and vivacity are neither necessary nor sufficient conditions for belief. We can believe without having occurrent feelings at all (as with dispositional beliefs), let alone vivid and forceful impressions. And we can have vivid and forceful feelings attached to ideas without believing them, as when we read a good novel or entertain a future possibility that would greatly alter our lives for good or ill. Nonetheless, Hume's is the first one to offer a psychology of belief and argue for the thesis that believing must be nonvolitional.

Finally, we must say a word about Hume's view of rational believing and the ethics of belief as it appears in his discussion of miracles in the *Enquiry*. Like Aquinas and Locke before him, Hume is a classical foundationalist, someone who believes that for a belief to be justified, it must be founded on a belief that is either empirical, present to memory or self-evident. 'If I ask you why you believe any particular matter of fact, which you related, you must tell me some reason; and this reason will be some other fact, connected with it. But as you cannot proceed after this manner, *in infinitum*, you must at last terminate in some fact, which is present to your memory or senses; or must allow that your belief is entirely without foundation' (E p. 48). In this regard Hume says that the 'wise man proportions his belief to the evidence' (E p. 110). While there is a spontaneous tendency to believe what testimony reports, the prudent person will suspend judgment and weigh the evidence. 'I weigh the one miracle against the other; and according to the superiority, which I discover, I pronounce my decision, and always reject the greater miracle' (E p. 116). As Passmore points out, this is Lockeian in tone. There are two sets of probabilities (pro and con) related to the possibility that a miracle has occurred. I weigh one against the other, discover that one is superior and then I 'pronounce my decision'.[7] It seems that Hume is implying that the will can enter into the believing process after all!

Note, however, while Hume has slipped into volitional language, unlike Locke Hume does not use 'ought' statements in conjunction with belief, nor does he have an ethics of belief. What he does have is counsels of prudence in belief-formation. We are told to apply rigorous checking monitors to our beliefs and proportion our beliefs to the evidence. But these mandates are hypothetical, not categorical. It is not the moral man who is to do these things, but the *wise* man (E p. 110f). He considers the evidence, weighs the opposite evidence in the balance and fixes his judgment to fit the sum of his weighings, the *probability*. Hume could make his counsels of prudence consistent with his nonvolitional account of believing by rephrasing his statements into counsels for prudent evidence-gathering, rather than believing. Likewise, Hume could be read to mean by 'decision' simply the sense of willingness which often accompanies a successful process, a believing willingly rather than a willful belief.

CHAPTER VIII

Kant and Kierkegaard on the Nature and Place of Faith

Kant's Concept of Faith

In Immanuel Kant (1724–1804) we have an interesting compromise of faith with reason. In his *magnum opus, The Critique of Pure Reason* (1781, henceforth 'K') Kant is, for the most part, concerned with knowledge and not believing. The distinction is between *philosophy*, which seeks apodictic certainty, and *philodoxy*, the area of belief, and Kant endeavors to drive a sharp wedge between the two. Here he seems to disparage anything less than knowledge as unworthy of a philosopher's serious attention. His overly simplistic schema is: where we have neither subjective nor objective sufficiency we have opinion; where we have subjective sufficiency but objective insufficiency we have belief; and where we have both subjective and objective sufficiency we have knowledge (K p. 645f). The notion of 'sufficiency', which is notoriously problematic is never explained.

Towards the end of this 'first critique' and more completely in the second critique, *The Critique of Practical Reason* (1783, henceforth 'CPR') Kant argues that while the traditional proofs for God's existence fail to give us knowledge of his existence, there still remains the distinct possibility that he exists. He sees himself as having denied reason in order to make place for faith. While theoretical reason neither proves nor disproves the existence of a Supreme Being, practical reason demands the postulate of such a being. Since all reasoning, including theoretical reasoning, is ultimately practical, we must pay close attention to the arguments that point towards a God. While Kant tries to steer clear of subjectivism (that reality ought to be as we desire it), his position seems a not-too-distant relative to that. The bottom line is that the postulate of God is necessary for having a united and coherent view of the world and for having a coherent view of morality. Kant tries to show that belief in God is necessary both for a coherent view of the universe and for a coherent view of morality. Stephen Evans sums up Kant's position this way:

> Kant's practical approach to theism represents a systematic, unified argument. From the standpoint of theoretical reason, he has argued that, though knowledge of God's existence or non-existence is both impossible and undesirable, the idea of God is a concept the reality of which reason must necessarily consider a possibility. The idea of a necessary being as the Supreme Condition of the world's existence is certainly a believable and cogent metaphysical interpretation of reality, even if it cannot be scientifically verified or logically demonstrated. It is a concept in which man has a rational interest. From the standpoint of practical reason, Kant has argued that the concept of God as a Moral Person is a postulate of rational, moral action. Here the rational interest which man has in God's existence takes the form of a necessary belief (C. Stephen Evans, *Subjectivity and Religious Belief*, p. 73).

In *Critique of Practical Reason* two arguments for religious belief are put forward. The first is his practical proof for the existence of God based on the reality of the moral law. The second is his proof for the immortality of rational beings based on our duty to become perfect moral beings.

Nothing is intrinsically good except virtue, doing one's duty without any ulterior motive. Everyone can always act virtuously and do his duty whether God exists or not. But, although virtue is the only intrinsic good, and the supreme good (*bonum supremum*), it is not the complete good (*bonum consummatum*). The complete good is composed of virtue accompanied by the exact measure of happiness that corresponds to the quality of the virtue in question. In this life we often see that virtue goes unrewarded and vice is rewarded. This ought not to be, but it ought to be the case that virtue, though disinterested, is, nevertheless, rewarded by happiness. But if morality has a legitimate basis, it must be the case that virtue and happiness are correlative states. There is nothing we are more sure of, on reflection, than the moral law, that we have duties and that goodness is the highest achievement of rational beings. So, since morality entails a correspondence between virtue and happiness, virtue and happiness must necessarily become correlated. But the only way it is conceivable that goodness could be rewarded with happiness is if a supremely powerful, benevolent, just Being intervenes into the scheme of things and causes the just resolution of the situation (CPR p. 128ff).

Similarly, Kant argues for immortality. The only supremely good thing is the good will. People may act from duty, and hence may manifest moral goodness, in a world where evil often prevails. But it is our duty to seek for the perfect good (*bonum consummatum*). The individual may help bring this about by striving to obey the categorical imperative, the moral law. But in order to do this perfectly, one needs to root out all inclinations to disobey the moral law, thus achieving a holy will. It is not possible in this life to reach such a state of perfection, but since it is our duty to reach this state, there must be another life, infinitely long, in which to strive and reach moral perfection. So, since we cannot doubt the reality of the moral law, we can reasonably believe in life after death (CPR pp. 126–8).

Belief in God, freedom of the will and immortality are necessary postulates of pure practical reason. Given the absoluteness and inner certainty of the moral law (almost a god within), the will is free to affirm these ideals.

> Granted that pure moral law inexorably binds every man as a command (not as a rule of prudence), the righteous man may say: I will that there be a God, that my existence in this world be also an existence in a pure world of the understanding outside the system of natural connections, and finally that my duration be endless. I stand by this and will not give up this belief, for this is the only case where my interest inevitably determines my judgment because I will not yield anything of this interest (CPR p. 149).

This is Kant's notion of rational faith. These beliefs cannot be proved speculatively, nor can it be commanded. In fact, contrary to what he seems to imply in calling these propositions 'necessary postulates of practical reason', we don't have a duty to believe them. It is a 'voluntary decision of our judgment to assume' the existence of God and 'to make it the foundation of further employment of reason, conducing to the moral (commanded) purpose and agreeing moreover with the theoretical need of reason, it is itself not commanded. It rather springs from the moral disposition itself. It can therefore often waver even if well disposed but can never fall into unbelief' (p. 151). Kant does not elaborate on the nature of this 'voluntary decision', but it seems that he supposes that belief is sometimes within our control, perhaps in those cases where the proposition in question is plausible but not compelling.

On the other hand, the motive for such volitional believing must be moral, not prudential. In *Religion within the Limits of Reason Alone* (henceforth 'R') Kant heaps contemptuous scorn upon those who follow Pascalian advice and believe out of expediency. 'The hypocrite regards as a mere nothing the danger arising from the dishonesty of his profession, the violation of conscience, involved in proclaiming even before God that something is certain, when he is aware that, its nature being what it is, it cannot be asserted with unconditional assurance' (p. 177).

However, the most important thing about Kant's notion of faith is that he subsumes it under two other categories: the category of hope, addressing the question 'What can be hope?' (for God, cosmic justice, and immortality) and, ultimately, the category of ethics. Ultimately, religious faith is transformed into a hopeful or optimistic ethics in what James Collins calls Kant's 'moral redaction of ethics'.[1]

While Kant was not the first one to develop an ethics of belief and apply it to religious belief (we have already seen this in Locke and a notion of doxastic prudence in Hume), he is the first philosopher (with the possible exception of the Stoics) to make a religion of ethics, to make moral conduct the alpha and omega of religion. Cured of ritual, revelation, encumbering dogma, and biblicism (which he demythologized), religion is finally reduced to morality, and the joys and passionate piety of his parents' faith is transplanted without loss into the domain of ethical consciousness. Although never ceasing to profess theism, God is largely seen, ex machina, as the judge necessary to enforce the moral law. While Kant calls God the great law-giver, the title is largely honorific, for within the structure of eternal reason itself is the adequacy of the moral law. Each autonomous being is, himself, a moral lawgiver. While God alone is morally perfect, the reality of moral goodness is logically separate from God. Even the holy one of Israel, the Son of God, must be judged by its norm.

Kant's treatment of morality is tantamount to the worship of God. The picture one gets is reminiscent of Plato's Good (read 'the Moral Law') which is Supreme. The God of theism resembles the Demiurge of the *Timaeus*, and is that which creates the world and carries out the enforcement of the Moral Law. True worship is directed to the Moral Law which even God must obey. To morality he writes such panegyrics as:

> O sincerity! Thou Astrae, that has fled from earth to heaven, how mayst thou (the basis of conscience, and hence of all inner religion) be drawn to us again?
> (R, p. 177).
> Duty, thou sublime and mighty name, that thou does embrace nothing charming or insinuating but requirest submission and yet seekest not to move the will by threatening . . . but only holdest forth a law which of itself finds entrance into the mind and gains reluctant reverence . . . what origin is worthy of thee?
> (CPR p. 193)

There is an immanentism in his later works that seems to identify God with the Moral Law itself. 'God is thus no substance discoverable outside of me but merely a moral relation within me.' He is a presence 'closer to us than breathing and nearer than hands and feet'.[2] The lawgiver is God who gives a law that is determined by reason, known to us in the categorical imperative. Each of us knows the law in his own conscience and is, in a sense, himself a lawgiver. 'The kingdom of God is within us! The conscience of moral freedom is the feeling of the presence of the Godhead in man.'[3] And finally:

> There is a God, for there is a Categorical Imperative of Duty, before which all knees do bow whether they be in heaven or in the earth or under the earth; and whose name is holy, without our having to suppose a substance which represents this Being to the senses (*Opus Postumum*, p. 820, quoted in Clement Webb, *Kant's Philosophy of Religion*, p. 197).

Kant's arguments from practical reason have been attacked from his own day (namely by Thomas Wizenman in 1787) until our own (especially by C.D. Broad, *Five Ethical Theories*), but he has had his defenders too. Recently, Allen Wood and Stephen Evans[4] have argued Kant was correct in arguing that human need for the kind of things that religion offers may be taken as decisive in justifying faith when the case for religion is plausible.

Kierkegaard on Faith

Sören Kierkegaard (1813–1855) is a watershed for our understanding of faith/belief in relation to religion. The father of existentialism and the grandfather of neo-orthodox theology, few have written as self-consciously of faith or have valued it as highly as he. Standing in the Kantian tradition, he continues where Kant leaves off. For, essentially, Kant's contribution to epistemology centers on his Copernican revolution of the structures of knowledge, not the nature of belief. Kierkegaard accepts the Kantian move, especially against Hegel, and proceeds to make faith, not knowledge, the highest attainment of the human subject. Faith, in its most salient form, is the highest attainment of the human subject. We cannot *know*, in any objective sense of that word, that God exists, that we are immortal and free, but belief in these postulates is necessary for the fulfillment of human personality. These truths edify, and, as such, the heart has need of them. As his pseudonym, Victor Erimita, puts it,

> Do not check your soul's flight, do not grieve the better promptings within you, do not dull your spirit with half wishes and half thoughts. Ask yourself, and continue to ask until you find the answer. For one may have known a thing many times and acknowledged it, one may have willed a thing many times and attempted it; and yet it is only by the deep inward movement, only by the indescribable emotions of the heart, that for the first time you are convinced that what you have known belongs to you, that no power can take it from you; for only the truth which edifies is truth for you (*Either/Or* II,
> p. 356)

But if Kierkegaard begins in the Kantian tradition, he goes much further, leaving Kant somewhere in the background. A 'religion within the limits of reason alone' is something Kierkegaard delimits to a lower stage of personal development. In seeing that religion goes beyond Kantian practical reason Kierkegaard seems strikingly Humean. Though the empiricism of Hume is about as far away from the Christian existentialism of Kierkegaard as one can imagine, there are fascinating points of convergence which make the comparison appropriate, indeed. First of all, Kierkegaard and Hume are in precise agreement on the relation of reason to the passions, and it could be said by either of them that 'reason is and ought to be nothing but a slave of the passions and must not pretend to any other office'. Both see in rationality an implicit self-deception and rationalization. Both agree that miracles and faith are irrational but necessary for Christian faith. Most interesting of all, the famous, ironic conclusion to Hume's essay on 'Miracles' (*Enquiry* Section X), which states that no one can believe in the paradoxical propositions of Christianity without a miracle to subvert one's reason, was read by the young Kierkegaard in a work of the Christian humorist, Hamann. Taking it to be a celebration of the radicality of faith in Hamann, Kierkegaard espoused it as a deep insight into the exact nature of faith. There is reason to suppose that the passage is pivotal in the development of Kierkegaard's notion of faith, and if so, there is an ironic connection between the two philosophers that has hitherto gone unnoticed.

No one writes more passionately about faith, nor values it more highly. Whereas, his predecessors have largely viewed faith as a necessary evil, a distant second to knowledge, Kierkegaard reverses the order. Knowledge about metaphysical issues is evil for us, because it prevents the most important virtue from developing. For him faith is the highest virtue precisely because it is objectively uncertain, for personal growth into selfhood depends on uncertainty, risk, venturing forth over 700,000 fathoms of ocean water. Faith is the lover's loyalty to the beloved when all the evidence is against her. Faith is the soul's deepest yearnings and hopes, which the rational part of us cannot fathom. Even if we had direct proofs for theism or Christianity, we would not want them; for they would take the venture out of the religious experience, without which the experience would be bland, indeed.[5]

Actually, Kierkegaard has, at least, seven different notions of faith/belief. They range from aesthetic faith through ethical commitment to religious faith and Christian religious faith, and they include 'opinion', belief as an organ of apprehension of the past, and faith as hope. There is no clear conceptual analysis of these terms, and the Danish word (*Tro*) for 'faith/belief' is similar to the English terms 'faith' and 'belief', including both the propositional aspect of 'belief' and the trustful emphasis of 'faith'. As with English there is only one verb for the concept, the Danish *'troer'*. Hence, there is a natural tendency to conflate and intermingle the various meanings of the word, and this we find in the father of existentialism.

Two aspects of Kierkegaard's thought should be introduced in order to help us understand his thoughts on belief. First, he thought that concepts were quasi-living or dynamic entities, God-given, which were multi-faceted, having a life of their own, as it were, and changing their meaning depending on their context. For our purposes, this means that the experience of faith changes as we develop into mature self-hood. The concept becomes transformed and means something different, though related, as we move from one stage of spiritual/psychological development to another.

This development of the self through the stages of life is the second aspect of Kierkegaard's thought which we need to understand. Each person is on a pilgrimage from innocence and immediacy in the naive egoism of the aesthetic (read 'sensual') stage through the ethical stage of personal commitment to others and the moral law to the religious stage, 'religiousness A' (the focus of existentialism), where the individual becomes fully autonomous and self-aware. If grace is afforded there is the possibility of reaching the Christian religious stage, religiousness B, where one believes in the paradox of the incarnation and lives in radical discipleship.

Faith changes its complexion throughout this development. In the aesthetic stage it is a seed, manifesting itself as animal intuition and a naive primitive trust. It has no opposite in reason, for the aesthete is not yet rational. In the ethical stage faith manifests itself as commitment to reason and the moral order which is the function or manifestation of reason in society. Ethical faith is a faith in reason to harmonize conflicts of interests and produce the social good. In religiousness A faith manifests itself as risk and venture in attaining the highest possibilities for selfhood. Like aesthetic faith it is intuitive and immediate, but it is so after reflection, as a 'second-immediacy'.

Finally, in the Christian religious stage the self believes by virtue of the absurd. In the words of Hume, the believer becomes 'conscious of a continued miracle in his own person, which subverts all the principles of his understanding, and gives him a determination to believe what is most contrary to custom and experience'. 'Faith is the objective uncertainty due to the repulsion of the absurd held fast by the passion of inwardness, which in this instance is intensified to the utmost degree' (*Concluding Unscientific Postscript*, p. 540). Grace is need to enable the individual to believe what is otherwise preposterous, but once grace is given, one is free to reject or accept the proposition. The will, which is involved in all non-contradictory types of belief-acquisition, is not able to believe what is fundamentally absurd. Grace is the miracle which enables us to 'subvert all the principles of our understanding' and allows us to believe what seems to others as an impossible proposition (viz., the paradox that Christ is both fully God and fully man).[6]

We need not spend much time with the fifth version of belief, opinion (*Mening*), for Kierkegaard is not interested in it and dismisses it as unimportant for his purposes. Opinion is probabilistic, commonsensical, the sort of psychological state necessary to get us to take our umbrella with us to work or take in less calories in our diet.

The sixth type of belief is 'the organ for apprehending history', which makes the past present to consciousness, involves the imagination and will in an act of recreation of the past (cf. 'Interlude' of the *Fragments*). In believing what happened in the past the will is active in recreating the scene or proposition. It takes testimony and reworks it, transforming the 'what' of the past into an active 'how' of the present, making the history contemporary. In this way belief is volitional. 'Belief in not so much a conclusion as a resolution. . . . Belief is not a form of knowledge but a free act, an expression of the will' (*Fragments* p.102f). The idea is that the imagination (of which nothing human is more free) takes over in belief attainment.

This is as radical a volitionalism as Descartes'. We are free to believe whatever we please and are responsible for all our beliefs. Believing is a fully autonomous act. It seems that Kierkegaard, who sought to work out a distinctively Christian epistemology, thought that this view was present in the *New Testament*, particularly in Paul's 'Epistle to the Romans', where he writes 'Whatsoever is not of faith is sin.' Paul seems to be talking about eating meat that was sacrificed to idols with a clear conscience, but Kierkegaard interprets this verse as having wider applicability. 'Belief (*Tro*), surely, implies an act of the will, and moreover not in the same sense as when I say, for instance, that all apprehension implies an act of will; how can I otherwise explain the saying in the New Testament that whatsoever is not of faith is sin (Romans 14:23)?' (*Papers* I A 36).

The final use of the concept of belief/faith in Kierkegaard is one found only late in his writings, mostly in his private papers. It sees faith, not as propositional belief, but as *hope*. Entirely consonant with the classic Christian text, Hebrews 11:1 ('Faith is the substance of things hoped for, the evidence of things not seen'), Kierkegaard speaks of the risk of faith which causes one to venture forth in spite of uncertainty. 'Without risk faith is impossible. To be related to spirit means to undergo a test, to believe, to wish to believe, to change one's life into a trial' (*Papers* X 2 A 408).

The aspect of possibility which is part of the concept of hope, over against belief (where *probability* is more important), is a defining feature of his concept of faith as hope: 'Faith is essentially holding fast to possibility' (*Papers* IX A 311). One comes to faith only when all other hopes fail.

> And now that in many ways I have been brought to the last extremity, now . . . a hope has awakened in my soul that God may desire to resolve the fundamental misery of my being. That is, now I am in faith in the profoundest sense. . . . I must never at any moment presume to say that there is no way out for God because I cannot see any (*Papers* VIII A 650, my translation).

The text seems to suggest that hoping is faith in its 'profoundest sense'.

In these later entries hope comes to replace the radical anti-rational believing that characterizes the pseudonymous (Johannes Climacus) works as the dominant concept in the Christian experience. Having faith is an 'infinite self-made care as to whether one has faith' (*Papers* IX A 32). It is living-as-if Christianity were true. The volitional quality is transferred from belief to active risking in hope, and one is allowed to maintain a tension between belief and doubt while planning one's life on the basis of a precious possibility.

Kierkegaard never developed his concepts in detail, but the twist and turns he gives to the notions of faith/belief are original and, often, insightful. Elsewhere, I have criticized the anti-rational element in some parts of his concept.[7] He seems to have too narrow a notion of reason, not realizing that intuition and testimony are forms of evidence which may be taken into the picture when assessing the merits of a proposition. We shall return to the volitional aspects of Kierkegaard's thought in the second part of this work.

CHAPTER IX

Clifford and James on the Ethics of Belief

Modern philosophy was founded on the doctrine, uncompromisingly formulated by Descartes, that to think philosophically is to accept as true only that which recommends itself to Reason. To be unphilosophical, in contrast, is to be seduced by the enticements of Will, which beckons men beyond the boundaries laid down by Reason into the wilderness of error. In England, Locke had acclimatised this Cartesian ideal. There is 'one unerring mark', he wrote, 'by which a man may know whether he is a lover of truth for truth's sake': namely, *'the not entertaining any proposition with greater assurance than the proofs it is built upon will warrant'* (J.A. Passmore, *A Hundred Years of Philosophy*, p. 95).

Perhaps no writings exhibit a faith in enlightenment rationality more than those of W.K. Clifford (1845–1879). Clifford believed that an analysis of the foundations of mathematics and science would lead to methodological principles which would enable us to arrive at a definitive body of knowledge and justifed, inductive beliefs. In his work 'The Ethics of Belief' (1877) Clifford sets forth his scientific foundations for rational believing, a normative account of how we are to go about arriving at a rational system. A concern for a normative relation between belief and evidence already existed in Locke and Hume, as we have seen, although for Hume, the 'ought' in the relation is mainly a prudential one. Clifford carries out the Lockean program with a vengeance, making the ethics of belief the touchstone of the civilized and upright citizen. There is a single rule to govern our doxastic states: 'it is wrong always, everywhere, and for anyone, to believe anything on insufficient evidence'.

75

Clifford begins his discussion with an example of a shipowner who sends to sea an emigrant ship. He knows that the ship is old and not well built, but he fails to have the ship inspected. Dismissing from his mind all doubts and suspicions of the unseaworthiness of the vessel, he trusts in Providence to care for the ship. He acquires a sincere and comfortable conviction in this way and collects his insurance money without a trace of guilt after the ship sinks, killing all passengers.

Clifford comments that although the shipowner sincerely believed that all was well with the ship, his sincerity in no way exculpates him because '*he had no right to believe on such evidence as was before him*'. One has an obligation to get oneself into a position where one will only believe propositions on sufficient evidence. Our beliefs are of the first importance because they are action guiding. Given our desires, we will try to reach our goals by the means specified by our beliefs. Because the shipowner held an unwarranted belief, he did not carry out the proper safety checks.

> It is not possible so to sever the belief from the action it suggests as to condemn the one without condemning the other. No man holding a strong belief on one side of a question, or even wishing to hold a belief on one side, can investigate it with such fairness and completeness as if he were really in doubt and unbiased; so that the existence of a belief not founded on fair inquiry unfits a man for the performance of this necessary duty (p. 41).

Because we can never know when a belief within our noetic structure may be called forth to affect our actions, we must guard the purity of our doxastic repertoire.

Furthermore, our beliefs are not private, but public, matters. The beliefs that we have eventually get communicated to the rest of society. They are its common property, 'fashioned and perfected from age to age; an heirloom which every succeeding generation inherits as a precious deposit and a sacred trust to be handed on to the next one. . . . Into this, for good or ill, is woven every belief of every man who has speech of his fellows. An awful privilege, and an awful responsibility, that we should help to create the world in which posterity will live' (p. 42). So we have a duty to guard ourselves from beliefs lacking sufficient evidence as from a 'pestilence, which may shortly master our own body and then spread to the rest of the town' (p. 43). In short, we must take care that we always believe on sufficient evidence and never violate this sacred obligation. Again 'It is wrong always, everywhere and for anyone to believe anything on insufficient evidence' (p. 44).

A few comments are in order. George Mavrodes has pointed out that the duty imposed by Clifford is different from the one imposed by Locke and Hume regarding believing on evidence. In Locke and Hume the duty is to *proportion the strength of one's belief to the preponderancy of the evidence.* That is, there is a notion of degrees of belief and disbelief which somehow must be correlated to objective probabilities. The proportionate rule of Locke and Hume gives way to a threshold principle in Clifford. Saying nothing about degrees of belief or evidence, he tells us simply not to believe unless we have sufficient evidence for the belief in question.[1]

These are two different principles and, Mavrodes points out, there are problems with both of them. Locke and Hume, while offering an interesting rule, do not tell us how to calculate the probabilities, nor how much evidence is needed to justify any given strength of belief. There is no advice given on how to correlate strengths of evidence with strengths of belief. On the other hand, Clifford does not tell us what is sufficient evidence for any belief. Do some beliefs demand more evidence than others before they are to be believed? Clifford's position is unclear, but given a broad enough interpretation of 'sufficient evidence', his philosophical enemy, William James, could actually agree with him.

Perhaps, it is misleading to call Clifford's theory an 'ethics of belief', for he does not fault the belief but the *way* it was arrived at. What he is advocating is an *ethics of investigation* or of intellectual inquiry. There are certain rules in evidence gathering which have moral significance: e.g., being impartial, gathering a wide sample of evidence, being open to criticism, and checking one's results. If one adheres to these processes, the likelihood is that one will have an optimal set of beliefs. Even if it turns out that some of our beliefs are false, we still maintain the integrity of truth seekers, and our experience is that in the long run this is the best way to insure true beliefs.

In William James (1842–1910) we have the classic response to the sort of rigid evidentialism that we find in W.K. Clifford. Whereas, for Clifford we all have a duty everywhere and at all times to believe anything only on sufficient evidence, in James the significance of believing is found in its practical consequences. We must live and pursue our goals. This is the first law of life. In order to act in ways that enable us to reach our goals we often need to believe that the goals are attainable and that we will reach them – even when we lack sufficient evidence for these beliefs. So long as we are convinced that our goals are legitimate, we are permitted to believe beyond what the evidence indicates. While James agrees with Clifford that normally we should base our beliefs on sufficient evidence, there are times when we have a duty or right to believe or try to believe in spite of insufficient evidence.

> Our passional nature not only lawfully may, but must, decide an option between propositions, whenever it is a genuine option that cannot by its nature be decided on intellectual grounds; for to say, under such circumstances, 'Do not decide, but leave the question open', is itself a passional decision, – just like deciding yes or no, – and is attended with the same risk of losing the truth (*Will to Believe* ['WB'] p.11).[2]

In 'The Sentiment of Rationality' (1879) he defines 'faith' as 'belief in something concerning which doubt is still theoretically possible; and as the test of belief is willingness to act, one may say that faith is the readiness to act in a cause the prosperous issue of which is not certified to us in advance'. In 'Will to Believe' (1896) he speaks of 'belief' as a live, optional hypothesis, which we adopt (p. 2). Such an option may be classified as (1) living or dead; (2) forced or avoidable; and (3) momentous or trivial. A genuine option is one which is 'forced, living, and momentous'. A 'living' hypothesis, as opposed to a 'dead' one, is one which appeals as a real possibility in that it is relevant to the individual and involves his willingness to act. A 'forced' option is one which entails 'a complete logical disjunction, with no possibility of not choosing'. A 'momentous' option, in contrast to a 'trivial' one, presupposes a unique opportunity of enormous personal significance (WB p. 4).

Such profound options are person relative. Believing in Mahdi (the guided one, a title taken by Mohammed Ahmed, who captured Khartoum in 1885) is not a *live* option for most Americans, but believing that God exists is. Taking our umbrella to work with us is a non-forced option, but 'either love me or hate me' or 'either call my theory true or call it false' are instances of *forced* options. As an illustration of a momentous option, he suggests the invitation to join an expedition to the North Pole. Religious faith for many of us partakes of all these characteristics and is, therefore, a 'genuine option'. In fact, there is no more momentously genuine option in life than believing in God.

If religion is a genuine option, then why should we not get ourselves to believe even though our purely logical mind has not been coerced by the evidence? Here James refers to Pascal's Wager, His rendition is: either you do or do not believe that God exists. Your reason cannot decide this for you. Weigh what your gains and losses would be if you should stake all you have on God's existence. If you win, you gain eternal happiness. If you lose, you 'lose nothing at all'. If the odds were infinitely against the one chance for God, you should still choose to commit yourself to God; for although there is the risk of finite loss, it is well worth the possibility of the infinite gain that would be your lot if God exists and you choose him. 'Go, then, and take holy water, and have masses said; belief will come and stupefy your scruples – Cela vous fera croire et vous abeitra' (p. 6).

James qualifies this crude analysis, saying that it only becomes morally acceptable if the option is truly living. The point is that it is precisely our volitional or 'willing nature' that determines whether religious propositions are live options in the first place. By 'willing nature' James means not only deliberate volitions which have established habits of belief, but all influences which make hypotheses possible or impossible – 'All such factors of belief as fear and hope, prejudice and passion, imitation and partisanship, the circumpressure of our caste and sect' (p. 9).

What divides the rigid evidentialist and the pragmatist is essentially a volitional commitment to two different epistemological stances, which manifest themselves as two separate laws regarding belief formation. The first law is 'We must know the truth' and the second is 'We must avoid error.' The Cliffordian positivist is so frozen with fear over being duped that he takes no risk with his belief-forming mechanisms; whereas the pragmatist following the Pascalian gambit, deems doxastic charity a splendid virtue. This is illustrated by religious belief.

> If religion be true and the evidence for it be still insufficient, I
> do not wish, by putting your extinguisher upon my nature
> (which feels to me as if it had after all some business in this

matter), to forfeit my sole chance in life of getting upon the winning side, . . . This command that we put a stopper to our heart, instincts, and courage, and *wait* – acting of course meanwhile more or less as if religion were *not* true – till doomsday, or till such time as our intellect and senses working together may have raked in evidence enough – this command, I say, seems to me the queerest idol ever manufactured in the philosophic cave (pp. 27, 29f).

James points out that there are times when we must choose between the chance of being wrong and the benefits that can only come in launching out in faith. Science itself would be far less advanced if it were not for the fact of pioneers risking themselves in speculative ideas.

A further reason of the need to will to believe rather than withhold assent is that often 'faith in a fact can help create the fact' (p. 25). A belief that your audience will like you often causes you to act in such ways that creates verification of the belief. In 'The Sentiment of Rationality' he offers the example of the climber in the Alps who find himself in a position from which he can only escape by means of an enormous leap. If he tries to calculate the evidence, only believing on sufficient evidence, he will be paralyzed by emotions of fear and mistrust. Without evidence of being able to perform this feat successfully, the climber would be better off getting himself to believe that he can and will make the leap. 'In this case . . . the part of wisdom clearly is to believe what one desires; for the belief is one of the indispensable preliminary conditions of the realization of its object. *There are then cases where faith creates its own verification*' (p. 96f).

Religion is an instance where Pascal's Wager applies. Essentially, religion says two things: (1) that 'the best things are the more eternal things, the overlapping things, the things in the universe that throw the last stone, so to speak' and (2) that we are better off believing the first affirmation. This seems inexact, for it is not simply that the best things are defined by endurance for if they were then Social Darwinism might apply to religion as well as morality. The holy would be defined as that which endured the longest. James wants to say that religion teaches us that the good will triumph over evil, that the world is governed by a benevolent hand, and that we shall survive death in eternal happiness. Later in the essay he speaks of the personal quality of the universe that is part of the gospel of religion.

> The more perfect and more eternal aspect of the universe is represented in our religions as having personal form. The universe is no longer a mere *It* to us, but a *Thou*, if we are religious; and any relation that may be possible from person to person might be possible here. For instance, although in one sense we are passive portions of the universe, in another we show a curious autonomy, as if we were small active centers on our own account. We feel, too, as if the appeal of religion to us were made to our own active good-will, as if evidence might be forever withheld from us unless we met the hypothesis half-way (p. 27f).

James's ideas on the will to believe have met with plenty of criticism. (1) His views have been attacked as converging belief with action. For it would seem that one need not actually believe the propositions of religion in order to live according to them. We may act *as if* the religion were true. James responds that this is an artificial separation, for since belief is measured by action, the skeptic also forbids us to act as we would 'if we did believe it to be true'. 'The whole defence of religious faith hinges upon action . . . The religious hypothesis gives to the world an expression which specifically determines our reactions, and makes them in a large part unlike what they might be on a purely naturalistic scheme of belief' (p. 30).

Peter Kauber and Peter Hare have drawn attention to the equivocation of the term 'belief' in James's work. Sometimes it is identified with action in a behaviorist manner, and sometimes it is defined as a disposition to act. It is not always clear which model James is using. Kauber and Hare show that in both cases James thinks that we have not only a right but a duty to *try* to believe certain propositions, i.e., those which would enable us to carry out our moral duties.[3]

(2) There is a problem about James's criteria for genuine options and their application. If the same odds apply to the Mahdi religion as Christianity, I don't see any legitimate criterion for excluding it as an equally valid genuine option. That religion claims to offer an equal or better way to eternal bliss than Christianity. Simply, because he has no immediate attraction to it is a poor excuse, for if it

promises him eternal blessedness (and unbelievers eternal damnation), James has every reason (on his logic of *willing to believe*
without evidence what has the best cost-benefit consequences) to
make a leap of faith there.

(3) Finally, there is an ambiguity in James's account of our
passional nature. Sometimes he seems to mean our ability to decide
what we shall believe and successfully choose it. At other times, he
seems to mean all those hopes, fears, prejudices, interests and
inclinations which enter into the belief acquisition process. The
nonvolitionalist need not deny the second meaning. He may also
admit that being passionate for the truth is a also a passion and
causes us to pay attention to the evidence and judge impartially.
What the nonvolitionalist denies is that we can obtain beliefs simply
by willing to have them or that this can be done indirectly without
great difficulty.

As noted above, George Mavrodes has pointed out that James
could accept Clifford's evidentialism without changing the logic of
his position. Where Clifford tells us not to believe anything on
insufficient evidence, James could agree, responding that for different types of propositions different levels of sufficiency are required. For the sort of beliefs he is talking about, where so much
supreme value is at stake, the threshold is much lower than say
believing that someone is guilty of murder.[4]

This is a valid point, but the spirit of James's epistemology is
radically different from Clifford's. For Clifford only objective
evidence counts in the justification process. Whether the belief is
edifying is beside the point. James, to the contrary, is willing to
allow for a pragmatic justification of beliefs. If it is likely to help
you, believe it. 'The true . . . is only the expedient in the way of our
thinking, just as the right is only the expedient in the way of our
believing.'[5] Here we are reminded of Kierkegaard's dictum: 'Only
the truth that edifies is truth for you.'[6]

Underlying James's radical pragmatism is a utilitarian assumption that we ought to satisfy all desires in a manner that maximizes
happiness. We shall be enabled to work towards this goal only if we
adopt the optimistic stance of believing that goodness will win over
evil. Since there is no way to determine this by looking at the
evidence, we have a right to believe in the enabling belief that good
will win. But, we may also have a duty to do so. The questions are
whether James's assumptions are necessary for the moral life,

whether his logic is coherent, and whether we might also have accompanying deontological doxastic duties which might off-set the teleological ones.

CHAPTER X

Modern Catholic Volitionalists: Newman, Pieper and Lonergan

Roman Catholic thought, from Augustine and Aquinas to modern times, has always had a volitional motif within its philosophical expression of faith. In the past one hundred years this motif been present in most Thomists. We shall view its expression in two Thomists (Josef Pieper and Bernard Lonergan) and in the thought of one non-Thomist, John Henry Newman.

In his *Essay in Aid of a Grammar of Assent* (1870) John Henry Newman sets forth the outline of an informal, non-rule governed mode of reasoning, called 'concrete reasoning', which purports to do justice to the great subtlety involved in religious belief. Newman's work may be seen as a rejection of the rigid rationalism of the Enlightenment, begun with Locke and culminating with the work of W.K. Clifford. For Newman there are three theses that characterize such a rationalism: (1) the notion of degrees of assent, so that we may give our assent to propositions in various degrees; (2) the notion of an ethics of belief which mandates that we assent to propositions exactly to the degree to which the evidence warrants; and (3) the notion of belief being identical with the conclusions of inferences, which makes assenting a passive phenomenon and excludes the will from any direct involvement in belief formation.

Newman rejects all three theses. Regarding the first thesis, Newman claims that there are no degrees to assenting, as there are to the conclusion of inferences. He separates inferring from assenting. In inferring one locates the amount of evidence for or against a proposition, reasoning from premises to conclusion, but in assenting, one accepts the proposition as true. As there are no degrees of truth (a proposition is either true or it is not), so there are no degrees in believing. Assent is 'in itself the absolute acceptance of a proposition without any condition' (p. 13). He claims that the conflation of the notion of degrees from the inference to the assent would altogether do away with the reality of assenting. If assenting is simply the arriving at a conclusion of the inference process, 'assent becomes a sort of necessary shadow, following upon inference, which is the substance; and is never without some alloy of doubt, because inference in the concrete never reaches more than probability. . . . Assent cannot rise higher than its source, inference in such matters is at best conditional, therefore assent is conditional also' (p. 159f).

Newman argues that this goes against the common experience of humankind which recognizes the separateness of assent as often going beyond the available evidence. Even Locke admits that certain 'probabilities rise so near to certainty, that they govern our thoughts as absolutely, and influence all our actions as fully, as the most evident demonstration' (p. 161). Besides, we often cannot say exactly what the evidence is that leads us to assent to a proposition and yet we do. Furthermore, in response to Locke's notion of an ethics of proportioning the strength of belief to the strength of evidence, Newman points out that the consensus of humanity is to reject this. In fact, it would make human intercourse impossible.

Here Newman develops his idea of the illative sense, an intuitive sense which engages in concrete reasoning and determines whether to give assent to the inferred proposition about concrete experience. It is a comprehensive mastery of a concrete field of knowledge.

> The sole and final judgment on the validity of an inference in
> concrete matter is committed to the personal action of the
> ratiocinative faculty, the perfection or virtue of which I have
> called the Illative Sense. . . . It is the mind that reasons, and
> that controls its own reasonings, not any technical apparatus of
> words and propositions. This power of judging and concluding,
> when its perfection, I call the Illative Sense (p. 345).

Newman illustrates this non-rule governed mode of reasoning by various examples: Napoleon's remarkable perceptions of military strategy (He could but look at a situation and conclude to the right course of action); a criminal trial, where there is evidence on both sides and talk of exact amounts or degrees is absurd; and the certainty we have that Great Britain is an island without really *knowing* that it is. On the last point he says:

Our reasons for believing that we are circumnavigable are such as these: – first, we have been so taught in our childhood, and it is so on all the maps; next, we have never heard it contradicted or questioned; on the contrary, everyone whom we have heard speak on the subject of Great Britain, every book we have read, invariably took it for granted; our whole national history, the routine transactions and current events of the country, our social and commercial system, our political relations with foreigners, imply it in one way or another. Numberless facts, or what we consider facts, rest on the truth of it; no received facts rests on its being otherwise (p. 294).

We may not be able to convince anyone who doubts these propositions, nor can we be said to have the sort of knowledge that Locke calls for before we can claim to be entitled to absolute certainty, yet it is quite obvious to all but the closet-dwelling skeptic that we are. The point is, that we must trust all sorts of informal evidences to build up a case for a proposition. In these cases 'it is the cumulation of probabilities, independent of each other, arising out of the nature and circumstances of the particular case which is under review; probabilities too fine to avail separately, too subtle and circuitous to be convertible into syllogisms, too numerous and various for such conversions, even were they convertible' (p. 288).

Not only is this cumulative type of reasoning not rule governed. It is person-relative. 'A cumulation of probabilities over and above their implicit character will vary both in their number and their separate estimated value, according to the particular intellect which is employed upon it. It follows that what to one intellect is proof is not so to another.' (p. 293).

Applying all this to religious belief, Newman argues that belief that Christianity, especially Catholicism, is true is a personal decision based on a cumulative case of many factors which cannot convince the non-believer. It is a result of our total interpretation, and yet it goes beyond the evidence in that it involves a volitional insertion of assenting. But all assenting involves decision, the will to bring a conclusion beyond the mere conclusions of an inference.

Assent is an act of the mind, congenial to its nature; and it, as other acts, may be made both when it ought to be made, and when it ought not. It is a free act, a personal act for which the doer is responsible, and the actual mistakes in making it, be they ever so numerous or serious, have no force whatever to prohibit the assent (p. 232).

Newman's arguments for volitionalism largely appeal to common human experience. We can be persuaded of the low probability of a conclusion based on inductive evidence and yet 'decide' to believe it. We are not merely logical beings but volitional too, and this volitional aspect is apparent on close introspection of belief states.

While Newman has generally been interpreted as being a direct volitionalist, Jamie Ferreira has recently shown that it is possible to offer an alternative view on the matter.[1] Ferreira contends that Newman is not, in fact, a direct volitionalist, but really is offering an alternative position between the paradigms of strict non-volitionalism with its view that all believing is passive and forced, on the one hand, and direct volitionalism with its view that the will can directly or by fiat cause a belief to form. Citing a passage from Newman's *Theological Papers*, she shows that Newman recognizes that the mind is affected by the evidence in forming a belief, but that the will still has some power in the relationship. The passage that she has in mind is the following:

[U]pon an inference of whatever kind there is a natural spontaneous act of the mind towards it of acceptance or the reverse, which I have above expressed under the word Assent, and said to be under the jurisdiction of the will . . . Certainty, which though it naturally follows upon conviction, is a making up the mind that a thing is true which is proved, and therefore is under the control of the will; that is, the will may suppress, extinguish the feeling (*The Theological Papers of John Henry Newman on Faith and Certainty*, p.14f, 1853).

Believing is both naturally spontaneous, which implies non-volitional, and under the jurisdiction of the will. Certainty is truth directed, which leaves out the will, and yet the will can veto the feeling. Perhaps, Newman wants an intermediate attitude such as 'accepting' a proposition as true without fully believing it or being certain. Newman does not give a close enough analysis of the issue for us to be certain, but his treatment seems to allow and encourage the role of the will in coming to believe. If he is not a direct volitionalist, he is close to it and certainly advocates the role of the will in affecting certainty.

Newman's notion of the illative sense and its response to the cumulative case have been generally recognized as major contributions to philosophy of religion and are developed by such philosophers as John Wisdom, John Hick and Basil Mitchell. However, his thesis that assent is absolute, degreeless and unconditional has never had a strong case made for it. Although Ferreira's recent study of his ethics of belief has shown that Newman's position may not be a clear case of direct volitionalism, nonetheless, he does seem to think that believing is under the direct control of our will, so that we are always responsible for our beliefs.

While Newman's view of the relation of willing to believing is unclear, the next two views seem to be more self-consciously volitional. We turn now to the notion of belief of two contemporary Catholic philosophers, Josef Pieper and Bernard Lonergan.

A contemporary rendition of a Thomistic, volitional analysis of religious belief is that of Josef Pieper's *Belief and Faith* (1963), a book that has been widely read and quoted as representative of modern Catholic thought. Pieper gives an approximate definition of 'belief'. 'To believe is equivalent to taking a position on the truth of a statement and on the actuality of the matter stated. More precisely, belief means that we think a statement true and consider the stated matter real, objectively existent' (p. 7). Belief differs from knowledge in that knowledge presumes a familiarity with the subject, whereas belief is always descriptive, and it differs from supposing in that the latter involves a conditional assent, whereas belief is an unconditional assenting or conviction. Belief cannot refer to what one sees, for one knows that; nor can it refer to doubtful testimony which one may only weakly think true, for this is a mere supposal (what Augustine and Aquinas labelled 'opinion'). Belief involves comprehension of what the thought entertains. As Aquinas says, 'Man could not believingly assent to any proposition if he did not in some way understand it' (p. 11).

As an example of believing, Pieper asks us to imagine that he receives a visit from a stranger who tells him that he (the stranger) has seen Pieper's brother, who has long been presumed dead, alive and well in a prison camp. Much of what the stranger says fits the description of Pieper's brother, though there is no way of checking the matter. After an amount of cross examination, a point must come where a decision is necessary: 'Am I to believe or not to believe the man's story?' (p. 14).

Three things stand out on this account. First, to believe something is always to believe someone, a person who is a witness, to treat him as an authority. At the furtherest extreme, this is to accept the witness of the authority unconditionally, accepting everything he says. It is ultimate trust. Secondly, belief in its proper sense really means *unqualified* assent and *unconditional* acceptance of the truth of something. Following Newman, Pieper avers that 'Believing to an extent' is not proper believing but merely supposing. The third thing that stands out in the example is that belief is always volitional.

> One can believe only if one wishes to. Perhaps the credibility of a given person will be revealed to me so persuasively that I cannot help but think: It is wrong not to believe him; I 'must' believe him. But this last step can be taken only in complete freedom, and that means that it can also not be taken. There may be plenty of compelling arguments for a man's credibility; but no argument can force us to believe him. . . . A free assent of will must be performed. Belief rests upon volitions (p. 25f).

The subject must have a motive for believing, as he does for acting. He must 'have insight that it is good to regard the subject matter as true . . . But it is the will, not cognition, which acknowledges the good' (p. 27). The will is actually more important than cognition in faith. 'We believe not because we see, perceive, deduce something true, but because we desire something good. . . . The believer believes because he wants to believe.'

Essentially, the will of the believer is directed not towards the proposition in question but towards the person of the witness, 'toward the warrantor'. Pieper goes so far as to say that the assent of the intellect to the witnessed truth involves 'participation in and communion with his insight, or in other words a spiritual union with him'. As Newman says, 'We believe because we love' (p. 31).

Pieper applies this to the Christian's faith. Genuine religious belief is an unconditional and volitional assenting to whatever the authority says, for it involves the unconditional trust and love of that authority. The authority is the consensus or core of the creeds, ultimately reposing in God himself, who has revealed himself to us in his word.

Pieper's thought is consonant with the Thomist tradition, but it seems to conflate too many concepts for the analyst's comfort.

Ought not 'trusting' and 'believing', even believing with unconditional conviction be kept separate? I need make no decision to
trust another human in any normal sense of that term in order to
believe what she says, if it seems to make sense. Furthermore, why
does believing have to be unconditional? I can believe that Ein-
stein's theory is true today, but also believe that after I take an
advanced Physics course, I may come to doubt it? I suppose that
Pieper would call this mere 'supposing', but doesn't he confuse
depth of ingress with degree of certainty? The depth of ingress or
existential import of a belief may be enormous for me while I have
only medium conviction about its truth. For example, it may mean a
lot to me to have assurance that my wife is faithful, but I may only
believe it moderately. Finally, what has love to do with belief? Can I
not trust someone whom I dislike? I believe that many of the things
my enemies and Adolf Hitler said were true, but I do not love them.

A second, and somewhat more sophisticated Thomist, who also
reflects a volitional stance on belief is Bernard Lonergan. In his
magnum opus Insight: A Study of Human Nature (1957) he gives the
concept of 'belief' short but careful analysis. According to him,
there are five stages in the typical process of obtaining a true belief,
namely:

1 preliminary judgments on the value of belief in general, on
   the reliability of the source for this belief, and on the accuracy
   of the communication from the source,
2 a reflective act of understanding that, in virtue of the
   preliminary judgment, grasps as virtually unconditioned the
   value of deciding to believe some particular proposition,
3 the consequent judgment of value,
4 the consequent decision of the will, and
5 the assent that is the act of believing (p. 708).

The preliminary judgment seems to be made up of a series of
smaller quasi-beliefs or opinions about the proposition in question.
Lonergan separates 'judgment' from 'belief'. It seems that judgments are nonvolitional, whereas beliefs are volitional. While a
judgment results necessarily from grasping the unconditioned
aspect of the proposition, the assent of belief is motivated 'by a
decision to profit by a human collaboration in the pursuit of truth'
(p. 709), though it can be made irresponsibly. The second step
involves both a comprehension of what is being asserted by the

proposition under consideration in the first step as well as something like a cost-benefit analysis of the value of believing the proposition in question (similar to Pieper's motive or interest).

The third act is the actual judgment on the value of deciding to believe that the proposition 'certainly or probably is true or false'. The fourth act is 'a free and responsible decision of the will to believe a given proposition as probably or certainly true or false. It is a reasonable act of the will, if it is preceded by a sincere and favorable judgment on the value of deciding to believe the proposition in question' (p. 709). It is like any other act of the will, except that it does not produce any bodily movements as they do. Rather the 'decision to believe is a decision to produce in intellect the act of assenting to a proposition or dissenting from it'. The fifth act is the act of believing itself. 'It is an act of rational self-consciousness that occurs within the general programme of a colaboration of minds in the advancement and the dissemination of knowledge of truth', though, again, it could be made without regard for truth.

Like Pieper, Lonergan gives us an essentially pragmatic view of believing. We can decide whether or not to believe a proposition depending on our motivation. Although it is good to be motivated towards the truth, there is no necessity in it. The differences between them are simply that Lonergan allows degrees of belief, underplays the role of believing someone in the act of belief, and supposes that there is a non-volitional state of judging which precedes believing. A non-volitionalist would argue that these are not two different states, but aspects of complex beliefs.

CHAPTER XI

The Contemporary Debate on Belief and Will

The Concept of Belief in Twentieth Century British Philosophy

In the first half of the twentieth century the problem of belief lost its importance as a dominant philosophical problem. Pragmatism and philosophy of religion, where the concept has a natural home, receded in importance and with it a whole series of issues which were once the life blood of philosophy (e.g., the question of the existence of God, freedom of the will, and ethics). Idealists were concerned with knowledge not belief and from a fundamentally different perspective the Logical Atomists and Logical Positivists were concerned only with logical relations and strictly verifiable empirical knowledge. In the *Tractatus* Wittgenstein reduces the scope of philosophy to logical analysis. Belief has to do with psychology, not philosophy. It is associated with speculative metaphysics, an area which atomism and positivism ruled out of the philosophical court as beyond its scope or as sheer nonsense. Almost to the same extent that metaphysics was rejected was belief seen as an uninteresting concept.

At Oxford University the early part of the twentieth century was dominated by the thought of John Cook Wilson and his followers, who placed the emphasis on knowledge as a simple, ultimate, indefinable experience, which is self-authenticating. In knowing anything one knows that one knows. Knowledge is the basis for belief but not the other way around. That is, in order to believe anything, one needs to have some first hand knowledge of facts. Essentially, knowing and believing are two different experiences. Knowledge is always infallible and belief is always fallible. Knowledge is reduced to present states of consciousness. For example, only I can know that I am in pain or having the sensation of seeing red. Everyone else only believes this of me. It follows, Wilson's disciple, H.H. Price, said, 'that it is impossible to know and to believe the same thing at the same time. If I know that A is B, I cannot at the same time believe that A is B, and if I believe it I cannot at the same time know it.'[1]

It follows that 'knowledge' is reduced to a very small segment of epistemology, excluding empirical statements, memory claims, and deductive conclusions not presently before the mind. The central question for this 'occurrentism' (the notion that a state of belief or knowledge is necessarily a conscious state) is, what happens to our knowledge when we are not thinking of it? Taken literally, the theory seems to suppose that one loses all of one's knowledge when one goes to sleep – for one is no longer conscious of it. Nor can I be said to know my own name nor know that '2 + 2 = 4' when I am not thinking about these things. Left with such epistemic poverty, it is no wonder that the such occurrentists as H.H. Price advocated that we get rid of the term 'knowledge' altogether and use instead a word to cover both knowledge and a lot of other things that seem certain to us. He suggested 'reasonable assurance'.[2]

Reduced to a narrow scope occurrentism drew strong reactions both in defining belief in terms of inductive probability and in moving towards a quasi behavioral or dispositional view of belief, wherein the 'feeling' or occurrent element in belief is minimized, if not altogether done away with. The move towards seeing the strength of belief in terms of probabilities was led by Frank Ramsey. The move against seeing belief defined in terms of feeling was led by Russell, Braitewaite and Kneale. It was Braitewaite who gave the alternative account, quasi-behavorism, its fullest defense.

The brilliant mathematician-philosopher, who died at the age of 27, Frank Ramsey (1903–1930) had written an article 'Truth and Probability' (1926)[3] which rejected Wittgenstein's doctrine that we have no grounds for non-tautological inferences. In its place Ramsey defended Peirce's contention that induction is a 'habit in the human mind', which, though it cannot be justified by any formal method, still seems reasonable to adopt as the basis for our judgments. Its justification is strictly pragmatic. It seems to work out well.

According to Ramsey there are no general beliefs, but only habits of singular beliefs. We do not believe that water is wet, but we have the habit of believing that each particular quantity of water is wet.

Singular beliefs are maps of the mind by which we steer and what we call general belief is only a habit of forming beliefs, a rule for forming singular beliefs. While Ramsey offers a causal account of belief in terms of degrees of probability, he does not embrace a wholly dispositional or behavioral account of belief, for he thinks that the difference between believing and not believing 'could well be held to lie in the presence or absence of introspectible feelings'.[4]

Although anticipated by Russell (*Analysis of Mind*, 1921) and Braitewaite ('The Nature of Belief', 1933), William Kneale's contribution was to challenge the whole enterprise of occurrent analyses of belief and knowledge, found in Hume, Bagehot, Cook Wilson and the early Price, as falsely resting on emotions. He pointed out that it is precisely when I have the deepest conviction that I feel no emotions at all. 'It is obvious', he writes in *Probability and Induction* (1949), 'that knowledge itself is not accompanied by confidence. When we realise that $2 + 2 = 4$, we do not sweat with any feeling of supreme intensity' (p. 15). Knowledge and beliefs do not need emotions at all for their reality. In fact we continue to know while we are sleeping or unsure of our knowledge (we need not know that we know in order to know). Both knowledge and belief are essentially dispositional.

The most anti-occurrentist movement of all was that of epistemological behaviorism. Although behavioral theories of belief begin with Alexander Bain (1818–1903), who in his *The Emotions and the Will* (1859), wrote that 'belief has no meaning except in reference to our actions', the most cogent and detailed defense of a modified behaviorism is that of R.B. Braitewaite's article 'The Nature of Belief' (1933). Braitewaite is the first philosopher since Plato to define 'knowledge' in terms of justified, true belief, reversing the Wilsonian dictum that belief was to be defined in terms of inscrutable knowledge.[5]

For Braitewaite belief consists in two aspects: (1) a subjective, cognitive attitude, 'entertainment in thought' and (2) a behavioral disposition to act as if *p* were true. It is the dispositional attitude that is the *differentia* of actual belief, separating it from mere entertainment of a proposition. This account is not wholly behavioral, for it recognizes conscious states: memory, the entertainment of propositions, and intentions; but it denies that beliefs are feelings and puts the accent on the 'readiness to act' aspect of belief. Indeed, we only find out whether we believe propositions by observing our actions.

'It seems to me that my belief in [the proposition that this is a pencil] consists, apart from its entertainment, in appropriate actions, e.g., in trying to write with the pencil; and that my reasons for believing that I believe it are inductive' (p. 36). Here he appeals to Ramsey's thought that belief can be defined in terms of probability. While we can only use this model with any exactness where a definite numerical probability is attributed to a definite event (as in a game of chance), the model serves as a guide for understanding belief as a sort of generalized betting (p. 39). This thesis, that we discover our beliefs by looking at our behavior culminated in Gilbert Ryle's *Concept of Mind* (1949).

While it is no doubt a significant contribution of the quasi-behaviorists to point out that believing has a non-occurrent aspect (e.g., that we need not 'feel' our beliefs as we do pains or emotions) and is linked with dispositions to act, there are several problems with this account. First, it seems counter intuitive. We do seem to be directly aware of our beliefs without having to look at our behavior. I believe my memory reports (e.g., that I had breakfast this morning) directly upon introspection without any observation of behavior. When asked whether I would like to go to the cinema, I report in the affirmative immediately and before I take steps to go (though, to be sure, my behavior may show that I have self-deceived myself). Furthermore, on the strong dispositional account the whole notion of weakness of will would not make any sense. If I said that it would be a good thing to stop smoking, but continued to smoke, the assertion would be discounted by my behavior. Again, in the behavioral account, it would be impossible to hold contradictory beliefs (which most of us believe that we have discovered in ourselves or others), for this view reduces beliefs to actions which cannot be contradictory (e.g., I cannot *do* and not *do* two contradictory actions at the same time).

Finally, on the quasi-behavioral account, intentions are given too scant attention. It is hard to see where they fit into the behavioral repertoire, for since it is only the behavior that finally counts, intentions might just as well not exist. But intentions are not only causally important. No account of action (as distinguished from mere behavior) seems complete without them. Often, we need to appeal to such subjective states to explain why someone did what he did, for any given behavior could have an infinite set of explanatory accounts. For example, I can take out a short-term life insurance policy either because I want to commit suicide and want to help my family by making them rich or because I want to harm them by spoiling them with material wealth that will lead to their damnation or because I think that there is a finite chance that I will die this year and want to insure against a financial catastrophe to my family. Strong dispositionalism does not give us guidance on adjudicating these points. It seems to be an overreaction to an exaggerated occurrentism. There seems no good reason to deny that we have access to our belief states directly through introspection.

It was H.H. Price (1899–1971), a disciple of Wilson, who brought moderation into the debate. Having been converted from occurrentism to dispositionalism, he never completely abandoned the occurrentist core of the concept of belief. Beliefs are dispositions and yet we have some direct access to our beliefs as we do other mental states. Price, more than any one else, is responsible for the kind of dispositionalism that enjoys a hegemony in philosophical circles today. In his 1960 Gifford Lectures (published under the title *Belief* in 1967) Price sets forth the most comprehensive treatise ever devoted to the concept of belief.

Price agrees with Braitewaite and Kneale that to say that 'A believes the proposition *p*' is to make a dispositional statement about A, and that this is equivalent to a series of conditional statements describing what he would be likely to say or do if such and such were to happen. But Price emphasizes that it also is tied up with emotions so that part of what it means to believe that *p* is to feel surprise when one finds that the proposition in question is false or to feel the strength of the belief when it is denied or challenged by others (pp. 20, 275–280). Furthermore, with regard to the 'feeling' aspect of believing, Price agrees that we need not have any feeling attached to belief so long as there is no 'conflict situation' involved, but once there is, we may well feel the tension between doubt and belief or surprise. In modifying dispositionalism to include the occurrentist notion of 'feeling', Price gives the concept a very wide sense. It is to be applied to

Any mental state or mental process which is introspectible. What is felt, in this sense, is what can be (though it need not actually be) an object of introspection; what we feel is just something which we 'live through'. . . . Sureness is a state of mind in which conflict or tension is absent. But it might still be a state of mind which is lived through or 'enjoyed' by the person who has it; and that, I suggest, is the sense which the word 'feel' has when a person says 'I feel sure'. . . . Feeling sure *is* rather like feeling calm, or feeling tranquil as Kneale puts it. But he is mistaken in supposing that feeling tranquil is just the absence of uneasiness. It is a positive state which we sometimes 'live through'. Should we wish to say that when a man feels well, the truth is only that he does *not* feel at all ill? (*Belief*, p. 288f).

Putting this all together, Price calls belief a 'multiform disposition' in that it may manifest itself in many different ways; 'not only in his actions, and his inactions, but also in emotional states such as hope and fear; in feelings of doubt, surprise and confidence; and finally in his inferences', both those in which a belief unconsciously just 'spreads itself' from a proposition to some of its implications and those which are self-conscious intellectual operations (p. 294). This is a compromise position. Belief is not a mental occurrence. It is a state of mind (including the sub-conscious mind), but belief acquisition, the realization of a belief, and the loss of a belief can all be mental occurrences.

Turning to the topic of volitionalism, Price in his Aristotelian Society paper, 'Belief and Will' (1954) shows that in some sense we can be said to choose which propositions we will believe and that some believing seems to be voluntary. This sense is reflected in our language 'I find that difficult to believe', 'I won't believe that', 'Try to believe me' and the like. There does seem to be an analogy between believing and practical reasoning in action. Just as I decide to act because of my wants, I decide to believe because of the evidence. When we acquire a belief it is often like coming down off a fence or taking a plunge.[6]

However, the preferential element in believing is not a voluntary choice. It is not a free choice at all, but a forced one. If you are in a reasonable frame of mind, you cannot help preferring the proposition which *your* evidence favors (p. 68). The voluntary element in believing is in our ability to direct our attention where we will. We may voluntarily cultivate beliefs or get ourselves to lose a belief by constant and persistent focusing of attention.

By such methods – by dwelling upon a proposition continually and repeatedly, by considering again and again what it would be like if it were true and imagining in detail what it would be like (if you can), by acting as if the proposition were true on all occasions to which its truth or falsity is relevant, and by increasing the number of these occasions whenever possible – by such means you will gradually get into a state of believing the proposition. You will wake up one fine day and find that you do believe it. Or if you believe it already, by these methods you will get into a state where you believe it almost unshakeably; a state in which you no longer have to bother about adverse evidence, or indeed about favorable evidence either ('Belief and Will', p. 71).[7]

In *Belief* he seems to modify this anti-volitional stance somewhat, saying that there is after all something we *do* in making an inference. 'There is indeed something voluntary about it. It is an exercise of our freedom. The initial suspension or inhibition is voluntary.' Furthermore, the attention we give to 'the logical connection between the proposition already believed and the other proposition to which our belief would have "spread" if we had allowed it to' is also under our direct control. Likewise, our freedom is prominent in our willingness 'to be guided by the strength . . . of the logical connection between the two propositions, and to conclude accordingly'.

For instance, we notice that *p* makes *q* very likely, but does not make it certain. Then, though we feel absolutely sure that *p*, we shall not allow ourselves to feel absolutely sure that *q*, but only to have a pretty confident opinion that *q* (*Belief*, p. 294).

Whereas Price modified his general position on belief over the years, he remains constant regarding the idea of an ethics of belief. There is none. Following Hume, rather than Locke and Clifford, he argues that there is only an *economics* of belief. His grounds for this position are largely utilitarian. In 'Belief and Will' he argues that to make belief-acquisition an ethical issue would leave ourselves open for inquisitorial consequences. For in implying that there are some beliefs (or methods of belief-acquisition) which we ought to believe, we open ourselves up to the idea of punishment; for if we are morally responsible for our beliefs, then we can be praised or blamed for them. But if we can be praised or blamed for them, it follows that we can be rewarded or punished for them. But it seems absurdly wrong to punish people for their beliefs, for by and large we cannot help believing what we believe. And even where we can affect beliefs through the will, each person should be allowed that personal freedom.

However, it is good to have a general policy of forming one's beliefs in accordance with the balance of the evidence, for in that way we are more likely to have true beliefs, and true beliefs are better guides to action than false ones. Hence, the 'ought' attached to the process of belief-acquisition is a prudential ought, not a moral one (p. 75f). In *Belief* the matter is put thusly:

> But even if it were in our power to be wholly rational all the time, it still would not follow that there is anything morally blameworthy about assenting unreasonably (against the evidence or without regard to the evidence) or that we ought to be chastised for doing so. There is nothing wicked about such assents. It is however true, and important, that unreasonable assent is contrary to our long-term interest. It is to our long-term interest to believe true propositions rather than false ones. And if we assent reasonably (i.e. in accordance with the evidence), it is likely that in the long run the propositions we believe will be more often true than false (*Belief*, p. 238).

Finally, we must look at Price's thought on religious belief, for being deeply religious, much of his concern about the concept of belief was generated by his struggle with faith and doubt. His thought falls into the British empirical camp, in the tradition of Paley and Locke, who try to show the reasonableness of Christianity and theism. In his early writings Price thought that while much of the relevant evidence pointed to agnosticism, parapsychology lent some support for a supernatural dimension. In *Belief* he discusses religious agnosticism and 'half-belief', where one alternates between belief and unbelief, where some facets of one's life reflect a believing attitude and others an unbelieving one. His main concern, however, is to defend an empiricist openness to the subject. 'Try it, and see for yourself what effect it has' (p. 480).

The agnostic's prayer 'O God, if there be a God, save my soul, if I have a soul', is a perfectly sensible one for a truth-speaking agnostic. What the doubter has to do is 'take the role' of a pious person, much as an actor puts himself into his part, and expose himself to the religious dimension. By opening oneself to the possibility of religious experience, one may experience what is deeply valid and yet imperceptible to normal eyes. Eventually, the matter can be decided by the will's freedom, not as a direct act of will to believe but more subtly through 'freedom of assent, which [may also be] a freedom to suspend judgement' (p. 484).

One of the most carefully analytic descriptions in his book is the chapter 'Belief-in and Belief-that' where Price wrestles with the problem of how far 'belief-in' statements can be reduced to belief-that statements. Essentially, they all can be so reduced to the idea 'it's a good thing that', but there are two very different ways in which this takes place. When I believe-in some thing or person, A, it can mean that I think that it is a good thing *extrinsically* or a good thing *intrinsically*. We believe-in our nation, hot-baths and our favorite car extrinsically, but we think that our trust in friendship and God, entail that the value here is intrinsic. What Price omits to discuss is whether belief-in entails belief that the object of belief-in exists. He simply takes it for granted that it does, but the issue seems in need of analysis. We shall be dealing with this problem in the second part of this work.

The Ethics of Belief in Contemporary Philosophy

No one has done more to provoke interest in and show the importance of epistemology in North America during the past three decades than Roderick Chisholm. At the heart of Chisholm's theory of knowledge we have an intricately developed system of an ethics of belief which takes seriously the concerns of W.K. Clifford without what James calls Clifford's 'somewhat too much robustious pathos'. In his *Perception* (1957) and 'Lewis' Ethics of Belief' (1968) Chisholm sets forth principles for a detailed ethics of belief. At the heart of Chisholm's theory is the Cliffordian principle that beliefs are subject to ethical appraisal. 'Belief' refers to a psychological act – 'to the fact that a man accepts a proposition, or takes it to be true . . . In this active sense of "belief", a belief . . . may be called wrong and in much the same sense as that in which a criminal act may be called wrong.'[8]

However, if Chisholm is no Jamesian doxastic Santa Claus, neither is he an epistemic Scrooge like Clifford. Unless a proposition is clearly evident (having adequate evidence in its favor) or unreasonable (having adequate evidence against it), it is epistemically indifferent, and so a permissible candidate for belief. Every 'proposition should be treated as innocent until proven guilty'.[9] Whereas Clifford has a threshold account of justified belief which determines that a necessary condition for believing that *p*, is that *p* have adequate evidence in its favor (i.e., is equivalent to Chisholm's notion of 'evident'), Chisholm optimistically places the threshold line over unreasonable propositions (those with adequate evidence against them) and allows anything above that line as doxastically permissible. We are permitted to believe all propositions which are epistemically indifferent. For Clifford no proposition is epistemically indifferent, for the skeptics all propositions are indifferent, but for Chisholm the range of indifference is between the zones of 'evidential' and 'unreasonable'.

Using the idea of the square of opposition, Chisholm sets four categories of propositions into the standard positions, thusly:

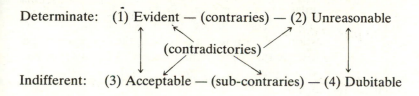

Determinate: (1) Evident — (contraries) — (2) Unreasonable

(contradictories)

Indifferent: (3) Acceptable — (sub-contraries) — (4) Dubitable

Evident and unreasonable propositions are epistemically determinate in that there is clear evidence one way or the other, but acceptable and dubitable propositions are epistemically indifferent and, as such, we are free to believe, withhold judgment, or disbelieve them. Actually, there seems to be a slight injunction to believe whatever is indifferent, since the principle of charity would incline us to accept what is innocent.

If epistemic states are to be subject to ethical appraisal, they must be under our control. Following C.I. Lewis, Chisholm claims that they are under our control. Believing is sometimes a voluntary act for which the believer is responsible. It is a mental motion to which the epistemic rules apply.

> If self-control is what is essential to activity, some of our beliefs would seem to be acts. When a man deliberates and comes finally to a conclusion, his decision is as much within his control as is any other deed we attribute to him. If his conclusion was unreasonable, a conclusion he should not have accepted, we

may plead with him: 'But you needn't have supposed that
so-and-so was true. Why didn't you take account of these other
facts?' We assume that his decision is one he could have
avoided and that, had he only chosen to do so, he could have
made a more reasonable inference. Or, if his conclusion is not
the result of deliberate inference, we may say, 'but if you had
only stopped to think,' implying that, had he chosen, he could
have stopped to think. We suppose, as we do whenever we
apply our ethical or moral predicates, that there was something
else the agent could have done instead ('Lewis' Ethics of
Belief', p. 224).

There is an isomorphism between moral argument which justifies
an act and epistemic argument which justifies a belief. Both refer to
free acts. Both actions and beliefs are justified as conclusions of
practical syllogisms. If we are challenged to defend our belief, we
respond in a similar way as we would in defending our action as
moral. 'The major premise will say that anyone having just the
evidence in question is warranted in accepting the conclusion; the
minor premise will say that I am in the position of having just that
evidence; and these premises will imply that I am justified in
accepting the conclusion.'[10]

The form of the argument is this:

1 Anyone having evidence e is justified in believing proposition h.
2 I have evidence e.
3 Therefore I am justified in believing h.

Not only are we irrational in refusing to believe h, but we are also
immoral.

The question, naturally, arises: why aren't we punished or rewarded for our beliefs the way that we are for our actions? Why
don't we put doxastic renegades in reform schools and prisons or, at
least, fine them? Lewis and Price thought that we refrained from
such behavior because our beliefs were of little importance to
others. But, Chisholm rightly objects, this is simply not the case. In
as much as beliefs guide our actions, they can be of immense
importance to others.

It is not the unimportance of our believings and concluding that
explain our failure to pass laws against, and to punish,
unreasonable believing and concluding. One reason for not

punishing a man who believes what he hadn't ought to believe may well be this: We do not punish a man for those ostensible actions that occur when 'he is not in his right mind' or when he is not behaving as a rational human being. But when a man fails to conform to the ethics of belief he is, *ipso facto*, behaving irrationally. On any occasion those beliefs we ought not to have and those conclusions we ought not to reach are precisely those beliefs and conclusions which would be unreasonable on that occasion. And another reason for not punishing those who fail to fulfill their epistemic obligations lies in the fact that such punishment would not be compatible with our right to freedom of thought – a right which, although it allows one to believe what one hadn't ought to believe, has compensating advantages in our present society ('Lewis' Ethics of Belief', p. 227).

The first reason for not punishing a person for his irresponsible beliefs (viz., they are not in their right mind) seems inconsistent with Chisholm's asseveration that believing is a free act, 'as much within his control as is any other deed we attribute to him.' The second reason for not punishing (that it is inconsistent with the right of freedom and thought) can be questioned also, for the notion of freedom of thought may not be an absolute right – especially if we could 'do' otherwise. Such a right seems to fare better within a nonvolitional system, where we cannot be said to have direct control over our beliefs.

Chisholm never tells us how he and Lewis know that beliefs are actions and not events. There is very little argument here. There is only one place where Chisholm argues for his position. It is in refuting Leibniz' argument against volitionalism. Leibniz thought that beliefs were not acts because they all consisted in remembering previous proofs or reasonings. Since memory is not within our power, neither can our beliefs be. But, counters Chisholm, even if this implausible thesis about beliefs being memories were true, there are respects in which our memory is dependent on the will.

If a memory judgment cannot be avoided, it may yet be altered. One can be persuaded that he mistakenly thought he remembered something. One may say: 'I thought I remembered once having visited him, but I realize now that I couldn't have been there.' Or one can be persuaded that some perceptual judgment upon which an (ostensible) memory depends was false. After saying 'I remember seeing him there', one may be led to concede, 'I certainly thought it was he at the time, but I realize now it couldn't have been', and hence to withdraw the original memory statement (ibid., p. 225).

But it may be questioned whether this is evidence for the thesis that remembering is within our control, is an act, for it could be accounted for equally well on nonvolitional grounds. It certainly doesn't seem to be evidence for the thesis that our believing and concluding contains all the 'main elements of moral conduct', as he approvingly quotes Peirce as saying.

There have been two significant criticisms of Chisholm's position in the literature. One is by Roderick Firth and criticizes Chisholm for committing a nonsequitor. The other is by Jack Meiland who criticizes Chisholm's evidentialist interpretation of the ethics of belief. We shall note briefly Firth's objection and then look at Meiland's position in more detail.

Firth, in his article 'Chisholm and the Ethics of Belief' points out that epistemic states or duties and moral states or duties may be analogous without being strictly entailed. That is, both may be classified as *normative* without being one a sub-set of the other. In proceeding directly from epistemic statements to moral judgments Chisholm neglects to notice the possibility that there may be other ways to evaluate a belief than simply on the basis of how close it follows evidential rules. For instance, it could be the case that the consequences of getting ourselves to believe against adequate evidence was morally justified.[11]

Jack Meiland picks up on this point and uses it to attack the whole enterprise of evidentialism. Although his criticisms are of evidentialism *tout court*, it includes Chisholm's variety. In his article 'What Ought We to Believe? or The Ethics of Belief Revisited' Meiland develops a radical position which claims that we have no special moral duties connected with epistemic states, but that every epistemic state must be judged from without from the perspective of morality. In all cases of belief-acquisition 'extra-factual considerations are relevant'.[12]

Whether it be Clifford's Scroogian evidentialism or Chisholm's Lady Bountiful version, evidentialism prohibits belief where the evidence is not sufficient. Fully justified belief is evidential belief. Anyone not believing a proposition where the evidence is sufficient is morally culpable. The conclusion of evidentialism is that no two persons having the same evidence regarding a given proposition could disagree in their doxastic state and still be rational. If both A and B are presented with the same argument regarding the existence for God and they differ, one of them must be irrational (though Chisholm is vague here, at times, allowing some difference within the area of 'epistemic indifference').

Meiland rejects evidentialism for it neglects important passional and volitional factors. He also rejects the Lockean variety of the ethics of belief which calls on us to tailor our beliefs to the evidence available. The only ethics of belief are ethical concerns *per se*. That is, *contra* Çhisholm, we have no special epistemic duties. The only duties there are are moral duties. Meiland argues on utilitarian grounds that it is often morally required that we act against so-called 'epistemic requirements' of sufficient evidence. He accepts a volitionalism which endorses acts of will to produce beliefs wherever a moral consequence is at stake. Here he is far more radical than James or Chisholm who allow voliting when the evidence is not sufficient, as a sort of tie breaker. Meiland holds that we may get ourselves (directly or indirectly) to believe propositions even when we have sufficient evidence to the contrary. However, he does not go as far as Kierkegaard in allowing for believing against conclusive evidence. There, it may not be in our power to obtain a belief by willing to have it.

The sort of 'sufficient evidence' for a proposition which we may believe against is illustrated by the example of the wife who finds lipstick on her husband's handkerchief, a blond strand of hair on his suit and a crumpled piece of paper with a telephone number on it in a woman's handwriting in his pocket. This would constitute sufficient evidence that the husband is having an affair with another woman and would normally cause the wife to believe that the husband is indeed seeing another woman. However, the wife sees that if she believes the evidence, their marriage will be ruined and great unhappiness will ensue, but that if she can somehow believe that her husband is innocent, the marriage will be saved. She believes that her husband will get over his craze and return to his marital commitment. Suppose that she has good evidence for this second belief. Should she not acquire the belief which would save her marriage? Perhaps she also knows that once she has obtained the 'unwarranted belief' and has saved the marriage, she will recall the process that led her to volit in the first place, so that no permanent damage will be done to her belief-forming mechanisms. Is it not possible that it is at least morally permissible to volit here?

I shall return to Meiland's paper in the second part of this work. But before closing this section we should briefly examine two other contemporary attempts to work out an ethics of belief. The first is contained in Richard Gale's 'William James and the Ethics of Belief'[13] and the second is J.T. Stevenson's theory in 'On Doxastic Responsibility'.[14] These two theses complement each other: the first offering an argument from personal autonomy and the second producing a broadly utilitarian argument. To these articles we now turn.

Richard Gale develops a deontological argument for evidentialism, which he calls the 'Scientific Credo', i.e., that it is morally wrong to get oneself to believe a proposition against sufficient evidence. The position he is attacking may be called volitionalism, which states that it is often morally permissible or obligatory to believe against or in the absense of sufficient evidence. Gale does not maintain that believing is under our direct control, but takes the rather uncontroversial position that it is often under our indirect control. Person S would like to believe that p, sees that doing a set of actions a is sufficient to produce a state of mind where he will believe that p, and does a, successfully bringing it about that S comes to believe that p. While indirect volitionalism is not in itself immoral (i.e., there may be cases where one does have sufficient evidence for p but cannot overcome some psychological quirk that prevents one from believing p), it becomes immortal where it violates the evidential warrant, causing belief in spite of the evidence. Ethical duties tie into epistemic duties via the 'Personhood Defense of the Scientific Credo' in that volitionalism violates 'an absolute moral stricture against undermining an individual's personhood' (p. 6). Reduced to its bare bones Gale's highly detailed argument is as follows:

1 It is a moral absolute that we ought never to diminish the free will of a person.
2 Acting on less than the best justified beliefs available diminishes the freedom of persons, reducing their autonomy, in that they do not have the best reasons available to them to guide their actions.

3 Volitional believing what is unwarranted by the evidence causes us to act on less than the best justified beliefs available.

4 Therefore, volitional believing against sufficient evidence diminishes the freedom of persons, reducing their autonomy, in that they do not have the best reasons available to them for action guidance. By (1.) such believing must be considered morally wrong.

By 'free will' Gale is neutral between compatibilist and libertarian accounts of freedom of the will. He uses the term to signify acting with maximal knowledge of possibilities. It seems to play the same role for him as 'rationality' does for Kant. 'To have free will is to behave as a morally responsible agent' (p. 6). A morally responsible agent, according to Gale's Kantianism, has 'Absolute value'.

The crucial premise in the argument is the first premise: that it is *always* wrong to diminish the free will of a person. But a follower of William James might object that there is no reason to accept Gale's absolutist stand here. If by voliting (indirectly, if not directly), I can bring it about that I could acquire a belief that would somehow cause me to act in such a way that I might save the lives of many fellow human beings, is it obvious that I ought not to do so?

At the end of his paper Gale admits that one may dissent from the Kantian absolutism of the personhood principle and suggests a possible weaker principle, viz., treating the personhood principle as a prima facie duty which might be overridden in extreme circumstances. It would seem that this principle would have a better chance of acceptance.

Appearing in a *Festschrift* (dedication work) for Roderick Chisholm, J. T. Stevenson's article 'On Doxastic Responsibility' makes a case for the social importance of highly justified beliefs that is consonant with the work of his mentor. Stevenson attempts to sail a course between the Charybdis of those who admit that we are responsible for our beliefs but claim absolute freedom of thought (he quotes H.H. Price and John Stuart Mill) and Scylla of those who say that we are never responsible for our beliefs in the first place (he quotes Thomas Jefferson and William Walwyn, p. 229f). Stevenson contends that we are responsible for our beliefs (if only indirectly, by focusing our attention on the available evidence, developing critical habits, accepting a stance of fallibilism), and, as such, we should be held responsible for them.

His first task is to undermine the position of Price that while we are responsible for our beliefs the 'ought' in the principle 'one ought to try to have the best justified beliefs' is purely a prudential ought. Price is wary of an ethics of belief on utilitarian grounds. He fears that holding that people deserve to be punished for their intellectual errors as well as for their moral delinquencies could lead to justifying 'all sorts of political and religious persecution'. Stevenson points out that 'persecution' means already suffering 'unjustly or outrageously'. We could have a system of punishment that was not persecutionary, but just. Furthermore, it is one thing to see the connection between doxastic responsibility and punishment and another thing to apply it in social situations. We may well accept a deterrentist or prospective view of punishment (even a Skinnerian approach which emphasizes positive reward) and, so, not misuse it.

The question that needs to be discussed is, 'What is the nature and justification of the practice of holding people responsible for their doxastic attitudes?' (p. 231). Stevenson believes that the acceptance of duties and accountability on the part of members of a group (his example is the crew of a ship) is a necessary condition for accomplishing any social project.

> The quasi-logical point [about the relationship of autonomy to accountability] is that responsibilities (duties and accountability) presuppose responsibility (agency) only of such a type as to make the responsibility system *work*. The responsibility system requires, for example, beings capable of understanding and acting in accordance with rules, but it does not require uncaused causes [the libertarian notion of free will]. It does not even require, I believe, beings capable of reflecting critically on the rules of the system; a responsibility system can be one of customs or habits which have grown and evolved without deliberate contrivance ('On Doxastic Responsibility', p. 242).

The point is that a society cannot get on without a notion of responsibility. Now it is fairly obvious that our actions are generated from our beliefs. We spontaneously act and speak on the basis of our beliefs. Many of our actions have significant social importance (here Stevenson discusses the role of shared knowledge in science). 'A community's survival and welfare depends in part on the stock of beliefs, hopefully knowledge, which it receives from past generations and which it transmits to future generations. Not all of this can or should be left to the stewardship of a special class; much of it will be generated, preserved and transmitted by members of the community at large. We all, then, have a stake in seeing that this communal heritage is not seriously corrupted' (p. 249). Since we can affect the kinds of belief we have through our actions, we must take responsibility for our beliefs. Since they have deep social import, that responsibility is not merely prudential but moral.

The concern for highly justified beliefs in important areas of life needs to be institutionalized both formally and informally. The chief formal means in society is the educational system 'in which youth is put under special tutelage, special accountability to their teachers, with a view not only to convey to them some part of the community's doxastic heritage as it stands at that time but with a view to making them on a permanent basis amenable to reason'. The informal means should involve expectations, habits, and attitudes which we bring to our general discourse with one another.

Stevenson admits that there is a need for experimentation with creative ideas and that individual creativity may flourish better where there is a large degree of freedom of opinion. 'What is to be opposed is that individualism which demands complete freedom of belief, which claims there is no justification for the imposition of obligations concerning belief, which denies that anyone can ever be accountable to others for his beliefs, which claims inviolable rights to mental privacy' (p. 251). Such a view may be found in some of J.S. Mill's work, when he calls for 'absolute freedom of opinion on all subjects'. Stevenson contends that our predilection with relatively unrestricted individualism needs to give way to a 'communalistic view which would restrict doxastic freedom to the *responsible* formation and expression of opinion and belief'.

While Stevenson's article deserves more attention as the most sustained defense of a social argument for an ethics of belief, one of the areas that it leaves relatively untouched is the problem of 'sufficient evidence'. Exactly, what does that mean and how do we determine it? He presupposes a relatively free society in his discussion, but one could use his arguments with their emphasis on 'communalism' to justify a benevolent despotism, a Platonic Republic. There is always the danger of the majority or privileged class imposing their standards onto weaker groups. The Gulag and 'hsi nao' (brain washing) are not inconsistent with Stevenson's position, even if they are with his motives.

But not only does it seem dangerous to contemplate moral control over our beliefs, it also seems impossible to decide whether they are justified. We cannot get to all the evidence and causal factors involved in belief formation in order to decide whether the beliefs are justified or not. We don't know enough about the unconscious belief forming mechanisms, nor can we bring in an accurate impersonal assessment of all the relevant evidence when there is ambiguous evidence or evidence on both sides of an issue.

The Volitionalism Debate in Contemporary Philosophy

Since the early 70's several articles on the relation between the will and belief acquisition have appeared, beginning with Bernard Williams' influential 'Deciding to Believe' (1972) and ending with Robert Holyer's provocative 'Belief and Will Revisited' (1983). In this section I shall describe some of the major arguments made in the ongoing discussion that takes place in these articles, offering, in passing, some general comments which will be developed in the second part of the book.

Bernard Williams' 'Deciding to Believe', which first appeared in *Language, Belief, and Metaphysics* (ed. Kiefer and Margolis, SUNY Press) in 1970, is largely responsible for the renewed interest in the question of whether the will directly causes belief acquisition. First, Williams offers a causal account of belief modelled on perception. While there must be some basic beliefs, most beliefs are founded on other beliefs in a causal way. For example, my memory belief that I ate cereal this morning is based on the fact that I consciously did eat cereal for breakfast. Belief in testimony implies that there is an information-chain which goes back somewhere near the facts themselves.

If we suppose that beliefs are causal, originating at the far end of information-chains or as perceptions, then it would seem that they are happenings like physical events. Hume was right to describe them as passive phenomena, events which happened to us. But there is something unsettling about Hume's account, for he writes as though it is merely a contingent matter that beliefs are event like. They could very well have been actions. Williams compares this to the activity of blushing. While we can not blush at will, we might have been made differently, so that we could accomplish this feat. Then he contrasts belief acquisition with blushing.

> Belief cannot be like that; it is not a contingent fact that I cannot bring it about just like that, that I believe something, as it is a contingent fact that I cannot bring it about, just like that, that I'm blushing. Why is this? One reason is connected with the characteristic of beliefs that they aim at truth. If I could acquire a belief by will, I could acquire it whether it was true or not; moreover I would know that I could acquire it whether it was true or not. If in full consciousness I could will to acquire a 'belief' irrespective of its truth, it is unclear that before the event I could seriously think of it as a belief, i.e. as something purporting to represent reality. At the very least, there might be a restriction on what is the case after the event; since I could not then, in full consciousness, regard this as a belief of mine, i.e. something I take to be true, and also know that I acquire it at will. With regard to no belief could I know – or, if all this is to be done in full consciousness, even suspect – that I had acquired it at will. But if I can acquire beliefs at will, I must know that I am able to do this; and could I know that I was capable of this feat, if with regard to every feat of this kind which I had performed I necessarily had to believe that it had not taken place? (p. 148).

Williams' argument rests on the idea that if I truly choose something, I must be fully aware of it. His second premise is that belief aims at truth. But if we rule out those self-verifying future-oriented beliefs discussed by William James, then we must recognize that 'believing never makes it so'. Hence, if I could obtain a belief by a fiat of the will, fully conscious of what I was doing, I would be recognizing that beliefs are necessarily truth-directed and that they need not be truth-directed, which is a contradiction. 'If I can acquire beliefs at will, I must know that I am able to do this; and could I know that I was capable of this feat', if I had to believe that it had not taken place?

Williams accepts that there may be indirect ways of getting oneself to believe what one desires to believe. Through hypnotism, drugs and other means I might eventually bring it about that I believe some proposition. Self-deception is a classic instance of getting oneself to believe what one wants to believe.

But, asks Williams, what is wrong with the idea of a conscious project to get onself to believe what one wants to believe? Here he distinguishes two applications of 'wanting to believe': those cases which fall under the class of 'truth-centered motives' and those which fall under the class of 'non-truth-centered motives'. Suppose a father has apparently lost his son in an accident. The evidence strongly suggests that he drowned at sea, but the man very much desires to believe that his son is alive. There are two ways he might want to believe this: (1) he might want to believe this based on the truth of the proposition, and (2) he might want to have the belief for his own peace of mind or other psychological benefit regardless of the truth. In the first case he has a truth-centered motive, where wanting to believe means 'wanting it to be the case'. In the second case he wants to believe for non-truth-centered reasons, where wanting to believe has to do with psychological states, being happy, comfortable, free from internal pain, and so forth. It is only in the second type of cases that it makes sense to go about getting oneself to believe by indirect means (e.g., going to the hypnotist or practicing autosuggestion) in order to obtain certain irrational beliefs.

However, this indirect non-truth-centered questing for beliefs is fraught with dangers. It opens up the possibility of chaos in one's noetic structure.

> [By] believing what is false . . . there is no end to the amount you have to pull down. It is like a revolutionary movement trying to extirpate the last remains of the *ancien regime*. The man gets rid of this belief about his son, and then there is some belief which strongly implies that his son is dead, and that has to be got rid of. Then there is another belief which could lead his thoughts in the undesired direction, and that has to be got rid of. It might be that a project of this kind tended in the end to involve total destruction of the world of reality, to lead to paranoia. Perhaps this is one reason why we have a strongly internalized objection to it. If we are not going to destroy all the evidence – all consciousness of the evidence – we have to have a project for steering ourselves through the world so as to avoid the embarrassing evidence. That sort of project is the project of the man who is deceiving himself, and he must really know what is true; for if he did not really know what was true, he would not

112

be able to steer around the contrary and conflicting evidence. Whether we should or should not say that he also believes what he really knows to be true, is one of the problems that surround self-deception (p. 151).

The sharpest critique of Williams' thesis that there is something contradictory about the thesis that we can obtain beliefs by direct fiats of the will is Barbara Winters' article 'Believing at Will' (*Journal of Philosophy*, 1979). Winters neither supports nor refutes the possibility of voliting in general, but she maintains that we can only rule out a certain type of direct volitionalism as logically impossible. Her thesis is that 'it is impossible to believe that one believes *p* and that one's belief of *p* originates and is sustained in a way that has no connection with *p*'s truth' (p. 243). She argues that this does not rule out the possibility that belief acquisitions are basic acts, as Williams tried to show.

In her analysis of normal belief acquisition she is in agreement with Williams that normally we acquire beliefs by being concerned about the truth of the proposition in question, rather than by willing to believe the proposition. Indeed, simply being confident that a belief has been formed through a non-volitional, truth-centered method gives us some reason to think that the belief is true (p. 245). If volitional believings are possible, we lack such assurance about our method of acquisition and are aware that the belief has no connection with the belief's truth – a liability which causes reflective disturbances.

Winters neatly distinguishes her moderate thesis from those of other philosophers who have written on the subject. Stuart Hampshire's position is that it is impossible for a person in full consciousness to believe that if his continuing belief of *p* would not be sustained by any truth consideration, he would no longer believe that *p*. But this seems to ignore the fact that we often are unaware of our beliefs.

In support of her own claim that we cannot in full-consciousness believe both that *p* and that *p* originates and is sustained apart from truth considerations, she offers some examples. The first is a modified example taken from Stuart Hampshire. A mesmerized subject is caused by a hypnotist to believe that he has an excellent singing voice. However, he later comes to realize that his belief has been caused entirely by the hypnotist's suggestion. Winters asks,

'Can the subject still think he holds this belief, now realizing that his current convictions about his musical talent have resulted only from the hypnotist's machinations?' (p. 248). In certain circumstances we could answer 'yes'. We could if, for example, the subject already had sufficient evidence for the proposition that he was an excellent singer but failed 'to achieve the warranted belief state owing to an inferiority complex'. But if the singer is unable to find such support for his belief, he cannot continue to believe that he believes that his voice is beautiful.

> As long as he remains fully conscious of the temptation's origin and cannot explain away the conflicting evidence, he will not be able to credit this feeling with the status of a belief. . . . He cannot regard himself as believing something while knowing that his belief did not stem from a source that made it in any way likely that the beliefs acquired from it were true (p. 248f).

Continuing to believe propositions after realizing that there is no truth connection for them is like continuing to hold to a dream after one wakes up in the morning and realizes that what has been experienced was only a dream. One cannot 'simultaneously in full consciousness' believe that the proposition in question is believed by the subject and yet hold that the proposition is not supported by the evidence.

Turning to Williams' analysis, Winters analyzes the passage quoted on p. 111 (above), where he maintains that we cannot acquire beliefs by will, because this would mean that we both must know and, at the same time, cannot know that we are able to acquire beliefs by will. Winters points out that there is a problem with Williams' argument, because he fails to distinguish between 'acquired at will' and 'sustained by will'. I may have formed the belief in a non-truth-centered way but now actually have good reason to hold it (as with the mesmerized singer). That is, the contradiction cited by Williams does not go through, because now I know that I believe the proposition for truth-directed reasons. If Williams' argument (on Winters interpretation) were to go through, 'I could not believe that my belief *b* arose from a basic act even if it did' (p. 254).

An article which attacks Williams from a similar vantage point but argues even more strongly for the possibility of volitional acts is that of Trudy Govier's 'Belief, Values and the Will' (*Dialogue* XV, no. 4, 1976). The article defends the thesis that 'logic and epistemology presuppose that there is some sense in which a person controls what he believes – some sense in which 'can' has a place in contexts where one comes to believe things' (p. 642). She sees herself critically following in the tracks of C.I. Lewis and R.M. Chisholm, clarifying and extending their notions of control in belief formation. Govier sets forth three different ways in which the will might be considered to function in belief formation: (1) belief by fiat; (2) Pascalian control, or indirect volitionalism; and (3) control by deliberation.

Concerning belief by fiat, she argues that philosophers such as Williams have failed to make their case that there is a logical inconsistency in the notion of believing just because one wants to. Her main thrust is to show that Williams' argument for the impossibility of believing by fiat has severe problems. First of all:

> It seems to rule out all believing for anyone with sufficient self-knowledge not to regard himself as infallible. Most people know that they have held beliefs which have turned out to be false and 'not representative of reality'; they nevertheless, in believing those things they do believe, believe these things to be true. Now if this is possible, then it would appear that Williams' argument contains some crucial flaw; for he is maintaining that *because* a person believing by *fiat* would know that he could believe irrespective of truth, believing by fiat is impossible. This argument is not sufficient. It might be buttressed up by adding that if one knew that a proposition was believed by *fiat*, one would know that it positively was not true. The problem with this stipulation is that one does not and could not uphold it in general, because something which one believed by *fiat* might be true by accident. One might know this in the particular case in which one was trying to believe by fiat in the face of compelling evidence against the proposition in question. Williams' argument could then be regarded as showing that belief by *fiat* was impossible in that kind of case, but not that it was impossible in general. But as it stands, Williams' first argument cannot support his conclusion (p. 647).

There seems nothing logically impossible about believing by fiat. If beliefs are immune from direct voluntary control, this may be not because of the nature of beliefs but, as Hume thought, because of human nature. We can imagine a creature, call it 'Super-Mind', who can change both his emotions and his beliefs simply by willing to be in a different state. 'Let us say that Super-Mind wills that there is another entity with a mind just like his own. Having decided to believe this proposition, he reflects on it, feels attached to it, acts as though it is true, and frequently asserts it. Believing it is believing that there is another creature with a super-mind' (p. 649).

Super-Mind is not a god, his wish is not father to the fact, so he cannot have inductive evidence to support a belief that his belief is self-verifying. So there will be some tension in Super-Mind's soul between his beliefs about the independent status of reality, the requirement that beliefs aim at truth, and his knowledge of his having willed to believe without evidence.

Williams' point is that this tension is radical. Super-Mind would experience no tension if he always forgot having willed to believe, but then he would be deprived of the knowledge that he was willing to believe. So he would not 'set out to believe by *fiat* if he did not know, or at least reasonably believe, that he was capable of doing this' (p. 650).

> The problem with belief by *fiat* within the kind of metaphysical framework we are dealing with is that it seems to require the following combination of beliefs on the part of the Super-Mind: (1) he cannot alter reality by mere acts of will; (2) there is another super-mind; and (3) he came to believe that there was another super-mind by *fiat*. There is a tension in this combination of beliefs, for the Super-Mind takes his beliefs to be true of reality and yet knows that one of them has been acquired without reference to reality, and solely in virtue of an act of his own will. This tension – which may or may not amount to an actual inconsistency – is internal to the combination of propositions. But whether there is a contradiction here or not, there is certainly no contradiction in the supposition that Super-Mind *believes* all of these propositions. He might believe all three, if he failed to be aware of the tension between them. If he did this, then he would have succeeded in believing by *fiat*, and believing by *fiat* would be shown to be logically possible. There is no contradiction in Super-Mind's performing this feat: hence I conclude that belief by *fiat* is logically possible. If it is impossible for human beings, it must be contingently impossible for them (p. 650f).

Not only does Williams fail to take this sort of situation into account, but his account fails to distinguish between coming to believe categorically (100%) and raising one's level of confidence in a proposition (e.g., from 55% to 65%). 'To strongly reject belief by fiat would be to claim that it is impossible even to raise one's level of confidence in any proposition by a mere act of will.' Govier concludes that the difficulties regarding believing by fiat are not logical ones but metaphysical. 'They arise from doctrines about belief and truth, truth and reality, and the concept of reality as something independent of direct control by a creature's will' (p. 651). Whether humans can perform such acts is an empirical question, and, as such, one on which philosophers ought to refrain from pronouncing a final verdict.

Turning to Pascalian Control, that we can affect our belief states by our actions, Govier does not think that this is controversial. We affect our belief states by getting ourselves into situations where certain evidence will be likely to affect us in a way that will cause us to believe what we would like to believe. This type of control over our belief states is admitted by virtually everyone who has written on the matter, but, Govier points out, what is the difference between the case where one believes by fiat and the case where one takes a few hours or days to obtain the belief? Merely a matter of time and intermediate actions. 'This difference would explain the fact (if it is one) that the first case is *psychologically* impossible, whereas the second is *psychologically* possible. But it would not explain any *logical* impossibility of the first case which failed to apply to the second, for an alleged logical impossibility would have to rest on some incompatibility in the combination of the concepts belief, truth, and decision. With respect to these concepts, the second case is the same as the first.'

Next, we turn to Govier's thesis that we can control our beliefs by deliberation. Sometimes the evidence is ambiguous and insufficient, or when one wants to check the matter more fully, one often makes a decision to seek further or to look at the evidence more critically or completely. These, while not decisions to believe either by fiat or in the Pascalian sense, are decisions which affect our belief states. One is making decisions in determining how much further evidence one is going to attempt to obtain. In a sense, one is 'deciding *what to believe*' (p. 654).

Control by deliberation can be illustrated by a person reflecting in order to reach a conclusion. In this situation one can direct one's reflection according to a variety of standards, only some of which are logical or epistemic (i.e., truth-oriented, rather than prudential, moral or aesthetic). A person can discover that he is biased in favor of a friend and so turn his attention to aspects of the case that would neutralize this factor in concern for veracity; or he can tell himself that he has a moral duty to be loyal to his friend and so turn his attention away from adverse evidence; or he can decide that he is too busy to investigate the matter further and so make a judgment on admittedly limited evidence.

> Control by deliberation is such that a person can choose to base his decision on epistemic and logical standards, or to base them on other standards. His choices here are comparable to moral choices where he may choose to act on one moral principle, on another, or on none at all (p. 658).

Finally, Govier agrees with Firth that those who (like Chisholm) equate epistemic appraisals with ethical ones or who infer ethical appraisals directly from epistemic ones without additional premises are in error because of the possibility of non-epistemic evaluations of states of belief. However, she agrees with Chisholm that there is an ethics of belief, and, as is the case with moral duties, sometimes we may have a conflict of duties involved with regard to belief states. In these cases we must simply make a decision, which again illustrates the place of the will in cases of conscious belief acquisition. 'Oughts' have a place here, and we have some substantial control over many of our belief states.

A direct response to Govier's position came two years later in a paper by H.G. Classen, 'Will, Belief and Knowledge' (*Dialogue*, 1979), in which the author argues that Govier has failed to make her case that 'it is possible to believe something by an act of will', for it goes beyond the acceptable premises of her argument, showing that we do have some control over our belief acquisitions. Having control, which may entail direct or indirect control, does not necessitate direct control. Classen does not offer any fresh arguments against volitionalism per se, but defends Williams' position by trying to neutralize Govier's arguments.

Classen argues that all who believe something have some authority for what they believe (p. 67). He does not dispute that there are many ways in which people can control not only the process leading to belief, but those processes leading to knowledge. He illustrates this point with the example of a widow who comes across a pile of love-letters of her late husband, implicating him in an adulterous affair. The widow immediately puts the pile to the pyre and thus precludes any knowledge of her late husband's paramour's name.

What Classen contests is that we can ever believe without authority (or evidence). The view that we can choose our criteria of assent (in deliberation), which he finds in O'Hear ('Belief and Will', *Philosophy*, 1972) and Govier, he finds indefensible, for this move only shifts the problem to another level. We must ask what is the authority for believing that one criterion is better than another?

With regard to Govier's Super-Mind, Classen argues that it could not have the sort of power of believing anything at all by fiat. For example, suppose that, on seeing Super-Mind B approaching his house, Super-Mind A tries to act surprised at Super-Mind B's visit, for he knows how much Super-Mind B loves to surprise people. He can 'act surprised' at the visit, but he cannot 'be surprised', for as Chisholm says, 'I think we may say that no one can believe falsely at any time either that he is surprised at that time or that he is not surprised at that time.' Coming to believe is no more an act or achievement than coming to know anything. 'Acts are what we do, and what we do we can, at least in logic, undo. But we cannot by an act of will "unknow" something that we knew. This is not a contingent aspect of belief and knowledge, but a necessary one' p. 72).

If Classen's counter-example is accepted, what it shows is that even Super-Mind would have limitations on what he could come to believe by willing to believe. He might just as well have used the Cartesian 'cogito', showing that we cannot will to doubt certain self-evident truths. He has not shown that Govier's thesis is invalid, only that it needs to be modified. There is a logic of belief that applies, at least, to some beliefs so that not every type of volitionalism is contingent.

An article has recently appeared, in the spirit of Govier's work, that points to a new emphasis in the volitional debate. Rather than focusing on whether belief by fiat is logically or contingently possible, Robert Holyer, in his article 'Belief and Will Revisited' (*Dialogue*, 1983), contends that the debate carried on by Price, Williams, Classen and myself has focused too much on whether we can obtain beliefs directly by a fiat of the will. In fact, Holyer says (but does not show), a careful reading of the work of the classic writers in support of volitionalism would show that they were 'really dealing with other issues' than direct volitionalism. Holyer sets forth the traditional distinction between the will's *directly* and *indirectly* influencing belief and states that this distinction has been made superficially clear-cut, when it is really quite complicated. Whereas direct volitionalism is contested, indirect volitionalism is uncontroversial. But the latter actually entails the former, so Holyer contends.

The importance of Holyer's article lies in the direction it takes. Pursuing themes found in Govier's article (above) and suggested before that by Anthony O'Hear, Holyer seeks to turn the discussion away from the problem of whether we can obtain beliefs by a fiat of the will to other ways in which the will does enter into belief acquisitions and sustainments. Quite radically, he wishes to abolish or greatly modify the traditional distinction between direct and indirect control the will has on belief formation.

In order to have a clear example of a deliberation process that leads to a belief, Holyer supposes a seasoned atheist who encounters a 'particularly persuasive religious believer'. In the course of their discussion the atheist finds, to his surprise, that the believer has some unusually cogent arguments for her position and is able to offset his strongest objections. Finally, he has to admit that the case for religious belief is impeccable. 'Yet, he does not at once assent; instead he goes away to mull the issues over in his mind, to search for other objections, to consult his atheist friends to see if they can shed new light on the matter, and to check the believer's facts and interpretations against reputedly expert opinion' (p. 276). It turns out that he cannot refute the believer's case and, 'at length, his conviction grows and he finally gives up his atheism to become a believer'.

Holyer thinks that this story illustrates how belief and *knowledge* are directly influenced by the will. He states that there are five senses in which 'knowledge as well as belief is voluntary' (p. 279). These are:

1 The atheist could refuse to examine the evidence which constitutes an element of direct control.
2 The atheist also exercises choice in that he selects certain epistemic norms or criteria by which to evaluate the evidence.

He suggests the criteria of 'coherence and agreement with historical fact' when he could choose others, such as that the believer was rationalizing his own self-interested concerns.

3 The atheist displays the capacity to withhold assent in the face of strong evidence, for he does not automatically assent to the religious propositions. 'Without this capacity to withhold assent . . ., he could not have exercised the caution and prudence demanded by his own personal integrity and the momentousness of the issue. Normally we would say that the atheist initially suspended judgment (note the *active* voice) and that he finally decided to believe – his will being exercised in both.' We can 'avoid assenting to strongly evidenced beliefs by not thinking about them' (p. 278).

4 The atheist exercises choice in that the termination of his deliberation is *to a degree* arbitrary. He could continue the investigation further before he concludes as he does. Logic alone does not tell us when to stop the process of deliberation; only the will does. More importantly, when we are deliberating, we are not believing, but suspending belief until we decide to believe.

5 'The atheist's initial reluctance to believe as well as his eventual assent may be described as the products of his will in that they were influenced by certain emotions over which he could exercise some control' (p. 278). Hope, fear, and desire can often play a deep role in the beliefs we end up with.

I have offered a critique of Holyer's proposal elsewhere.[15] Briefly, I try to show that all the essential challenges that Holyer makes can be met by a non-volitionalist in such a way that preserves the traditional distinction between the direct and indirect causal effects of the will on belief formation. For example, senses 1 and 4 have to do with the process of investigation and paying attention. This can be accounted for by a traditional interpretation of indirect influence, for we can focus attention, carry on an investigation, and deliberate about propositions without necessarily believing them. The investigation and deliberation are within our control (to some extent), but this does not entail that belief itself is within our direct control. If, by doing A voluntarily, I effect B, it would seem that only A is a basic act, not B. I can directly control the movement of my arm or leg simply by willing to move them in one way or another, but in moving them in the requisite ways while in my car, I only indirectly control the movements of the car. Likewise, I can directly control my operation of my eyes by opening and shutting them or by looking in one direction rather than another, but I cannot control what I see when I open them. While there is a close causal relation between deliberating and believing, and while deliberating may be a basic act, there is no reason to suppose that believing is.

Regarding 2, I doubt whether we do choose our criteria in a directly volitional way. Our criteria are already standards that we believe to be applicable to areas of judgment (e.g., we believe that the criterion of imagination is correctly applicable to works of poetry). If Holyer means that we can experiment with norms in some hypothetical way, I would agree that we can do this, but not in the way he imagines. Our atheist may say, 'Let's see what the situation would look like if I interpreted all that the believer said from a Freudian perspective', without believing that criterion of assessment – or believing it very strongly. However, after applying it, he may be struck by the explanatory power of the criterion (non-volitionally, I might add) and so acquire a belief in the Freudian interpretation.

Sense 5 can also be explained by the indirect influence of the will on belief formation. In fact, Holyer's examples and discussion could easily be accommodated to the standard non-volitional account. Our emotions, desires, hopes, fears, and imaginings often affect our noetic structure. Auto-suggestion and self-deception are classic cases of the indirect influence of the will on belief. Perhaps, there is a more direct component, but Holyer has failed to demonstrate this. It is sense 3 (the ability to withhold assent through turning away from the evidence) which may be Holyer's strongest point. I shall postpone discussion of this point until the second part of this work.

CHAPTER XII

The Contemporary Debate on Faith and Reason: Fideism and Rationalism

Wittgensteinian Fideism: Norman Malcolm

'God exists' is not a statement of fact. You might say also that it is not in the indicative mood. It is a confession – or expression – of faith. This is recognized in some way when people say that God's existence is 'necessary existence' as opposed to the 'contingency' of what exists as a matter of fact; and when they say that to doubt God's existence is a sin, as opposed to a mistake about the facts (Rush Rhees, *Without Answers*, p. 130).

Although Ludwig Wittgenstein (1889–1951) said very little about religion, his philosophy of language, as well as his remarks on certainty and religious language, have formed the basis of an interesting and influential position on the subject of faith and reason. It is a position that takes a suspicious view of external justification of religious beliefs and tends to locate all meaningful discussion of religion within a distinctive mode of discourse or form of life. Understanding a form of life, such as a religion, depends on meaningful participation in it. There is no objectively neutral place from which a philosopher can relevantly criticize whole modes of discourse, for each mode of discourse or form of life has its own internal logic and criteria of rationality. Philosophy cannot validly criticize religion. All it can do is reveal that inner logic. Essentially, one must be a believer in order to take part in the critical enterprise, for the non-believer and the believer do not mean the same thing when they use the same words. They take their meanings out of different conceptual contexts or language games.

Prominent adherents to this position are D.Z. Phillips, Peter Winch, G.E. Hughes, and Norman Malcolm.[1] While these philosophers differ among themselves on some points and their focus is different, they all share the internalist methodology and epistemology mentioned above. Because he is the clearest example of Wittgensteinian fideism, I have chosen Malcolm as the focal point for the discussion of this view. His article, 'The Groundlessness of Religious Belief' ('GRB'), will serve as our primary material.

Malcolm contends that religious beliefs are not hypotheses, since they are never held tentatively by religious believers, as though the evidence could possibly discredit them. They are regulative axioms that are groundless. They cannot and ought not to be justified, for they form the criteria of all other justification. They are comparable to other groundless beliefs, such as (1) our belief that things don't vanish; (2) belief in the uniformity of nature; (3) one's knowledge of one's intentions; and (4) our belief in the law of induction. These basic beliefs belong to the framework of our thinking about the world.

> Framework principles such as the continuity of nature or the assumption that material things do not cease to exist without physical cause belong to what Wittgenstein calls a 'system'. He makes the following observation. . . . : 'All testing, all confirmation and disconfirmation of a hypothesis takes place already within a system. And this system is not a more or less arbitrary and doubtful point of departure for all our arguments: no, it belongs to the nature of what we call an argument. The system is not so much the point of departure as the elements in which arguments have their life' (GRB, p. 146).

A 'system' provides the boundaries *within* which we ask questions, investigate and justify. 'Hypotheses are put forth, and challenged, *within* a system. Verification, justification, the search for evidence, occur *within* a system. The framework propositions of the system are not put to the test, not backed up by evidence.' Here, Malcolm cites Wittgenstein's remarks in *On Certainty* ('OC'): 'Of course there is justification; but justification comes to an end' (OC, 192) . . . and 'Whenever we test anything we are already presupposing something that is not tested' (OC, 163). 'We grow into a framework. We don't question it. We accept it trustingly.' And we do all this in a nonvolitional way. 'We do not decide to accept framework propositions. We do not decide that we live on the earth, any more than we decide to learn our native tongue' (p. 147). The principles are the common ways of speaking and thinking that the community takes for granted and passes down to its posterity. As such, they are not looked upon as contingent propositions whose credibility might rise or fall on the basis of evidence. They are viewed as non-contingent, as necessary truths.

Religion is one form of life among others. It is language embedded in action, a 'language game'. 'Science is another. Neither stands in need of justification, the one no more than the other' (p. 156). While science has a wider acceptance in our culture (especially among academics), this in itself has no bearing on the issue of justification. For there can be no understanding of a form of life without participation in that form. Only those who have religious experiences can appreciate the role of the language.

The very notion of separating belief *that* God exists from belief *in* seems strange to Malcolm. Criticizing Roger Trigg, Malcolm thinks this to be an artificial distinction. He drives a wide wedge between 'religious belief' and 'religious doctrines'. The faith of the believer is different from the formalized creed. This is the same point that Rhees is making in the statement quoted at the head of this chapter, 'God exists is not a statement of fact', but a confession or expression of faith made from within a form of life. The believer uses the term God *in* the religious activities of worship, prayer and service, while the theologian and philosopher talk about an abstraction which is removed from the essential language games of religious discourse.

John Hick makes this point more clearly when he writes: 'faith consists of a voluntary recognition of God's activity in human history, consisting in seeing, appreciating, or interpreting events in a special way'.[2] The man of faith does not merely see a mountain, but sees God's marvelous handiwork. Faith is fundamentally interpretive.

Wittgensteinian fideism has been criticized from many sources. Some have argued that this position neglects the fact that there has been a strong apologetic strain in traditional religion and that this strain seeks to provide some justification for religious beliefs.[3] Others have pointed out that religious beliefs are not universal in the way Malcolm's other groundless beliefs are. That is, our belief in induction and that things don't disappear enjoy virtually universal acceptance, and it is hard to imagine any form of life without them, whereas religious beliefs which are peculiar to times and specific cultures, are more particular.[4] Kai Nielsen has argued that the fideist position reduces 'God-talk' to 'witch-talk', for neither offers external criteria that would root it in our common experience.[5]

In the sharpest examination of Wittgensteinian fideism known to me, Gary Gutting has pointed out that if the meaning of religious language is entirely *sui generis* in the way that the fideists sometimes claim, 'then there are no *religious* answers to our basic human questions about suffering, death, love and hope', for an 'answer must share a context of meaning with the question to which it responds. On the internalist construal, religion does not answer our questions; it changes the subject.'[6] Gutting also points out that in spite of the telling insights made by Malcolm, Phillips and others with regard to religious language, they themselves have done very little toward developing a detailed account of the nature of God-talk, and 'for this reason, Wittgensteinian philosophy of religion remains embarrassingly programmatic'.[7]

We shall return to Wittgensteinian fideism in Part II (chapter XV) and before that we shall examine a position similar to it, which is not so language dependent, and which avoids many of the objections made against it. But before we turn to Plantinga's reformed religious epistemology, we need to examine the exact opposite of Wittgensteinian fideism, the rationalism of Richard Swinburne.

Modern Evidentialism: Richard Swinburne

Whereas fideism treats religious belief as entirely regulative of one's life and non-contingent, Swinburne locates religion as an explanatory hypothesis of the world. If, for the fideist, faith is against reason, for Swinburne, it is based entirely on reason. Whereas, for the fideist, all justification must be internal to the system, Swinburne is an externalist, allowing the deliverances of reason to make whatever case it can. In an impressive attempt to work out a comprehensive philosophy of religion, Swinburne's recent Oxford University Wilde Lectures constitute a cogent defense of theism. It is mainly Swinburne's third series of lectures, now published under the title *Faith and Reason*, that shall occupy us in this section.

Swinburne separates belief from faith. Belief is defined in terms of probability. Normally, to believe that some proposition *p* is true is to be in a dispositional mental state which judges that *p* is more probable than not (p. 4). However, he offers a weaker form of believing in which the subject merely believes that p is more probable than any of its alternatives (e.g., I might only believe that Smith has a 40% chance of winning the election, but since I believe that the other two candidates, Jones and Brown, each have only a 30% chance of winning, I can be said to believe weakly that Smith will win). The importance of believing is that it is action guiding. We need beliefs in order to reach our goals. Beliefs and wants together determine action. If I believe that p is more probable than q and entails that doing some act A_1, will bring about a desired goal, X, whereas q would mandate doing A_2, then I will do A_1 rather than A_2. Beliefs are dispositional, tendencies to act, but they are also mental states of which the 'subject is aware or can be made aware by self-examination' (p. 15).

Swinburne's account is nonvolitional. Believing is an event, not an action. Against Aquinas and on the side of Hume, he argues that we cannot choose our beliefs. Agreeing with Williams in opposition to Hume, however, he believes that this impossibility is not merely contingent, but logical. Using a similar argument as we found in Williams, Swinburne argues that since believing is a function of basic propositions and inductive rules, which precludes voluntary acquisition, our beliefs cannot be under our direct control. Of course, we can get ourselves to believe propositions by looking selectively at the evidence or trying to forget the selective character of our investigation. Indirect volitionalism involves an intervening action.

Swinburne next develops a foundationalist account of rational believing. Rational believing is based on evidence in the right way. Our basic evidence or beliefs are 'initial propositions' (sense experience, mental states, and memory reports) and 'prior propositions' (truths known a priori, such as the laws of logic or that '2 + 2 = 4'). From these we reason deductively or inductively to conclusions. A problem in deciding what constitutes rational believing is the fact that we differ on inductive standards. Although all people reason inductively, we may read the evidence quite differently (e.g., the gambler who has just become a father of a baby boy may bet on a horse called 'Sonny Boy', thinking it an omen). Nevertheless, Swinburne is optimistic that we can reach broad agreement on generally relevant inductive standards. Rationality, then, becomes a function of applying one's inductive standards to available evidence. Ideal rational belief is having a belief based on past investigation which has been carried out on the best inductive standards at one's disposal. One believes according to the evidence and with the degree of confidence warranted by the evidence.

Applying this notion of rational believing to religion, we see a fallibilist position emerge. While Swinburne believes that a cumulative case can be made for theism and Christianity, it is not a strong case, so that one may differ with it. The atheist and the believer may both be viewing the data at their disposal from different inductive bases. Each may be rational. Here, Swinburne introduces the notion of treating religion as an experimental hypothesis. Since religion offers us values in terms of a worthwhile life and eternal happiness, it is worth pursuing even in the face of doubt. Theism is so important, that even if one cannot positively believe it is true one may still have reason to live as if it were so. 'Weak belief' in theism is living on the assumption of its truth, believing that one is more likely to achieve the goals of religion in so doing.

At this point Swinburne introduces the notion of faith as trust and discusses it in relationship to belief. Whereas for Aquinas belief seems the dominant attitude in regard to religious propositions, for Luther, the aspect of trust or faith is stress, though it clearly entails propositional belief that God exists. However, there is a third position, perhaps found in William James, wherein faith as commitment to a way of life entails only a weak belief in the existence of its object.

> The pursuit of the Christian way may . . . appropriately be described as acting on the assumption that there is a God who has certain properties and has done certain things and provided certain means of salvation. For the pursuer is doing those actions which he would do if he had a stronger belief. In pursuing the way to attain his salvation or that of others or to ensure that God is properly worshipped and obeyed, he is acting on the assumption that if he pursues the way God will ensure that these purposes are achieved (p. 167).

Swinburne's treatment has been criticized as misunderstanding the nature of belief and of religion. His definition of belief (and hence of rational belief) is subject to the objection that it depends on a formal notion of probability, whereas one can believe that *p* without considering that *p* is more probable than any alternative.

Related to this criticism is whether the concept of probability applies to comprehensive world views. Hick, following a point made by Peirce, has argued that it does not, because there are not other worlds with which to compare this one. There are only different ways to view the world as a whole, different visions.[8]

W.D. Hudson, in his review of *Faith and Reason*, argues that the religious belief may be more regulative than Swinburne realizes and that treating religion as an hypothesis may be a fundamental misconception.

> The logical role of basic religious beliefs is not determined by whether or not everybody subscribes to them; nor yet again, by whether or not certain kinds of argument appear to some people to prove, or disprove, them. It is determined by the answers to such questions as: Given the way we talk about God, is it more coherent to conceive of religious experience as giving religious belief its probability, or of religious belief giving religious experience its character? And again, can anything be conceived as a theistic question or answer – as distinct from one *about* theism – unless God's existence is its presupposition in somewhat the same way that the uniformity of nature is the presupposition of all scientific questions and answers? It seems to me that Swinburne's cavalier dismissal of . . . the regulative interpretation of religious belief uncharacteristically confuses empirical considerations with logical ones (*Religious Studies*, March 1983).

We shall return to this issue in the second part of our work. Now we must turn to a work that combines some of the insights of Wittgensteinian fideism with a Calvinistic epistemology.

Reformed Epistemology: Alvin Plantinga

One of the most innovative, brilliant and controversial contributions to the debate on faith and reason is the theory set forth by Alvin Plantinga that claims that belief that God exists is rational even though it is not based on prior evidence. In a series of articles Plantinga has juxtaposed what he calls 'Reformed epistemology' (or Calvinist epistemology) with classical foundationalism (which he finds in Aquinas, Descartes, Locke, Hume and many others) and has concluded that the theist is rationally justified in believing in God without further evidence.[9] Plantinga finds classical foundationalism wanting, but he himself seems to prefer a revised version of foundationalism as the best available epistemological theory. In this section I shall exposit Plantinga's arguments, using his latest article, 'Reason and Belief in God', as the focal point of my analysis. After this, I shall discuss two criticisms of his position.

Classical foundationalism, which is found in Aquinas, Descartes, Locke and others, is the doctrine that all justified beliefs must either be properly basic by fulfilling certain criteria or be based on other beliefs which eventually result in a tree-like construction with properly basic beliefs resting at the bottom, or at the foundations. According to a typical classical foundationalism:

> A proposition p is properly basic for a person S if and only if p is either self-evident to S or incorrigible for S or evident to the senses for S (p. 59).

Foundationalists may differ about the exact makeup of the definition (Descartes accepting only the first two disjuncts but Aquinas and Locke accepting all three), but they all agree that justified beliefs must be based on foundations having some of the above components. Self-evident propositions are those that a person just sees as true immediately, such as 'that $1 + 2 = 3$' or 'that nothing all green is all black' or that the law of non-contradiction is universally valid. Incorrigible propositions are those about one's states of consciousness in which one cannot mistakenly believe what is not true, such as 'that I seem to see a red ball' or 'I think, therefore I am' or 'I am in pain.' Aquinas and Locke add a third type of proposition, that which is evident to the senses, such as 'that I see a tree' or 'I see a red ball.' The goals of the classical foundationalist is to protect our belief systems from error by allowing only solid or absolutely certain beliefs to make up the foundations of our belief systems.

Next, Plantinga develops the notion of a *noetic structure*. 'A person's noetic structure is the set of propositions he believes together with certain epistemic relations that hold among him and these propositions' (p. 48). Plantinga analyzes the noetic structure from the point of view of foundationalism in general. There are three ways of classifying the contents of our noetic structure: (1) in terms of basicality; (2) in terms of degree of belief; and (3) in terms of the depth of ingress of a belief.

(1) Basicality refers to the dependency relationship of all other beliefs on basic beliefs. The relationship is irreflexive (it can't be justified by itself), one-many (non-basic beliefs may depend on more than one belief), and asymmetric (if belief A depends on belief B, belief B cannot legitimately depend on belief A).

(2) We believe propositions in various degrees. Classical foundationalists like Locke and Hume would define rationality in terms of believing propositions according to the strength of the evidence, but, whereas Plantinga agrees that we do believe in varying degrees, he rejects any attempt to work out an exact correlation of degrees of evidence and degrees of belief. He does so because the only candidate is some sort of quantification test, which he rejects as unworkable.

(3) Regarding the matter of depth of ingress, Plantinga says that beliefs play different roles within our noetic structure. Some of our beliefs are more central and some more peripheral to our doxastic system, so that losing some beliefs will have a greater effect on us than losing others. We are less worried about being wrong about the trivial proposition that there are x number of steps in the city of Dallas than about the proposition that the snake we are about to handle is non-poisonous.

Applying this theory of classical foundationalism to religious claims, we see that, according to it, belief in God has no legitimacy. The thesis excludes the belief from the foundations of one's noetic structure, for it is neither self-evident, incorrigible, nor evident to the senses. Furthermore, because it does not seem possible to get from the types of propositions allowed in our noetic structure by these conditions to the conclusion that God exists, the present-day foundationalists tend to reject the belief that God exists as unjustified or irrational.

But classical foundationalism is not without problems. First of all, it seems that 'relative to propositions that are self-evident and incorrigible, most of the beliefs that form the stock in trade of ordinary everyday life are not probable – at any rate there is no reason to think they are probable' (p. 59). Such propositions as that there are enduring physical objects, other minds, and that the world has existed for more than five minutes 'are not more probable than not with respect to what is self-evident or incorrigible for me'. Nor are the propositions that there are other minds or that the world existed five minutes ago evident to the senses.

Furthermore, many propositions that do not meet the criteria of classical foundationalism seem properly basic for me. 'I believe, for example, that I had lunch this noon. I do not believe this proposition on the basis of other propositions; I take it as basic; it is in the foundations of my noetic structure. Furthermore, I am entirely rational in so taking it, even though this proposition is neither self-evident nor evident to the senses nor incorrigible for me' (p. 60).

The most devastating criticism of the formula of classical foundationalism, however, is that it is self-referentially incoherent. For the statement that we are rational only if either it is properly basic or derived from statements that are does not seem to be either properly basic or derived from other statements which are properly basic. To be properly basic, the statement must be either self-evident, incorrigible, or evident to the senses. But the statement that prescribes such rules does not seem to be any of these. Nor does it seem to be derived from statements that are. Hence, it seems irrational to accept it by its own standards.

Plantinga's alternative to classical foundationalism is rooted in the Reformed theological tradition which contains the core of a non-evidentialist epistemology. The Reformed thinkers have eschewed the attempt to demonstrate the existence of God. From the outset such theologians as Calvin, Bavinck, Warfield, and, more recently, Barth have seen dangers in trying to prove theism, have recognized that arguments are not the source of the believer's confidence, and have insisted that they are not needed for rational justification. As Scripture 'proceeds from God as the starting point,' so should the believer. In this sense, belief that God exists is like belief in other minds or that I have had lunch this noon. It does not need argument before it can be properly basic. Starting from that premise, the theist could then go on and adhere to foundational rules (1) In every rational noetic structure there is a set of beliefs taken as basic – that is, not accepted on the basis of other beliefs; and (2) In a rational noetic structure nonbasic belief is proportional to support from the foundations (p. 72).

Plantinga does not offer criteria for proper basicality, but he does want to protect Reformed epistemology from certain objections. Specifically, his position should not be confused with the view that any belief may be part of one's epistemic foundations, nor does he

want to say that it is groundless. It is not a version of Wittgensteinian fideism. Some objectors have complained that Plantinga's
views open the door to all sorts of irrationality in the foundations of
our noetic structure. Why cannot belief in the Great Pumpkin be
considered properly basic? Plantinga's answer is that the Reformed
epistemologist agrees with Calvin that 'God has implanted in us a
natural tendency to see his hand in the world around us; the same
cannot be said for the Great Pumpkin, there being no Great
Pumpkin and no natural tendency to accept belief about the Great
Pumpkin' (p. 78).

Plantinga does not give any criteria to help us distinguish unacceptable from acceptable candidates for proper basicality, but he
suggests that the manner of arriving at such will be broadly inductive.

> We must assemble examples of beliefs and conditions such that
> the former are obviously properly basic in the latter, and
> examples of beliefs and conditions such that the former are
> obviously *not* properly basic in the latter. We must then frame
> hypotheses as to the necessary and sufficient conditions of
> proper basicality and test these hypotheses by reference to
> those examples (p. 76).

But there is a certain relativity in the process of searching for criteria
for proper basicality. Each community will assemble a different set
of examples of beliefs and accompanying conditions, so that there is
no reason to assume that everyone will agree on the examples.

> The Christian will of course suppose that belief in God is
> entirely proper and rational; if he does not accept this belief on
> the basis of other propositions, he will conclude that it is basic
> for him and properly so. Followers of Bertrand Russell and
> Madelyn Murray O'Hare may disagree; but how is that
> relevant? Must my criteria, or those of the Christian
> community, conform to their examples? Surely not. The
> Christian community is responsible to *its* set of examples, not
> theirs (p. 77).

It may well be the case that we shall never arrive at universal
agreement regarding the conditions for proper basicality. This does
not mean that there is no truth in this area, but simply that at least
one set of criteria is wrong. It is important to point out that

Plantinga is not stating that no argument could ever cause the theist to give up his belief in God, but that the objector has yet to give any such argument. Argument for proper criteria is important, but until good reasons are given why the believer should not accept belief in God into the foundations of her noetic structure, there is no reason for the believer to be troubled. Plantinga distinguishes *weak justification*, where one is in one's epistemic rights in accepting a proposition, from *strong justification*, where one has what amounts to knowledge. He suggests that the believer may only have a weak justification for belief that God exists, but indicates that, in the absence of a successful defeater, it is rational to believe in God. One is *prima facie*, but not *ultima facie*, justified in so doing (p. 84f).

Regarding the objection that Reformed epistemology makes belief in God groundless, Plantinga answers that the belief is properly grounded in other beliefs, such as 'God is speaking to me' and 'God forgives me', which are properly basic. They are analogous to perceptual beliefs (e.g., 'I see a tree'), memory beliefs ('I had breakfast this morning') and beliefs ascribing mental states to other persons (e.g., 'that person is in pain'). In proper circumstances (e.g., where there is no reason to believe that my noetic structure is defective), my having an experience of a certain sort confers on me the right to hold the belief in question (p. 79). In like manner, having the experience that God is speaking to me or that God is forgiving me are properly basic in the right circumstances. In this sense, 'it is not wholly accurate to say that it is belief in God that is properly basic'. It is really these more experiential beliefs that are properly basic. They in turn entail that God exists. The proposition that God exists is a relatively high-level general proposition that is based on these other more basic propositions.

Finally, Plantinga's proposal is to be distinguished from fideism. Plantinga accepts the definition of fideism as 'exclusive or basic reliance upon faith alone, accompanied by a consequent disparagement of reason and utilized especially in the pursuit of philosophical or religious truth' (p. 87). Extreme fideism disparages and denigrates reason, while moderate fideism simply prefers faith over reason in religious matters.

The Reformed epistemologist rightly rejects the extreme fideism of a Kierkegaard (who makes faith in the *absurdity* of the eternal entering time a necessary condition for being a Christian) and Shestov (who holds that one can attain religious truth only by rejecting the proposition that $2 + 2 = 4$ and accepting instead $2 + 2 = 5$). If we understand the deliverances of reason to include basic perceptual truths, incorrigible propositions, certain memory propositions, certain propositions about other minds, and certain moral or ethical propositions, then the Reformed epistemologist would say that belief in God fits into this scheme as properly rational, rather than being an instance where faith overrides reason. There is a 'tendency or nisus' to apprehend God's existence and to understand something of his nature and actions. 'This natural knowledge can be and is suppressed by sin, but the fact remains that a capacity to apprehend God's existence is as much part of our natural noetic equipment as is the capacity to apprehend perceptual truths, truths about the past, and truths about other minds' (p. 90). Hence, belief that God exists is among the deliverances of reason as much as these other basic beliefs, and hence, the theist need not be a fideist of any sort.

Plantinga is one of the growing number of philosophers of religion who is sensitive to the matter of volitionalism and the ethics of belief. He rejects direct volitionalism as a plausible account of belief formation. We cannot get ourselves to believe propositions by fiat. Beliefs are not normally, at least, within our control. But if they are not under our control, how can we be said to have duties to believe rationally or according to the evidence?

Plantinga begins his answer by appealing to almost universal beliefs about moral responsibility. Nearly all of us have a deep belief that we can be held morally responsible for our actions even when they are based on what we presently believe. Sincere, false belief does not excuse us from moral condemnation. The anti-Semite, who believes that she is following the evidence to the abhorrent conclusion and who acts on the conclusion that Jews are bad, is morally culpable. A person who believes that it is morally proper to arrive at beliefs carelessly or who is sincere in rejecting morality is still morally guilty. This is because we believe that there is an objective morality which each normal person could know if she cared to.

While we cannot get ourselves to believe just anything at all by willing to believe it, we can affect our doxastic repertoires by paying attention to the evidence, in this case, to our inner moral prompting. The implication of this is that we may also be responsible for whether we believe in God. Perhaps the non-believer is one who has defiled his natural tendency to see God in nature.

Among the critiques of Plantinga's position, that of Gary Gutting stands out as meriting special attention.[10] Gutting is troubled by the ease with which Plantinga dismisses the views of those who differ from him, his epistemic peers, who do not find the proposition 'God exists' as properly basic. Let us take an instance of disagreement among epistemic peers.

> Suppose a mathematician has reflected long and hard on a given proposition (e.g., the axiom of choice) and, although he is not able to derive it as a theorem or even to put forward strong plausibility arguments for it, has come to an entirely firm conviction of its truth. He just 'sees' that it is true. However, when he proposes his proposition to his equally competent colleagues, he meets mixed reactions. Some share his intuitive acceptance of the proposition, others do not. In such a case, is he entitled to continue believing the proposition or should he withhold judgment on it? (p. 85).

It would seem that the mathematician ought to take account of his opponents' views. He should see whether they have any good arguments against his views and, if he concludes that they do not, 'he must see if there is any reason to trust his opponents' judgment (intuition) rather than his own on this point'. But even if there is no reason to prefer their judgment to his own, he should be moved from his certainty by the fact of their difference. To cling tenaciously to his intuition rather than weakening his hold on the proposition is to be guilty of 'epistemological egoism' which is just as 'arbitrary and unjustifiable as ethical egoism is generally regarded to be' (p. 86). That is, there is something like peer review of important propositions within any given field. While such review may not always cause us to give up a belief that we cannot defend, it ought, at least, to cause us to loosen our grasp on the belief, to realize that we could be wrong, and to hold with a lesser degree of certainty than before.

A second criticism, which has been made by Robert Audi[11] and others, is that Plantinga has not shown us why almost anything cannot be allowed into the foundations of one's noetic structure. In letting belief in God in as properly basic, he seems to be permitting belief in the Great Pumpkin and much more – and this, in spite of his asseverations that there are limits on what is acceptable. His response that 'God has implanted in us a natural tendency to see his hand in the world around us; the same cannot be said for the Great Pumpkin, there being no Great Pumpkin and no natural tendency to accept belief about the Great Pumpkin' (p. 78), seems circular, for the Pumpkin theologian could claim the same as the reason there are not more followers of the Pumpkin. Is Plantinga making 'a natural tendency to believe something' a criterion for proper basicality? If so, belief that God exists does not seem to have that property. At least it does not have it to the extent that beliefs in other minds or in modus ponens has it. If there is a strong person-relative aspect to rationality, why can it not be the case that someone comes to believe some strange things about the Great Pumpkin? Plantinga's point seems to be that there is no reason to worry about fictions like the Great Pumpkin which are not serious candidates for proper basicality, but he has not shown what is wrong with such a belief. Likewise, someone could well believe that God is evil or that Satan is the creator of heaven and earth and claim this belief as properly basic. I've met people who believe this and that God is a sadist who is out to harm them. As Plantinga himself points out, it may turn out that we will not find clear criteria to separate the theist's beliefs from the atheist's or Satanist's beliefs. It may be that the different sets of criteria which characterize what is properly basic for different groups and persons will never be entirely harmonized, but it may also be true that rationality directs us to be deeply respectful of our epistemic peers and moderate our judgment in matters where we have great differences and cannot give good reasons for preferring our positions. Belief that God exists or that he is speaking to me is not, after all, subject to the almost universal confirmability of the statement 'I see a tree'.

Conclusion

At this point, in 1986, the debate in Philosophy of Religion is largely between the evidentialists, both theists and non-theists, on the one side, and fideists or neo-fideists like Plantinga, on the other side. We have noted that the strongest evidentialist, Swinburne, has made a cumulative case for the existence of God. Taking all the evidence into consideration, the cosmological, teleological and argument from religious experience, the case for theism has a slight edge. Swinburne's controversy with the agnostics and atheists looks like a family quarrel compared with Plantinga's work on religious foundationalism, which rejects the notion of needing arguments for one's belief in God. God is the beginning point for the religious person, not something that we arrive at by argument. The role of philosophy of religion becomes very limited, at best a negative enterprise of marshalling attacks that will be met by a polite rebuttal by the theist who will not let anything come in the way of his faith in God. Plantinga's work is, at present, the central focus of debate.

The verificationist and falsificationist attacks of the 40's and 50's are now mostly a matter of history (except, oddly enough, in certain theological apologetics where some theologians are still using them as the whipping post), and the extreme versions of fideism no longer hold prominence. Classical foundationalism (the view that a belief is properly basic if and only if it is either self-evident or incorrigible or evident to the senses) has been undermined by such counter-examples as memory beliefs and beliefs in other minds and by the embarrassing fact that no version of it has been devised that is not self-referentially incoherent, that is, the principle itself is neither self-evident, evident to the senses, nor incorrigible. Plantinga and others have put forward a version of weak foundationalism with greater latitude in what is to be allowed as properly basic and which includes belief in God as properly basic. The question is whether his version is too broad or whether a narrower version may be constructed which is not open to some of the problems that Plantinga's version is.

One such attempt, which seems compatible with the concerns of Gutting and Audi, is found in Anthony Kenny's recent lectures at Columbia University, now published as a book, *Faith and Reason*. Kenny has been influenced by Plantinga and agrees that classical foundationalism is dead. However, he thinks that Plantinga's version of allowing belief in God into the foundations of one's noetic structure opens the door for letting in any proposition whatever, including the proposition that there is no God. Kenny's alternative version of foundationalism, which escapes both the self-referential incoherence of classical foundationalism and the latitudinarianism of Plantinga, states that a belief is properly basic if and only if it is: 'self-evident or fundamental, – evident to the senses or to memory, – defensible by argument, inquiry or performance' (p. 27).

By 'fundamental' Kenny means such universal beliefs as that

there are other minds, that cats do not grow on trees, that the earth has existed for many years, and the like. By being defensible by inquiry, Kenny merely means that sometimes we ourselves do not have the requisite evidence at our finger tips but are ready to take steps to get it. By being defensible by performance, he means such situations where the person always gets the right answers even though he may not himself know how, e.g., the water diviner who knows but can't tell how he knows that there is water in certain places. Kenny believes that this reconstructed evidentialist version of foundationalism escapes the liabilities of classical foundationalism, as well as the attacks by the anti-evidentialists. Whether it does or not will doubtless be the subject of forthcoming work in the area of faith and reason.

PART TWO

Belief, Will and Justification of Religious Belief

CHAPTER XIII

Direct Descriptive Volitionalism

Introduction: Varieties of Volitionalism

In this part of my book I shall work out my theory of religious belief and the will, endeavouring to show the right and wrong relationships between the various concepts involved. First, I shall treat the relationship between believing and willing. In later chapters I shall work out the relationship between belief and the will as it relates to faith.

It is a widely held view that we can obtain beliefs and withhold beliefs directly upon performing an act of the will. This thesis is sometimes identified with the view that believing is a basic act, an act which is under our direct control. Often it is said that only some beliefs are under our direct control, the beliefs which are not irresistible or forced upon us. I shall call the thesis that some of our beliefs are basic acts of will 'Direct Volitionalism'. I shall contrast this view with the thesis that some beliefs arise indirectly from basic acts, acts of will and intentions. This thesis I shall refer to as 'Indirect Volitionalism'.

There is another distinction that I wish to make at the outset regarding the relation of believing to willing in belief acquisition: that between describing volitional acts and prescribing them. I shall call those types of volitionalism 'descriptive' which merely describe the process of coming to believe through 'voliting' (i.e., obtaining a belief directly upon willing to have it). I shall call those types of volitionalism 'prescriptive' which include a normative element. Direct Prescriptive Volitionalism states that it is permissible or obligatory to acquire certain beliefs directly by willing to have them. Indirect Prescriptive Volitionalism states that it is permissible or obligatory to take the necessary steps to acquire beliefs based on non-epistemic considerations. A schematic representation of the various theses I have in mind looks like this:

	Direct	*Indirect*
Descriptive	(1) One can acquire beliefs directly simply by willing to believe certain propositions.	(2) One can acquire beliefs indirectly by willing to believe propositions and then taking the necessary steps to bring it about that one believes the propositions.
Prescriptive	(3) One can acquire beliefs directly by willing to believe propositions, and one is justified in so doing.	(4) One can acquire beliefs indirectly by willing to believe propositions as described in (2), and one is justified in purposefully bringing it about that one acquires beliefs in this way.

This schema is not meant to be an exhaustive set of relations between believing and willing, but it is intended to classify some of the important theses that we have noted in our study of the subject of belief and will in the history of philosophy. One might add a fifth way of acquiring beliefs: non-volitional belief acquisition, where the will plays no decisive role (or no role at all) in the obtaining of the belief. This type of belief formation will be referred to in the course of this work as the standard mode of belief acquisition, for even most of the volitionalists agree that ordinarily beliefs come unbidden, without being willed.

Direct Volitionalism has to do with the nature of believing and the type of control that we have over our belief states; Prescriptive Volitionalism has to do with the ethics of belief, with our duties with regard to the acquisition and sustainment of beliefs. In what follows I shall discuss these two types of volitionalism both in their direct and indirect forms, contrasting them with the standard mode of belief acquisition. In this chapter I first briefly classify the various volitional positions of the first part of this study. In the second section I offer an analysis of belief. Then, in the two main sections, I set forth the criteria which a fully successful volitional belief acquisition (a 'volit') would have to meet and show why we should be skeptical about whether any instances obtain. I offer two arguments against Direct Descriptive Volitionalism. The first argument is the Phenomenological Argument, which procedes on the basis of an introspective account of the nature of belief acquisition, and shows that, while there are anomalies, obtaining a belief occurs, normally, if not always, in a non-volitional manner. The second argument, the Logic of Belief Argument, shows that there is a conceptual connection between believing and non-volitional states, so that even if someone came to believe a proposition directly upon willing to have it, the person could not in full-consciousness believe that his belief was solely based on an act of will and still continue to hold the belief. In developing these arguments I consider two important qualifications to my thesis that direct cognitive volits do not occur: (1) the claim that there is a veto phenomenon of the will in prohibiting belief formations and (2) the claim that the will is active in self-creating beliefs, where faith in the possible fact helps create the fact. In Chapter XIV I turn to Indirect Prescriptive Volitionalism and the matter of ethics of belief. In Chapter XV I develop a rationalist perspective of religious faith in line with what has gone on before, and in Chapter XVI I work out the implications of my study for faith, doubt and hope. First, however, we must classify the various philosophers studied in the first part of this work. We have seen that the issues have been hotly debated since the 17th century but that they appear in the literature long before that time.[1]

The theses outlined in the schema above, showing various causal relationships between willing and believing, have all been held by philosophers in the history of Western Philosophy. As we have seen, there are traces of Direct Volitionalism in the early Church fathers, especially in Iranaeus, Clement of Alexandria and Augustine, but the first relatively clear case of the position seems to be that of St. Thomas Aquinas, who describes believing as an act of the intellect moved by the will.[2] This direct causal relationship between willing and believing has generally been asserted by Catholic philosophers since Aquinas. Descartes holds that the will is absolutely limitless in relationship to belief acquisition, and he uses the thesis as a counter to the argument from evil against the existence of God. False belief, quasi-sins, are caused when people use the will to make judgments which they should not make; hence we are solely responsible for our errors of judgment, judgment being an act of the will. If we were not responsible for errors of judgment, God would be, which is tantamount to blasphemy in that it makes God into a deceiver.[3]

We saw that other Catholic philosophers, while not so liberal in their volitionalism as Descartes, accept direct volitionalism. Cardinal Newman writes, 'Assent is an act of the mind, congenial to its nature; and it, as other acts, may be made both when it ought to be made and when it ought not. It is a free act, a personal act for which the doer is responsible.'[4] Bernard Lonergan agrees that believing is 'a free and responsible decision of the will'.[5] And Pieper enlarges on the issue, treating belief formation as a result of our having a free will. 'One can believe only if one wishes to. . . . A free assent of will must be performed. Belief rests upon volition.'[6] Because these philosophers make the sharp Platonic-Cartesian distinction between knowledge and belief, they are confining volitionally acquired beliefs to those propositions which are based on a testimony or memory. They are not talking about perceptual states or logical beliefs, which they would consider as knowledge.

Among the non-Catholic philosophers we have studied, Soren Kierkegaard is the most radically volitionalist, deeming every belief acquisition as a resolution of the will. Kant is sometimes sympathetic to volitionalism. Williams James holds to a variety of volitionalism, but it is not clear to what extent he holds it. He seems to prescribe it mainly for future states of affairs, where faith in the fact will help create the fact. Even W.K. Clifford holds a form of volitionalism, since he urges us to reject any proposition not evidential, as though it were optional. Among contemporary philosophers Laurence Bonjour, Roderick Chisholm, H.H. Price, Trudy Govier, and Jack Meiland are the most prominent volitionalists, Meiland holding the strongest thesis, that we can sometimes obtain beliefs by voliting even when we see sufficient evidence against them. We have seen that philosophers like Spinoza, Locke, Hume, and Bernard Williams reject volitionalism in all of its standard forms.

Of course, one may be a direct descriptivist without being a prescriptivist; that is, one could allow for the possibility that we can sometimes obtain beliefs by voliting without recommending it. Indeed, one could have an ethic of belief which prohibited our using the will in this way, but our study has not turned up any direct descriptivists who are not also prescriptivists.

Prescriptivists are even more numerous than direct descriptivists. Some prescriptivists would deny that we can volit (by fiat) but contend only that indirect descriptivism is possible, that we can only come to believe via the will indirectly. Pascal seems to fall into this group. Often the tenor of the recommendation is: get to believe this proposition by whatever means available. One can find passages as far back as the New Testament which seem to treat believing as an action which is somehow virtuous and for which we are responsible.[7] The Athanasian Creed, along with many others, makes propositional belief a necessary condition for salvation, the implication being that it's in one's best interest to get oneself to believe that the doctrine of the Trinity is true by whatever means possible. Likewise, in calling for heretics to recant their beliefs, the Inquisition espoused a variety of descriptive and prescriptive volitionalism, for how else could we reject our beliefs but by being able to cease believing them? Pascal makes self-interest the motive in his Wager Argument for getting oneself indirectly to believe in the existence of God. 'Make believe that you believe . . . by taking holy water, by hearing masses, etc. This will naturally bring you to believe, and will calm you.'[8]

It would seem that William James accepts descriptive volitionalism, though what he says could be completely covered by a form of prescriptive indirect volitionalism. C.I. Lewis and Roderick Chisholm allow for descriptive volitionalism and prescribe it in cases where the evidence is approximately counterbalanced.[9] Jack Meiland goes even further, saying for any (non-coerced) belief, practical considerations are always relevant in determining whether one should believe according to or against sufficient evidence.[10]

I need not say very much about Indirect Descriptive Volitionalism. Virtually every philosopher accepts the role of actions and intentions as indirectly operative in belief acquisition. I may focus on certain parts of the total evidence with the intention of obtaining or sustaining a belief. I may purposefully put myself in a situation where I am likely to acquire or reinforce a given belief. No one doubts that this can and does happen. The interesting question is whether it should, and that leads to the matter of prescriptive volitionalism, which we have already discussed.

It might be helpful to break down our classifications even further. Let us list the relevantly possible relations between believing and willing in belief acquisition and sustainment. Consistent with the analysis that will follow, I shall analyze the varieties of volitionalism in terms of whether they are basic or non-basic acts, done in full-consciousness or less than full-consciousness, and whether evidence (or truth considerations) is decisive in the belief formation. The following list emerges:

Non-Volitional Modes

(1) The Standard Mode. The belief acquisition just occurs. It is unbidden, spontaneous (even though a period of deliberation may have gone on before). It is evidential, based on other beliefs or basic to our noetic structure. It occurs after we entertain the proposition in full-consciousness or it occurs immediately upon being entertained, perhaps so quickly that the moment of entertainment cannot be separated from the belief happening.

(2) Quasi-Standard Mode. The acquisition spontaneously happens (or so it seems) but the event occurs in less than full consciousness. Perhaps we are not aware of the acquisition, but simply find ourselves believing a proposition.

Volitional Modes

DIRECTLY VOLITIONAL

(3) Non-evidential, but in full consciousness, a basic act.
(4) Non-evidential, with less than full consciousness, a basic act.
(5) Evidential, in full consciousness, but needing a basic act to perform (doxastic incontinence).
(6) Evidential, in less than full consciousness, but needing a basic act (doxastic incontinence).
(7) Against the evidence, in full consciousness, by a basic act.
(8) Against the evidence, in less than full-consciousness, by a basic act.

INDIRECTLY VOLITIONAL

(9) Indirect, evidential, less than full consciousness, not a basic act but an act (or acts) causes the belief to come about, as in possible forms of doxastic incontinence.

(10) Indirect, non-evidential, less than full consciousness, not a basic act but an act (or acts) causes the belief to come about, e.g., as in self-deception.

(11) Indirect, against the evidence, in less than full consciousness, not a basic act but an act (or acts) causes the belief to come about.

The following chart may be useful to diagram the volitional positions described above. Let the number refer to the type described above. Let 'F' stand for 'full consciousness'; 'V' for 'vague' or 'less than full consciousness; 'N' for 'No'; 'Y' for 'Yes'; 'A' for 'Against'.

	Direct Volitionalism					Indirect Volitionalism			
Number	/ 3 /	4 /	5 /	6 /	7 /	8 /	9 /	10 /	11
Conscious	F	V	F	V	F	V	V	V	V
Evidence	N	N	Y	Y	A	A	Y	N	A
Basic act	Y	Y	Y	Y	Y	Y	N	N	N

In our historical study we saw 3 represented in Augustine, Aquinas, Descartes, Kierkegaard, Newman, Pieper, Lonergan and Meiland. We saw 4 exemplified in Price, Govier, and Holyer. We saw 5 or 6 exemplified in Gale. We saw 7 and/or 8 exemplified in Tertullian, Descartes and Kierkegaard. William James seems to hold something like 3 or 4, but it is not clear which. 9 is uncontroversial. Virtually every epistemologist admits that our actions influence the beliefs we finally end up with, and virtually everyone admits that 10 happens. Many philosophers, especially Locke and Clifford, speak against it, while Pascal, James, Chisholm, and Meiland speak in favor of this mode of belief acquisition on pragmatic grounds. All of these with the exception of Chisholm would prescribe 11.

An Analysis of Belief

A brief look at ordinary language shows conceptual connections between belief and will. We say, 'I choose to believe what he says', 'Please believe me' (as though it were optional), 'That's hard to believe', 'I find that difficult to believe', and the like. On occasions we even hear people say, 'I can believe that' or 'I can't believe *that*' (implying that it is beyond normal volitional abilities), but perhaps the most perplexing locution is, 'I cannot and will not believe that', for the statement appears self-contradictory. If will implies ability, then we can believe, and it makes no sense to speak of not being able to do so. Another perplexing expression is, 'I can't believe some things that I ought to believe.' If *ought* implies *can*, there is something wrong with this statement, too. The task of analyzing the deep structure of such doxastic, volitional sentences has yet to be done, but it seems clear that many everyday uses of 'belief' are connected with volitional expressions. As Stuart Hampshire has remarked, there is a 'whole range of idioms that assimilate belief to action'.[11] It is almost as if William James had found his way into ordinary language (or is the ideal reflection to it). It seems to me that this is a paradigm case of where ordinary language can be shown to be (on the surface, at least) plainly misleading. Perhaps one of the problems is that we use 'belief' and its cognates to perform a variety of roles, or perhaps the term 'belief' refers not to one concept but to a whole family of concepts. At this time it seems impossible to give a non-circular and non-trivial definition of the term.

What is it to believe? When someone comes to believe some statement, what precisely takes place? When Sam believes that there is a chair in the room, what is the state of Sam's mind? What happens to Sam in acquiring such a belief? In what ways may he acquire such a belief? Must he be conscious of the acquisition, by noticing the chair and then realizing that he notices it? Can he acquire the belief without realizing that he has done so? Or are our belief forming mechanisms like tollbooth guards who first scrutinize all proposed luggage before allowing the traveller in? Even if the tollbooth model were true, it is clear that we have forgotten the origins of many of our belief acquisitions.

Perhaps the clearest type of belief acquisition is occurrent believing, where someone entertains a proposition and judges it to be true. Our occurrent beliefs are those which we are conscious of having now. I am now conscious that there is a typewriter in front of me and that I believe that it is a reliable machine. If, suddenly, it were to break down, I would be mildly surprised, because I had mild confidence in its reliability. The degree to which we believe a proposition can be measured by the degree of surprise that we would feel if it turned out that our belief was false. An occurrent belief is usually accompanied by feeling. Hume identified belief with that feeling. However, that seems wrong. A belief is often sustained even when you are not thinking about it, when you have no feeling about it at all, when you have forgotten it, and when you are sleeping. The Humean analysis has been rejected by many philosophers as simplistic or positively misleading. In its place has been set a dispositional analysis which has no need of feelings.

One might be tempted to react to the introspective model's weaknesses by taking a purely materialist view of the mind and short cut the problem of believing by identifying belief states with brain states, but one infelicity of this move is that we might have to say that permanently comatose people and dead people still have beliefs – in as much as the brain states may remain long after the individual dies. Under this description many things we have 'forgotten' would still be believed – since there is a brain state corresponding to the 'forgotten belief'. But such beliefs are not action guiding and the equation seems unhelpful.

A theory that is attentive to the action guiding aspect of believing that also rejects Humean occurrentism is dispositionalism. An extreme dispositionalist is the behaviorist who rejects introspective accounts of belief in favor of dispositions to behave in certain ways. Bain, Braitewaite, Ryle, and Audi[12] omit the introspective element and concentrate entirely on the tendency to act. As Bain wrote, 'Belief has no meaning, except in reference to our actions. . . . An intellectual notion, or conception, is likewise indispensable to the act of believing, but no mere conception that does not directly or indirectly implicate our voluntary exertions, can ever amount to the state in question.'[13] Audi is more subtle than Bain and Ryle here, realizing the need for wants in his dispositional theory, but both forms of the theory are vulnerable to certain objections. The pure form of Bain and Ryle suffers from the weakness that it does not include wants in the action assessment. But belief, wants, and actions form an interconnected web. In many cases, we cannot account for one of these without taking into consideration the other two. If we begin with beliefs and see Sue acting in a certain way, we are likely to infer that Sue must have some object or desire in mind. Of course, we may not be sure which action, belief, or desire is operative in any behavior. If we see Sue registering for college, we may infer that she has some belief about college being a means to some long-range goal, but we may be misled here. She may simply want to please her parents, or get away from home, or she may be registering under duress, or she may have nothing better to do. Actions are explained by beliefs and desires, and they are unintelligible apart from them. Likewise, desires are blind without beliefs, but beliefs need desires in order to motivate action.

However, Audi's theoretical construct analysis which analyzes beliefs in terms of wants and actions is open to objections also, for it omits something that seems essential to our understanding of having a belief – the possible awareness of its possession. For example, suppose that at t_1 I believe that I shall not confess under torture. However, a moment later at t_2, as soon as I begin to be tortured, I confess. Under Audi's conditions, I could be said to believe that I would confess at t_1, for any torture would cause me to confess. In fact, it turns out on this account that I can never believe falsely about my immanent behavior because the tendencies and wants are the sole factors in defining the belief. But, surely, we can have such false beliefs, nor are they always self-deceptive. Our intentions may be honorable, but our actions incontinent. We suffer from weakness of will, which cannot be easily accounted for under Audi's conditions without the inclusion of an additional item, that of assenting or introspective reports. Such a mental nod or 'yessing' to the proposed truth of a proposition is primitive, something like Hume's feeling, but it may come without clear emotion, as a simple 'acknowledgement' or sense of fitness, imperceptible and without any observable marks.

Dispositional accounts help us understand belief-behavior, for if I want to get to goal G and believe that action A will be the best (or adequate) means of getting G, then I will doubtless try to do A. But I may never have an opportunity to exercise my belief in action, or I may never want to act on my belief. But this is no reason for not attributing many beliefs that I 'feel' that I have.

H.H. Price may be right when, in the spirit of conciliation, he calls belief a 'multiform disposition' which is manifested or actualized in many different ways.

> It should now be clear that if 'A believes that p' is a dispositional statement about A, the disposition we attribute to him is a multiform disposition, which is manifested or actualized in many different ways: not only in his actions and his inactions, but also in emotional states such as hope and fear; in

feelings of doubt, surprise, and confidence; and finally in his inferences, both those in which a belief just 'spreads itself' from a proposition to some of its consequences (certain and probable) and those in which the inference is a self-conscious and self-critical intellectual operation (*Belief*, p. 294).

Price's statement is appropriate because it recognizes the complexity of having a belief: that it includes a Humean element of feeling, that it is essentially dispositional, and that it includes the obvious entailments of our conscious beliefs as beliefs. It does not exactly define belief, but only characterizes this complex propositional attitude as having both external and internal aspects. Something like Hume's occurrentist awareness of assenting to a proposition seems to be at the heart of what it means to believe, but belief is more than this. It is dispositional, so that even when we are not aware of our beliefs, we may be said to be guided by them.

In this respect Frank Ramsey's metaphor is apposite. Beliefs are maps by which we steer. D.M. Armstrong enlarges upon this description to read: particular beliefs are maps by which we steer, and general beliefs are dispositions to extend the original belief-map according to rules.[14] Beliefs are by their nature causative of action, and the importance of having accurate beliefs can largely be explained in terms of the action-guiding aspect, which the map metaphor brings out.

Beliefs are not all-or-nothing states in the way that Newman supposed. We believe in degrees as was illustrated by the statement of President Ronald Reagan in a recent Fourth of July speech, when he said, 'I believed as a boy, and believe even more today, that [July fourth] is the birthday of the greatest nation on earth.' I believe that my wife is an utterly honest person to a greater degree than I believe that my neighbour is. I believe most of the propositions based on first-hand empirical evidence than I do those based on testimony or the deliverances of memory. We each have our own peculiar noetic structure wherein evidence (even where it seems to be 'the same') is believed to warrant conclusions in different ways and to different degrees. In your noetic structure the teleological argument may lend no support for the existence of a supreme being but in mine it may lend weak support, while in our friend's it may give strong support.

It may be possible to classify many of our beliefs on a continuum of subjective probability. Each one of us will have his or her own belief system ranging on a scale from 0 to 1 with 0.5 being doxastic indifference, neither believing nor disbelieving. As long as we agree that there is a state of positively believing with utmost conviction that p, a state of withholding belief that p, and the notion of degrees of belief, we have all we need for a classified belief system. For if we let the number 1 stand for the state of absolute conviction, 0 will stand for its opposite state, a conviction that p is false. 0.5 will stand for the state of uncertainty or withholding of belief and between 0 and 0.5 and 0.5 and 1 will be all the rest of our belief states. We may not be sure of the exact numbers to give to these belief states and our degree of conviction may vary from time to time, but we may be able roughly to quantify our beliefs.

One way to test the degree to which you believe a proposition is to imagine how surprised you would be if your belief turned out to be false. We might also imagine some future society with a highly developed lie detector-type of machine for measuring the degree to which we believed. We can imagine a Belief Meter which has two rubber walls wired to it, and which, when the balls are squeezed, measures the pressure of the squeezes. The subject holds a ball in each hand and is instructed to squeeze the ball in his right hand when he believes that the proposition in question, to squeeze the ball in his left hand when he believes the contradictory of the proposition and to refrain from squeezing when he believes neither proposition. In addition the subject would be instructed to squeeze the appropriate ball with a pressure appropriate to the degree with which he believes the proposition. A certain amount of experimentation may be necessary to work the correlations out, but accuracy will be approximated by the help of a truth serum. In this way we might be able to quantify our beliefs into a roughly ordered system. Such a system might do wonders to exhibit the actual degrees to which preachers, politicians, and patriots actually believe their assertions.

Not only do we believe propositions to varying degrees, but we have complex emotional or valuational attachments to our beliefs. We may call this feature 'the depth of ingress' of our beliefs, a phrase first given to me by Alvin Plantinga. Some of these emotional or valuational attachments are connected with our self-understanding or our sense of purpose in life. Normally, a belief that it will rain this afternoon or that the New York Yankees will

154

win the pennant may be undermined without too much havoc to our noetic structure (though I've known exceptions to this, where one's self-understanding is dependent on an athletic team's success), but the defeat of a belief in one's friend's loyalty, one's spouse's fidelity, one's child's innocence, the existence of God or an objective moral order may bring personal chaos. We value beliefs to varying degrees even as we believe in varying degrees. If we would quantify these aspects, we might say that Sam's degree of belief that p is 0.6, whereas his depth of ingress index with regard to p is 0.9. The proposition plays a mightier role than many of the propositions which he never doubts but hardly cares about.

Belief is typically manifest in assertions but an assertion is neither a necessary nor a sufficient condition for having a belief. One can believe without ever asserting, and one can assert insincerely. Still one may argue that there is a conceptual connection between asserting and believing. We learn what believing means through assertions, and occurrent believings have the phenomenal property of inward assertions, assentings, feelings of affirmation or yesness.

While the clear cases of belief acquisition often involve the entertainment of a proposition, a weighing of the evidence, and a conclusion, we may believe without any intermediate step of entertaining, as in normal perceptual beliefs where 'seeing is believing'. Furthermore, we probably are not aware of all our belief acquisitions, for we take in enormous amounts of information which seem to make up our noetic structure without our being conscious of ever acquiring the belief. If on being asked the color of the wall of the room I've left, I give the right answer without ever consciously entertaining it, should it not be said that I believed all along it was that color, though I did not realize it? I think that I have believed that 100 is more than 3.5 though I don't remember entertaining that proposition before this moment. The 'obvious' entailments of some of our beliefs must themselves be classified as beliefs. The tollbooth model of belief seems too rigid and counter-intuitive.

Belief is typically related to evidence which supports it, unless the belief in question is a basic belief, in which case it provides evidence for other beliefs in an inverted tree like construction (i.e., a second level belief has branches rooted in one or more basic belief). Basic beliefs are generally self-evident or evident to the senses (e.g., the analytic belief that '2 + 2 = 4' or the empirical belief 'I see a tree' or the memory belief 'I remember eating dinner this evening'). Beliefs claim implicitly to be connected to the world, to represent the way the world is and hence imply a direct or indirect relation to the world. In memory beliefs, for example, there is the belief that what I am recalling at the moment is connected in a chain like manner with what part of the world was like a few hours ago. In testimony belief there is the implied belief that what I am now accepting is causally connected with the world that my neighbor saw and is reporting to me.

This brings us to the central question of our study: what role does the will play in forming a belief. Is belief formation in some sense within our direct control? Or does the judgment come naturally as a spontaneous response to the total evidence (including background information and assumptions)? If receiving evidence in entertaining propositions can be likened to placing weights on balanced scales, can the will enter in to influence the outcome. On the standard model of belief acquisition the judgment is not a separate act but simply the result of the weighing process. It is as though the weighing process exhibited the state of evidence, and then the mind simply registered the state of the scales. On the volitional model the judgment is a special action over and above the weighing process. It is as though the mind recognized the state of the scales but was allowed to choose whether to accept that state or to influence it by putting a mental finger on one side or the other, depending on desire. The non-volitionalist need not deny that desire unconsciously influences our belief-acquisitions, but he does resist the notion that beliefs can be formed by conscious acts of will. The volitionalist, on the other hand, need not maintain that such acts of will (volits) can occur any time one wants them to. There may be times when it is impossible to move the weights through any effort of the will. Here the analogy with freedom of the will is apposite. The libertarian need not say that no act is determined or that every act is within our control, only that some significant acts are. Likewise, the doxastic libertarian need only say that some significant beliefs are acts, fully within our control. It is sometimes possible to place the mental finger on the doxastic scales and influence the formation of a judgment or belief.

In what follows I shall attempt to show that there are problems with the volitional notion of belief formation. Although it is not possible to prove that no one ever volits or that it is impossible to do so (as Bernard Williams mistakenly claims), I shall offer two arguments to undermine the thesis that we acquire beliefs through willing consciously to have them. I will also indicate the legitimate role the will does play in the belief acquisition. My first argument is called 'The Phenomenological Argument Against Direct Descriptive Volitionalism'. It involves an introspective analysis of the phenomena of belief acquisition. The second argument is called 'The Logic of Belief Argument Against Direct Descriptive Volitionalism'. In it I shall try to show that there is a conceptual connection between belief and truth, so that there is something incoherent about holding that a particular belief is held decisively on the basis of wanting to have that belief. Along the way I shall take up the matter of the veto phenomenon (i.e., the will's ability to prevent a belief from forming) and the matter of self-verifying beliefs (beliefs which help to create states of affairs that correspond to the beliefs in question). We turn now to the first argument against direct descriptive volitionalism.

The Phenomenological Argument Against Direct Descriptive Volitionalism

First of all we must understand what is involved in direct volitionalism (in this section 'volitionalism' will stand for direct descriptive volitionalism unless otherwise stated). The following features seem necessary and jointly sufficient conditions for a minimal interesting thesis of volitionalism:

(1) The acquisition is a basic act. That is, some of our beliefs are obtained by acts of will directly upon being willed. Believing itself need not be an action. It may be dispositional. The volitionalist need not assert that all belief acquisitions occur via the fiat of the will, only that some of them do.

(2) The acquisition must be done in full consciousness of what one is doing. The paradigm cases of acts of will are those in which the agent deliberates over two courses of action and decides on one of them. However, acts of will may take place with greater or lesser awareness. Here our notion of will is ambiguous between two meanings: 'desiring' and 'deciding'. Sometimes we mean by 'act of will' simply a desire which manifests itself in action, such as my being hungry and finding myself going to the refrigerator or tired and finding myself heading for bed. We are not always aware of our

desires or intentions. There is difference between this type of willing and the sort where we are fully aware of a decision to perform an act. If we obtain beliefs via the will in the weaker sense of desiring of which we are only dimly aware, how can we ever be sure that it was really an act of will that caused the belief directly rather than the will simply being an accompaniment of the belief? That is, there is a difference between willing to believe and believing willingly. The latter case is not an instance of acquiring a belief by fiat of the will, only the former is. While there are interesting relations between the will and belief (cf. our discussion of Govier and Holyer towards the end of Part One), in order for the volitionalist to make his case, he must assert that the acts of will which produce beliefs are decisions of which we are fully aware.

(3) The belief must be acquired independently of evidential considerations. That is, the evidence is not what is decisive in forming the belief. Perhaps the belief may be influenced by evidence (testimony, memory, inductive experience, and the like), so that the leap of faith cannot occur just any time over any proposition, but only over propositions that have some evidence in their favor but are still inadequately supported by that evidence. They have an initial subjective probability of, or just under, 0.5. According to Descartes, we ought to withhold belief in such situations where the evidence is exactly equal, whereas with Kierkegaard religious and existential considerations may justify leaps of believing even when the evidence is approximately equally weighted but where existential considerations call for a decision. We saw that William James prescribed such leaps only when the option was forced, living and momentous.[15] It may not be possible to volit in the way Kierkegaard prescribes without a miracle of grace, as he suggests, but the volitionalist would have to assert that volitional belief goes beyond all evidence at one's disposal and hence the believer must acquire the belief through an act of choice which goes beyond evidential considerations. Recurring to our earlier metaphor of the weights, it is possible to place our volitional finger on the mental scales of evidence assessment, tipping them one way or the other.

In sum, then, a volit is an act of will whereby I acquire a belief directly upon willing to have the belief, and it is an act made in full consciousness and independently of evidential considerations. The act of acquiring a belief may itself not be a belief but a way of moving from mere entertainment of a proposition to its acceptance.

There is much to be said in favor of volitionalism. It seems to extend the scope of human freedom to an important domain, and it seems to fit our experience of believing where we are conscious of having made a choice. The teacher who sees that the evidence against a pupil's honesty is great and yet decides to trust him, believing that somehow he is innocent in spite of the evidence, and the theist who believes in God in spite of insufficient evidence seem to be everyday examples confirming our inclination towards a volitional account of belief formation. We suspect, at times, that many of our beliefs, not formed through fully conscious volits, have been formed through half-aware desires, for on introspection we note that past beliefs have been acquired in ways that could not have taken the evidence seriously into consideration. Volitionalism seems a good explanatory theory to account for a great deal of our cognitive experience.

Nonetheless, there are considerations which may make us question whether on reflection volitionalism is the correct account of our situation. I will argue that it is not the natural way in which we acquire beliefs, and that while it may not be logically impossible that some people volit, it seems psychologically odd and, even conceptually incoherent. In this section we shall look at the psychology of belief acquisition and in the next the logic of that experience. We turn then to The Phenomenological Argument Against Volitionalism, which schematically goes as something like this:

1　Phenomenologically speaking, acquiring a belief is a happening in which the world forces itself upon a subject.
2　A happening in which the world forces itself upon a subject is not a thing the subject does (i.e., is not a basic act) or chooses.
3　Therefore, phenomenologically speaking, acquiring a belief is not something a subject does or chooses.

This describes the standard mode of belief acquisition and, it will be urged, is the way all beliefs occur. The first premise appeals to our introspective data and assumes that acquiring a belief has a spontaneous, unbidden, involuntary or forced aspect attached to it. The second premise merely points out the active/passive distinction, that there is a difference between doing something and having something happen to oneself. Hence, the conclusion states that as a happening believing is not something one does or chooses. The Phenomenological Argument asks us to look within ourselves in order to see if acquiring a belief is not different from entertaining a proposition, the latter of which can be done at will. The first premise is based on the view that beliefs are psychological states about states of affairs. They are, to use Ramsey's metaphor, mappings in the mind by which we steer our lives. As such the states of affairs which beliefs represent exist independently of the mind; they exist independently of whether we want them to exist. Insofar as beliefs presume to represent the way the world is, and hence serve as effective guides to action, the will seems superfluous. Believing seems more like falling than jumping, catching a cold than catching a ball, getting drunk than taking a drink, blushing than smiling, getting a headache than giving one to someone else. Indeed, this passive aspect seems true on introspection of most propositional attitudes: anger, envy, fearing, suspecting, doubting, though not necessarily of imagining or entertaining a proposition, where an active element may often be present.

The heart of the argument is in the first premise and that premise can only be established by considering a number of different types of belief acquisition in order to see if they all exhibit this passive or non-volitional feature: having the world force itself upon one. While such an investigation might never end, we can, at least, consider typical cases of belief formation of various types. Let us begin with perceptual beliefs. If I am in a normal physiological condition and open my eyes, I cannot help but see certain things, for example, this piece of white paper in front of me. It seems intuitively obvious that I don't have to choose to have a belief that I see this piece of white paper before I believe I see it. Here seeing is believing. This is not to deny a certain active element in perception. I can explore my environment, focus in on certain features, turn from others. I can direct my perceptual mechanism, but once I do this the perceptions I obtain come of themselves whether or not I will to have them. I may even have an aversion to white paper and not want to have such a perception. Likewise, if I am in a normal physiological state and someone nearby turns on loud music, I hear it. I cannot help believing that I hear it. Belief is forced on me.

Consider, next, memorial beliefs. The typical instances of believing what I seem to remember require no special choosings. I may choose to search my memory for the name of my friend's spouse, but what I finally come up with, what I seem to remember, comes of itself, has its own weight attached to it. I do not choose to believe my memory report that my friend's spouse's name is Pam. Normally, I cannot help believing it. There may be times when we only faintly recollect, but the fact that we only weakly believe our memory reports does not imply a volitional element in the belief formation. Although there are times (especially when considering events in one's distant past or one's childhood) when we are not sure whether what we seem to remember actually occurred, even here it seems that it is typically the evidence of the memory which impresses us sufficiently to tip the scales of judgment one way or the other.

This analysis can be extended to abstract and logical beliefs. Very few volitionalists affirm that we choose to believe that the law of non-contradiction has universal application or that '2 + 2 = 4'. These sorts of beliefs seem almost undeniably non-volitional and some volitionalists would even withhold the designation 'belief' from them, classifying them as cases of knowledge *simpliciter*. In any case, all agree that in these cases, if one understands what is being asserted, one is compelled to believe (or know) these propositions. They are paradigms of doxastic happenings which force themselves upon us regardless of whether we will to believe them.

It seems to me that a similar process is at work regarding theoretical beliefs, including scientific, religious, ideological, political and moral beliefs. Given a whole network of background beliefs, some views or theories are simply going to win out in my noetic structure over others. We sometimes find ourselves forced to accept theories which conflict with and even overthrow our favorite explanations. Accepting a theory as the best explanation or as probably true, doesn't entail that we must act on it. We may believe an explanation to be true but find it so unedifying or personally revulsive that we are at a loss for what action to take. Such might be the case when a libertarian finds herself forced by argument to accept the doctrine of determinism or when a person whose entire world view and moral system is connected with an essentialist's view of personhood suddenly is converted to Hume's theory of personal identity. When doxastic revolutions break out, chaos results, and we suddenly find ourselves without relied-upon anchors to stabilize us or maps to guide us.

We can also accept a theory as the best explanation among a set of weak hypotheses without believing it. There is an attitude of accepting a proposition, acting on it as an experimental hypothesis, without assenting to its truth. A behavioral analysis would conflate such acceptance with belief, but there is no reason to accept behaviorism. Sometimes we accept a theory little by little as evidence from various parts of it makes sense to us. At other times, it is as though we suddenly saw the world differently, what was once a cosmic duck is now seen as a cosmic rabbit. The term 'seeing' is appropriate, for even as we do not choose what we see when we look at an object (though we can focus in on part of it, neglect another part, and so forth), so we do not choose to believe a theory and by doing so believe it to be true. Rather, we cannot do otherwise in these cases. Nothing I have said, of course, is meant to deny that the will plays an indirect role in acquiring such beliefs.

Finally, and most importantly, there is the matter of testimony beliefs that arise on the basis of reports of others. This is the kind of belief that is emphasized by Pieper and Meiland. Certainly, this seems a more complex type of believing than perceptions or memory beliefs. Often we read reports in newspapers or hear rumors or predictions and hesitate before siding one way or the other. Sometimes the news seems shocking or threatening to our whole noetic structure. Here one may have the phenomenal feel, at first glance, that a decision is being made by the agent. For example, I hear a report that someone I know well and esteem highly has cheated his company of $50,000. The evidence seems the sort that I normally credit as reliable, but I somehow resist accepting it. Have I willed to withhold belief or disbelief? I don't think so. Although I am stunned by the evidence, I have a great deal of background evidence, which I cannot immediately express in detail but which I have within my noetic structure, subconsciously, but which plays a role in putting the fresh data into a larger perspective.

Perhaps I find myself believing willingly that, in spite of the evidence, my friend is innocent. Does this 'believing willingly' against the evidence constitute an act of will? I don't think so. Here the reader will recall the distinction between (1) willing to believe and thereby believing and (2) believing willingly, where one feels drawn towards a belief state and willingly goes along with it. One can identify with and feel good about what one comes to believe, but in neither case is the will directly causative. In addition, there is the experience of viewing the objective evidence as roughly counterbalanced, but where one feels inclined one way or the other.

162

Here something like our intuitions or unconscious processes play a decisive role in belief formation, but these are not things we have direct control over. Within our noetic structure are dispositional beliefs and dispositions to believe which influence belief formation. There is no need to appeal to acts of will to explain instances of anomalous belief acquisition.

Normally, however, I find myself immediately and automatically assenting to testimony. If I am lost in a new neighborhood and looking for a supermarket, I may ask someone for directions. Under favorable circumstances I will believe what she tells me because I have learned through experience that normally people will give reliable directions if they can. Even if I have to deliberate about the testimony, wondering whether the witness is credible, I don't come to a conclusion on the basis of any willing to believe one way or the other but because the complex factors in the situation incline me one way or the other. One of these factors may be my wants and wishes which influence my focus, but once the belief comes, it comes as produced by the evidence and not by the choice.

I have been arguing that acquiring a belief is an event in which the world itself forces itself upon me. Nevertheless, there may be instances in which our paradigms do not entirely fit. Gary Gutting has offered an interesting counter-example of a person, Sue, who has been raised in a white racist community, and who still has a very strong tendency to assent to the proposition that blacks are inferior to whites.[16] She often finds herself automatically and involuntarily assenting in her mind to this claim. Suppose, however, that she wages a continuing and successful battle against this disposition by deliberately denying the claim on every occasion that she finds herself involuntarily assenting to it. This seems to show that belief is not always an involuntary assent.

How should we treat this sort of case? Perhaps it comes under the designation of self-deception or doxastic incontinence. If Sue has no evidence to move her from her original belief but is motivated to dislike having a racist belief by the fact that having one keeps her from smiling spontaneously when she is supposed to be making cosmetic sales to black women, then she probably is deceiving herself in thinking that she has denied her original inegalitarian belief.

On the other hand, if she really believes that there is evidence for an essential equality of blacks with whites, then this may be a case of doxastic incontinence, of not being able to assent to what the evidence clearly points to. Her upbringing has deeply affected her noetic structure to the point where evidence itself may be insufficient to affect it, or where the influence of the evidence is in constant tension with the background conditions. There is the strange experience of feeling oneself being of two minds about something, as though we were split personalities or made up of subselves which laid different claims to our allegiance.

If we treat this case as an instance of self-deception, we may explain it by saying that Sue is repressing her first belief (viz. the racist one) and focusing on different evidence (e.g., all the bright black people she knows, the testimony of those friends who assert that blacks are truly equal to whites), so that she is able to have, temporarily, an egalitarian belief. However, she really believes that this evidence is contrived or selective, so its power to influence her is limited and transient. This could be a case in which beliefs alternate very rapidly. When she looks at some of the evidence in a certain way, she believes one way. When she looks at other evidence or allows her instinctual belief to arise from within, she believes another way. Alternating belief states are a common phenomenon. Consider the case of wondering whether a friend has lied to you about an important matter. The mental turmoil is considerable. On the one hand, your past experience with your friend counts heavily in his favor. On the other hand, the evidence that he lied is very strong. You alternate between believing the circumstantial evidence and believing what his over-all character suggests. When you look into his face, you are filled with the chaotically ambivalent emotions of deep pain, embarrassment at your distrust, fear that he may truly have deceived you, torment at your uncertainty and confusion. In times like these you want to flee his gaze, and yet you want also to resolve the issue one way or the other. But, while something like a decision may occur, it does not occur through directly willing to believe that he is innocent (or guilty) but by focusing on the friend's character and face or on the circumstantial evidence against him. The belief may have been caused indirectly by willing to have a belief in his innocence, but it was still broadly evidential.

If we treat Sue's case as an instance of *doxastic incontinence*, where she somehow cannot believe what the evidence points to, we have a more difficult problem. It may well be the case that our background and upbringing have so deeply affected us that we find it hard to assent to what the evidence suggests. It may be the case that the feeling element in assent is absent, but we may still have a cognitive recognition of the weight of the evidence. In these cases, it seems, to recognize the evidence is to have a belief in what the evidence points to. If Sue really believes that the evidence – taken as a whole, including her culture's testimony – points to equality of blacks with whites, then, even if she has a difficult time admitting this, she does believe that blacks are equal to whites. On the other hand, intuitions are to be taken into account as part of the total evidence, so that if Sue finds herself assenting to the statement that blacks are inferior in spite of the evidence, she may be warranted in suspending judgment on the matter or even trusting in the original intuition until she can understand why it should be overthrown. She has an obligation to investigate the grounds or causal mechanisms for the inegalitarian intuition, but, as an intuition, it still counts as prima facie evidence. Such cases of doxastic incontinence push one away from a simplistic model of belief and towards a behavioral or dispositional one, though as we have seen, there are also problems in putting too much weight on those models. Nevertheless, although behavior such as Sue's suggests difficulties in accounting for the phenomena of alternating beliefs, nothing in this behaviour warrants our believing that the beliefs are directly caused by acts of will. Sue looks at certain selective evidence in a certain light and that causes the belief. The belief comes indirectly by a process involving the will.

It may be that given enough time and resources we can come to believe almost anything indirectly through willing the appropriate means and acting upon them. For example, we believe that the world is spherical and not flat, and no amount of effort seems sufficient to overturn this belief; but perhaps if we had good prudential reasons to do so (e.g., someone offered us a million dollars if we could get ourselves to believe that the world was flat), we might go to a hypnotist, take drugs or use elaborate auto-suggestion until we actually acquired the belief.

Perhaps the volitionalist will respond that there is really little difference between a case of auto-suggestion and a case of volition. Consider the following cases which progressively tend towards a state of successful auto-suggestive belief acquisition:

1 It might be virtually impossible for anyone to use auto-suggestion to come to believe that one does not exist.
2 It may take several days for the average person to get herself to believe through auto-suggestion that the earth is flat.
3 It may take several hours to get oneself to believe that one's spouse is faithful where there is good evidence to the contrary.
4 It may only take several minutes for a garden-variety racist to get into a state of believing that people of another race are full human beings.
5 It may take some people only a few seconds to acquire the belief that the tossed coin will come up heads.
6 With practice some people could get themselves to acquire the belief that the tossed coin will come up heads in an imperceptibly short amount of time.
7 Some masters at auto-suggestion may be able to acquire beliefs about tossed coins without any time intervening between the volition and the belief formation.

Perhaps it is strange, stupid, or even perversely immoral to engage in such auto-suggestive belief acquisition, but cases 2 and 5 seem psychologically possible (to leave to the side for the moment the likely damage to our belief-forming mechanisms and our noetic structure as a whole). It is conceivable that 6 and 7 obtain. In throwing dice, one sometimes has the feeling that the lucky (unlucky) number will turn up in a way that resembles this sort of phenomenon. Perhaps there are some people who can believe some propositions at will the way people can blush, wiggle their ears and sneeze as basic acts. If 7 is psychologically possible, then the first premise and the conclusion of the Phenomenological Argument must be altered to take account of these anomalies, so that the revised argument would read as follows:

1 Acquiring a belief is *typically* a happening in which the world forces itself upon a subject, and
2 Happenings in which the world forces itself upon a subject are not things the subject does or chooses.
3 Therefore, acquiring a belief is not *typically* something a subject does or chooses.

However, while we can never entirely rule out such behavior, it seems dubious whether we actually do perform such acts. It is hard to know whether such a case would be a case of imagining a state of affairs or believing a proposition, for the distinction is blurred at this point. At some point to imagine that *p* becomes a belief that *p*. For most of us, most of the time, however, such belief-acquisitions will not be possible. For consider the proposition that 'this coin will land heads'. Do you have any sense of yesness or noness, assent or dissent regarding it? Or suppose that the local torturer holds out his two fists and says to you, 'If you choose the fist with the penny in it, you will receive $100,000, but if you pick the empty fist, you will be tortured for the next week. The only stipulation on your choosing the correct fist is that when you choose it, you must not only point to it but *believe* that the coin is in that hand and not in the other (a lie detector will monitor your reaction).' I take it that most of us would be in for some hard times.

The last illustration nicely brings out the difference between acting and believing. It is relatively easy to *do* crazy things if there are practical grounds for them. We can easily act when the evidence is equally balanced (e.g., call heads while the coin is in the air), but believing is typically more passive in nature, not a doing, but a guide to doing. The Phenomenological Argument shows that volitionalism is abnormal and bizarre, but it does not rule out the possibility of acquiring beliefs by voliting.

Veto Phenomena

There is another possible use of the will regarding belief acquisition which needs to be addressed: the veto phenomenon. We already saw indications of this form in Locke and Holyer in our historical part of this work. These philosophers hold that the will can act as a veto on belief inclinations, halting would-be beliefs in the process of formation. This is a negative type of volition, for it does not claim that we can actually attain beliefs by the fiat of the will, only that we can prevent some from getting hold of us by putting up a doxastic road-block just in the nick of time. What seems to occur is this:

1 S entertains proposition *p* (This is sometimes under our direct control).
2 S is inclined to believe that *p* or S suspects that *p* (This is not normally under our control).

3 The veto phenomenon occurs by raising doubts, suspending judgment or 'tabling' the proposition under focus.

4 S looks at further evidence or looks at the old evidence in a fresh light and forms a judgment (While the 'looking' is under our direct control, the 'seeing' or judgment is not).

Is the veto-event under our direct control, or is it caused by a counter claim, a sense that there is counter evidence, or a sense that there is something wrong with our first inclination? For example, I am interviewing candidate A for a vacant position in our department and have a strong inclination to believe her to be the right person for the job, but, suddenly, I remember that we still have two candidates to interview and realize that my inclination to believe 'that A is *the* best candidate for the job' is founded on insufficient evidence. I must modify the proposition to state that she is a good candidate. Here it seems that another belief (viz., that there are other good candidates still to be interviewed) comes into play and forces the other belief aside. No act of will is present to my consciousness. But even if I do feel a will to believe or withhold judgment in these sorts of cases, it doesn't follow that the will causes the belief. It may well be an accompaniment. Nevertheless, there are other types of vetoing where I may clearly prevent a belief from forming on the basis of the evidence. Consider the situation where John tells Joan that her father has embezzled some money from his company, and before he is finished presenting the evidence Joan stops him, crying, 'Stop it, please, I can't bear to hear any more!' It seems plausible to suppose that something analogous to her stopping John from providing the incriminating evidence which would cause a belief to form may also occur within us when we begin to consider evidence for a position which we deplore. We may inwardly turn away from the evidence, focus on something else, and so fail to form a belief in the matter. Perhaps this is similar to self-deception, but in any case, the veto-power seems to be sometimes under our direct control. Nevertheless, it does not show that we actually can acquire beliefs by voliting, but shows only that the will has a negative role to play in preventing beliefs from fixing themselves in us.

Cartesia

Although our analysis hasn't ruled out the possibility of voliting, it does support the claim that there is something peculiar about the phenomenon. If voliters exist, they are like people who can wiggle their ears, blush, vomit or regulate their heart beat at will. But unlike these volitional phenomena, believing at will seems to involve a conceptual confusion. Typically, I take it, believing is representational in nature, purporting to mirror our world and our relations with the world, so that every instance of volitional-nonrepresentational believing deviates from that relationship in a fundamental way. To see this better imagine a society, Cartesia, whose members all volit. They attain beliefs as we engage in coughing, both voluntarily and involuntarily. Regarding every proposition voliting will be a serious consideration. When a member of Cartesia hears that her spouse has been unfaithful, she must ask herself, not simply what the evidence is for this charge but whether she has an obligation to believe that her spouse is faithful in spite of sufficient evidence. Such people have no difficulty in making Kierkegaardian leaps of faith against sufficient evidence, let alone where the evidence is counterbalanced. For example, when they throw coins up into the air, they form convictions about the way the coins will land. No doubt they will have a strong normative component regarding voliting in order to regulate the activity. There will have to be elaborate classification systems covering obligatory volits, permissible volits, little white volits, immoral volits, and illegal volits punishable by the State.

Such a society is hard to imagine, but in it there would have to be a distinction between voliting-type beliefs and nonvoliting-type beliefs. The latter alone would be treated as reliable for action guidance, voliting types of belief being tolerated mainly in the private domain, where no public issue is at stake. In other words, the nonvoliting belief acquisitions would be treated very much the way beliefs are treated in our society, as action guides which, as such, should be reliable mirrors of the evidence.

One is tempted to give an evolutionary account of the nonvolitional nature of belief acquisition. In order to survive, animals need a fairly accurate and spontaneous representation of the world. The cat's action of catching the mouse and the primitive human's running away from the bear would not be aided by intervening volits between the representations of the mouse and the bear and the beliefs that the representations were accurate, nor would it be helpful for us to have to decide to believe our perceptions under normal conditions. Basically, we are credulous creatures. For most believings, most of the time, *contra* Descartes and Kierkegaard, the will has nothing to do with the matter. Beliefs come naturally as that which purports to represent the way the world is so that our actions may have a reliable map by which to steer.

The Logic of Belief Argument Against Volitionalism

The Phenomenological Argument gets its force by attacking the second characteristic of an act of voliting: the act must be done in full consciousness. If my analysis is correct, voliting must be a highly abnormal phenomenon, if it exists in any positive form at all. However, I have not ruled out the possibility of some people voliting. In this sense, my analysis has resembled Hume's account in which it is a contingent matter that we do not obtain beliefs by fiat of the will. A second argument, close to, but avoiding the problems of, that put forth by Williams and Swinburne, now will be put forward which attacks volitionalism primarily on the basis of its third characteristic, i.e., that it must be done independently of evidential or truth considerations (I use these terms synonymously to stand for evidence in the broad sense of the term, including the self-evidence of basic beliefs). I call this argument 'The Logic of Belief Argument'. It states that the notion of volitional believing involves a conceptual confusion, that it is broadly a logical mistake. It argues that there is something incoherent in stating that one can obtain or sustain a belief in full consciousness simply by a basic act of the will. It does not rule out the possibility of obtaining beliefs by voliting in less than full consciousness (not truly voliting), but asserts that when full consciousness enters, the 'belief' will wither from one's noetic structure. One cannot believe in full consciousness 'that *p* and I believe that *p* for other than truth considerations'. The statement has a similar incoherence as Moore's paradox 'I believe that *p*, but *p* is false', in that while neither are strictly speaking contradictions, they are logically odd. Perhaps we can say that they involve broadly logical contradictions given our notion of first

170

person statements. My argument only applies to propositions over which I have no control, to what I call 'standard cases of belief'. It omits 'self-creative beliefs' (sometimes called 'self-verifying beliefs') where belief in a proposition actually helps bring about the proposition's truth (I deal with this at the end of this chapter). The argument against the coherence of voliting is this:

1 If A believes that *p*, A believes that *p* is true (by analysis of the concept of belief).
2 In standard cases of belief, the truth of *p* is wholly dependent on the states of affairs, S, which either corresponds to *p* (and makes *p* true) or fails to correspond to *p* (and makes *p* false).
3 In standard cases of belief, whether or not the appropriate states of affairs S that corresponds to *p* obtains is a matter that is independent of A's actions and volitions.
4 In standard cases of belief, A subconsciously or consciously believes or presupposes premise 3 (i.e., we recognize intuitively that wishing doesn't make it so).
5 Therefore, in standard cases of belief, A cannot both believe that *p* and that A's belief is presently caused by his willing to believe that *p*. Rather A must believe that what makes his belief true (if it is true) is state of affairs S, which obtains independently of his will.

Several comments are in order to defend this argument. In premise 4 I am claiming that rational beings (i.e., those with a minimal understanding of the primitive notion of 'belief' and who include children) at least tacitly comprehend that the logic of belief involves the passive element in the belief acquisition. For example, when the child believes that the block that she has been playing with is still behind her a minute after she has placed it there, she tacitly understands that mere wanting it not to be there has no effect on the facts. Wishing never makes it so; but even if it did, there would still be a nonvolitional difference between the world before the wish and after the wish which even the wish couldn't overcome without a complete abandonment of our understanding of time and space.

The phrase 'presently caused' in premise 5 is necessary to rule out such cases as the following: A believes that *p* by a volition and later comes to believe that *p* on the basis of the evidence. Now A believes that he obtained the belief by a volit, but he sustains the belief by the evidence. It is the failure to recognize this sort of situation that creates a problem with Williams' formulation, as Winters shows. The logic of the above argument shows that while a person may have obtained a belief through self-deception, he cannot knowingly or in full-consciousness acquire a belief or continue to hold it simply by willing to believe the proposition. He must believe that there is some evidence for it in virtue of which it is true.

The point is that because beliefs just are about the way the world is and are made true (or false) depending on the way the world is, it is a confusion to believe that any given belief is true simply on the basis of being willed. As soon as the believer discovers the basis of his belief – as being caused by the will alone – he must drop the belief. In this regard, saying 'I believe that p, but I believe it only because I want to believe it', has the same incoherence attached to it as Moore's paradoxical, 'I believe p but it is false that p'. Structurally, neither are strictly logical contradictions, but both show an incoherence that might be called broadly contradictory.

Robert Audi has objected that my argument only has merit if one supposes that the believer is rational, for an irrational believer could continue to believe that p in some other sense. That is, one's believing that p does not entail that one's belief is *based* on evidence. I agree that we may not notice the evidential connection of our beliefs. Children, animals, and all of us some of the time believe without formulating our beliefs (as when one spontaneously dodges an opponent's fist, in which case one 'believes' a fist is coming but does not notice that he possesses a belief about a fist coming). What I want to urge, however, is that there is a tacit recognition of a putative truth-connection in having any belief. That is, the very concept of having a belief entails the belief that if the belief is true, there must be some connection between it and states of affairs in the world. While a child may not have the concept of 'evidence' or 'truth', his state of consciousness can correctly be described as tacitly recognizing these features. Using the term 'evidence' in a broad sense (to include evident to the senses, self-evidence, and spontaneous recognition of states of affairs), we may say that to believe anything entails evidence for the belief.

My formulation builds minimal understanding of the concept of belief and truth or evidence into its premises, but if the reader is sympathetic to Audi's criticism, we can modify our formula to apply only to rational believing (leaving aside whether irrational believing *in this sense* is possible) by adding premise 5' and conclusion 6':

5' Rational believing is defined as believing according to the evidence and completely rational believing is defined as believing solely because of the evidence.

6' Therefore, in standard cases of belief, A cannot in complete rationality both believe that *p* and that his belief is presently caused by his willing to believe that *p*. Rather, if rational, A must believe that what makes his belief true is a state of affairs S which obtains independently of his will.

Wayne Davis has objected that all that we are doing is applying our normal concept of rational believing – the notion that we ought not to believe against (or without) sufficient evidence.[17] All non-evidential believing is irrational. This is true, but volitional believing is not simply irrational believing, but a special variety of it. It is not simply a failure of induction but a failure in principle. It is incoherently irrational in a way that normal inductive reason is not, for it represents a confusion at the very heart of the concept of belief. In volitional believing I not only believe without decisive regard for the evidence, but I do so for no other reason than because I want to (i.e., I don't believe because of misreading the evidence but because of the desire itself which has nothing to do with the evidence).

Davis has also objected that there could be a case of rational voliting involved in doxastic incontinence. Suppose Ann has good evidence for *p* and, moreover, she knows that she has good evidence for *p* but still is unable to believe that *p*. Ann believes that she can volit and obtain the belief that *p* and by continuing to will to believe, she can continue to sustain her belief (though not on the evidence, but simply because she wants to believe the evidence).

Here my inclination is to say that Ann already believes *p*, for to believe that evidence E entails *p* and to believe E, is, following *modus ponens*, simply to believe *p*, if one considers the proposition at all. While it is possible for a person not to believe that she believes propositions so inferred, I think there is reason to doubt that the belief about her unbelief is a true belief. It seems similar to a self-deceptive belief where we have an inherent confusion in our doxastic repertoire. Sometimes we have feelings of doubt attached to belief states which are as disturbing as they are puzzling. Some people worry whether they believe strongly enough that their spouses are faithful or that God exists, and sometimes we forget the evidence that caused our belief in the first place or we turn away from the evidence which supports our beliefs and temporarily seem to lose them; but so long as we see the logical connection and consider the belief, it seems more reasonable to say that we believe the proposition (at least dispositionally) although we waver (occurrently) regarding it.

But even if the believer can believe that it is his will that is causing the belief in cases of doxastic incontinence, the revised argument (above) would show that the believer could not believe that his belief was being caused or sustained in the right way. The rational believer, in full consciousness, would see that there must be a truth connection between states of affairs and the beliefs by virtue of which the belief is true, so that the will is essentially unnecessary for the belief – although it may be necessary in order to get into a proper state of mind where he will be able to perceive the evidence perspicuously. Just as there is an instrumental relation between opening one's eyes and seeing whatever one sees, but an intrinsic relation between states of affairs in the world and what one sees, so likewise there is only an instrumental relationship between willing to believe *p* and believing *p*, whereas there is an intrinsic relationship between state of affairs S by virtue of which *p* is true and my belief that *p*. Once Ann realizes that willing never makes it so, she must give up the belief that it is the will that is decisively or intrinsically sustaining her belief that *p*, though she may believe that there is an instrumental relationship. At least, she will not be able to believe that the will *alone* is causing her to believe that *p*, but that it is the evidence that is the deciding factor.

My argument could just as well be stated using the concept of the will as the point of departure rather than the concept of belief. It would run as follows:

1 In standard cases of willing the agent cannot will to do an action which he has no control over and which he knows he has no control over.
2 Many states of affairs (all those that occurred in the past, and which exist in the present or will occur in the future but not connected to our actions) are out of our control and are believed by us to be beyond our control.
3 But in standard cases of belief acquisition, the acquisition is an event in which the subject aims to obtain a representation

of states of affairs which he believes to be beyond his control to effect.

4 Therefore, a subject cannot consciously will to believe that a proposition, which could only be made true by his action but is beyond his control, is true.

There is a clear difference between acting, which is volitional, and acquiring a belief, which is not volitional, but an event or a happening. Believing is evidential, in that to believe that p is to presuppose that I have evidence for p or that p is self-evident to the senses. I need not have a developed concept of evidence to believe this. Children do not have a full concept of belief, but they tacitly suppose something like this. On reflection, rational adults seem to recognize the connection between a belief and objective states of affairs. In a sense, belief that p seems to imply the thought of a causal chain stretching back from the belief to a primary relationship with the world and so faithfully representing the world. We may have more or less confidence about the preciseness of the way our beliefs represent the world, but some degree seems implicit in every belief state.

Another way to make this same point about the evidentiality of belief is to define propositional belief in terms of a subjective probability index. All believing is believing to a degree of confidence. You may test the approximate degree to which you believe that a proposition by imagining how surprised you would be if you found out that the particular belief in question turned out to be false. If the reader will recall the idea of measuring our beliefs by means of a Belief Meter, mentioned in the section on p. 149, we can conceive of attaining a rough subjective probability index. For example, it might turn out that Ann discovers that she only believes that God exists to a probability of 0.6 (on a scale of 0 to 1 where 0.5 represents withholding assent), whereas she believes that it will rain today to a probability of 0.8. It might also turn out that Ann believes that she believes that God exists more strongly than she believes that it will rain today; but when she sees the evidence on the Belief Meter, she may be forced to change her mind – although it is also possible that she doubt that the Belief Meter is working properly or is an accurate index of her belief states.

In principle I see no reason why something like this could not be done, but the point is that we already have a rough notion of subjective probability in terms of the relative degrees with which we believe propositions. If believing were the result of our immediate willings, it would not be about the probability of states of affairs obtaining, but simply about our desires. It would be the case that I could come to a judgment that the probability of p on the evidence E was 0.5 and via a volit conclude that it was 0.6. Could one in full consciousness make such a leap? It seems as possible as believing that '2 + 2 = 4' and then deliberately believing at the same time that '2 + 2 = 5'.

It may be objected that this argument implies that one must have a concept of probability, but I think that we all do have a notion of degrees of belief which entails a rough notion of subjective probability in the manner that I have described. If this argument is sound, the interesting thing is that not only can we not volit a belief, but we cannot even volit a change in the degree with which we believe a proposition. We cannot increase the strength of our belief that p from 0.6 to 0.65 simply by fiat of the will.

The Logic of Belief Argument has not ruled out the logical possibility of voliting but simply rules out as logically odd (in the wider sense of the term) the possibility of acquiring a belief in full consciousness by a fiat of the will without regard to truth consideration. It does not rule out the possibility of obtaining the belief in less than full consciousness or indirectly. The phenomena in these cases seem similar to that of self-deception where one is not fully aware of what one truly believes. Once one discovers that one has self-deceived oneself, the logic of the discovery seems to entail the giving up of the false 'belief' (the one that the person thought she had on a conscious level). Likewise once one realizes that the only basis for believing that p is one's wanting p to be true, the belief must wither. Hence, if one could come to have a belief through directly willing to have it, once he reflected on the acquisition and discovered its illegitimate origin, the person would give it up (unless, of course, he now had evidence for it). He would see on reflection that the purported belief reflects only the content of his will. It has the same status as a product of the imagination.

Consider this similarity between imagining and willing to believe. Take for example, Vivid Imaginer Imogene who gets so carried away with her imagination that she sometimes believes her imagination reports. While sitting bored to death in her logic class, she fantasizes that she is swimming in the Bahamas or is being embraced by Warren Beatty. She imagines these things so vividly that for the moment she believes that they are really happening, until the teacher rudely calls on her and breaks the spell of her daydream, thus shattering her transient 'beliefs'. Perhaps many of our beliefs are formed through the imagination which are more subtle than this and which we never discover, but when we do discover that a belief has its basis in the imagination, we discard it as worthless – and we do so automatically and not by a volit. But voliting and imagining seem to display the very same logic regarding belief acquisition. Both are acquired independently of evidential considerations.

Of course, it is possible that a person regard his wants about reality as counting as *evidence* for propositions. For example, someone might say, 'I have found that whenever I want a proposition to be true, amazingly it generally turns out to be so'. Here wanting would indirectly cause belief, but not by voliting, but rather by being regarded as reliable evidence, a type of credible testimony. It would still be the case that what causes the believer to believe is evidential and not simply the will's fiat.

If my analysis is correct, there is a deep conceptual confusion in self-consciously believing of any proposition that it has originated through a volit and/or that what sustains one's belief is one's will. I regard this analysis as a correction of Bernard Williams' earlier account (above, ch. XI) which has been criticized by Barbara Winters for confusing the state of acquiring a belief in full consciousness with presently sustaining that belief. Williams forgets that while I may have acquired a belief through a volit, once I discover this I may still hold on to the belief just so long as I now believe it for truth considerations. However, I disagree with Winters when she denies that we can have a sound argument against the coherence of direct volitionalism. If one takes the notion of full consciousness and links it appropriately with an implicit evidential relationship, then it turns out that most forms of volitional belief acquisition as well as sustainment are shown to be incoherent.

Self-Creative Beliefs

There is one final objection to my thesis that we do not (normally) acquire beliefs by voliting. This objection centers on the phenomenon of self-creative or self-verifying beliefs, the activity described by William James in his classic article 'The Will to Believe', whereby one's deciding to believe is causally operative in creating a state of affairs which makes the belief true. This, the objector claims, seems like a normal case of volitionalism. Suppose you are going to play a game of chess. Your using auto-suggestion to get into a state of mind where you believe you will win actually plays a causal role in your winning (it may, of course, have the reverse effect through causing over-confidence). James' own example (with my filling out an interpretation) is of a person trapped at the edge of a crevasse, overlooking a yawning gorge. He calculates that a successful leap is improbable, but it will increase in probability in proportion to his convincing himself that he must get himself to believe what an impartial look at the evidence will not allow. So he volits the belief. Or consider a student who loves philosophy and whose self-identity is centered on the goal of being a good philosopher. She doubts whether she will ever become such, but believes that her chances of becoming good will be increased by believing that she will reach that goal. So she apparently volits and believes without sufficient evidence that she will become a good philosopher. Because of this confidence, she succeeds where she would have otherwise failed. These sort of cases have been used as counter-examples to the arguments against volitionalism.

There are two things to be said about these kinds of cases. The first is that they are not counter-examples to the thesis that we cannot acquire beliefs by fiat of the will. It seems reasonable to say that a deliberation process went on in each of these cases in which the will *indirectly* caused belief by refocusing the mind on favorable evidence rather than on the unfavorable evidence. No volit is necessary.

For example, caught as I am before the yawning gorge, I ask myself, how in the world am I to attain the presumably necessary belief (which I don't have) that I can jump the gorge. I cannot just acquire it by a fiat, so I hit upon the idea of thinking of all the successful long jumps I made in grammar school. I then imagine myself a great Olympic track star. Perhaps a little hypnosis helps here. I focus on appropriate successes (real or imaginary), block out negative thoughts (if I can) and finally, self-deceive myself to the point where I believe that I believe that I can leap over the crevasse. But all this illustrates is a case of indirect volitional control, not direct control over believing. I have a goal, plan a policy of action and indirectly come to attain that goal.

The second thing to say is that this example seems to be an instance where a form of self-deception has salutary effects, but this leads us to the next chapter where we shall discuss indirect prescriptive volitionalism and the ethics of belief.

I conclude this chapter. Voliting seems (following Hume) psychologically aberrant and (following Williams and Swinburne) conceptually confused. It is psychologically problematic because of the feature of demanding full-consciousness which attaches to acts of will. It is conceptually confused because it neglects the evidential aspect of conscious belief acquisition and sustainment.

CHAPTER XIV

Indirect Volitionalism, Prescriptive Volitionalism and the Ethics of Belief

Indirectly believing does involve the will. I have argued that we cannot normally believe anything at all simply by willing to do so, for believing aims at truth and is not a basic act or a direct product of the will. If we could believe whatever we chose to believe simply by willing to do so, belief would not be about reality but about our wants. Nevertheless, the will does play an important indirect role in believing. Many of the beliefs that we arrive at are finally the results of our policy decisions. Although believing itself is not an act, our acts determine the sorts of beliefs we end up with. It is primarily because we judge that our beliefs are to some significant degree the indirect results of our actions that we speak of being responsible for them. Although we cannot be said to be directly responsible for them, as though they were actions, we can be said to be indirectly responsible for many of them. If we had chosen differently, if we had been better moral agents, paid attention to the evidence, and so forth, we would have different beliefs than we in fact do have.

To be sure, we are not responsible for all our beliefs, and the degree of responsibility seems to vary in proportion to the amount of evidence available at different times and our ability to attend properly to that evidence. For example, the person who pays attention regarding a certain matter often comes to have more accurate beliefs than the inattentive person. Attention is generally within our direct control (to some degree). As long as we agree that the inattentive person could have acted differently, could have been attentive if he had really wanted to, we can conclude that the inattentive person is responsible for not having the true beliefs which he might have had. In the same way we can conclude that the attentive person is responsible for the beliefs that she has.

Being (indirectly) responsible for our beliefs indicates that praise

180

and blame attach indirectly to our epistemic states, that indirectly beliefs are morally assessable. It may be the case that I have many beliefs which I ought not to have. If I had been a better person, learned to investigate certain matters with the right categories, I might now be endowed with a more accurate system of beliefs and believe many of my present beliefs in different degrees of confidence than I presently do.

We saw that some philosophers reject the notion of an ethics of belief. Mill, James and Meiland believe that there are no special doxastic moral duties. Hume and Price thought that there were only counsels of prudence. Price puts it thusly:

> But even if it were in our power to be wholly rational all of the time, it still would not follow that there is anything morally blameworthy about assenting unreasonably (against the evidence or without regard to the evidence) or that we ought to be chastised for doing so. There is nothing wicked about such assents. It is however true, and important, that unreasonable assent is contrary to our *long term interest*. It is to our long term interest to believe true propositions rather than false ones. And if we assent reasonably (i.e. in accordance with the evidence), it is likely that in the long run the propositions we believe will be more often true than false (*Belief*, p. 238).

The only 'ought' regarding belief acquisition is a prudential ought. A person is free to seek whatever goals he desires: happiness, salvation, convenience, aesthetic pleasure and so forth. It is simply in one's long term best interest generally to seek to have true beliefs. However, if you find yourself inclined to sacrifice truth for some other goal, you have every right to do so. We may call this the *Libertarian View of Doxastic Responsibility*. It affirms that believing is a purely private matter. Mill says that each person must be accorded 'absolute freedom of opinion on all subjects practical and speculative'.[1]

One may readily recognize the virtues of this position. Not many of us want to see government intervention into personal beliefs, totalitarian thought reforms and brainwashing in order to help others acquire 'true beliefs'. The Libertarian position is right to emphasize human autonomy with regard to our private selves, and it may even be the case that it is a good thing to have a plurality of opinions in a society. Nevertheless, I believe that there is something seriously deficient in this libertarian-prudentialist strategy. *It sells the truth short*. It does so on two counts. It underestimates the significance of truth for the individual himself, and it ignores the social dimension of truth seeking. Personhood, involving a high degree of autonomy, entails respect for highly justified beliefs. Socially, truth seeking is important, for unless a society has accurate information, many of its goals are not likely to be reached. I shall develop these ideas in the following analysis.

Perhaps the clearest account of a volitional stance on the ethics of belief is Jack Meiland's article 'What Ought We to Believe? or the Ethics of Belief Revisited', which we briefly noted in chapter 11. There Meiland argues that not only is it sometimes morally *permissible* to believe against the evidence, but that it is sometimes morally *obligatory* to do so. In all cases of belief-acquisition 'extra-factual considerations are relevant'.[2] It is worth our while in working out an ethics of belief to examine Meiland's arguments at greater length than we did in chapter 11. After presenting Meiland's against a strict evidentialism and in favor of prescriptive volitional belief-acquisition, I shall attempt to show what is wrong with Meiland's position, showing that what is new is not true and what is true is not new. Specifically, I shall contend that there is a more moderate form of evidentialism which escapes Meiland's criticisms and thus provides a middle way between the two extremes of rigid evidentialism and volitionalism. I shall outline what such a moderate evidentialism with regard to the ethics of belief looks like.

Rigid evidentialism states, following Meiland's interpretation, that one ought to believe propositions if and only if they are backed by sufficient evidence. This position, which, according to Meiland, is found in Descartes, Locke, Clifford and Chisholm, is largely impervious to subjective factors in belief formation. Chisholm's formulation is cited as a clear expression of this position:

1 Anyone having just the evidence in question is warranted in accepting the conclusion.
2 I am in a position of having that evidence.
3 Therefore, I am justified in accepting the conclusion (p. 19).

On this account, everyone is epistemically required to come to the same conclusion, given the same evidence. The argument for this position can be spelled out as follow. Suppose person A is justified on the evidence E in believing that *p*. Suppose, further, that person B has exactly the same evidence as A has but believes that not-*p*. On the face of it, it seems contradictory to say that although A is justified in believing that *p* on E, B is justified in believing that not-*p*, but this defies our very notion of justification. Hence, the evidentialist concludes that not both A and B can be justified in believing what they believe on E. If A is justified in believing that *p* on E, then B is not, and vice versa. On the other hand, anyone who has the evidence A has is in the same state of being justified as A is, whether he knows it or not.

What this argument for evidentialism neglects is a notion of the larger context into which apparently similar evidence comes. Just as a farmer, a real estate dealer and an artist, looking at the 'same' field, may not see the same *field*, so evidence always is relative to a person's individuating background beliefs, capacities to interpret data and expectations. Meiland, rightly, points out that subjective factors play a strong role in our interpretation of evidence and in the formation of beliefs, but he may go too far when he interprets this subjectivism to include direct volitionalism, the acquisition of beliefs through conscious choices. Classical evidentialism may be too rigid in its notion of justification. It neglects psychological factors which enter into every belief acquisition. All believing is believing from a perspective, and any type of evidentialism which neglects this perspectivial element may be designated 'rigid' in that it lacks a proper appreciation for the complexity of evidence gathering and assembling.

A second important feature of Meiland's position on the ethics of belief is his subsuming epistemic duties under the heading of general ethical duties. That is, we have no special epistemic duties that are not already covered by ethical principles *simpliciter*. If we claim that someone has a duty to believe some proposition, we must give moral reasons for that duty, not epistemic ones. Meiland argues on utilitarian grounds that it is often morally required that we act against so-called 'epistemic requirements' of believing according to sufficient evidence. Here Meiland holds a stronger position than James, Chisholm or Nathanson, who allow for voliting only when the evidence is insufficient, as a sort of a tie breaker.[3]

Meiland maintains that we are sometimes obligated to get ourselves to believe propositions even when we have sufficient evidence to the contrary. However, he does not go as far as Kierkegaard in allowing for believing against even conclusive evidence. When we have conclusive evidence, it is not in our power to believe against the evidence.

The sort of sufficient evidence for a proposition against which we may believe is illustrated in the example of the wife who finds lipstick on her husband's handkerchief, a blond strand of hair on his suit, and a crumpled piece of paper with a telephone number on it in a woman's handwriting in his pocket. This would constitute sufficient evidence (on the rigid evidentialist account) that the husband is having an affair with another woman and would normally cause the wife to believe that her husband was being unfaithful. However, the wife may have good reason for rejecting the evidence even though she admits that it is sufficient to justify belief in her husband's unfaithfulness. She rejects the belief, however, for pragmatic reasons. Suppose that the wife closely examines the evidence and decides that if she comes to believe what it points to (or continues to believe that her husband is unfaithful), their marriage will be ruined and great unhappiness will ensue. If, on the other hand, she can get herself to believe that her husband is faithful, in spite of the evidence to the contrary, the marriage probably will be saved. She reasons that her husband will very likely get over his infatuation and return to his marital commitment. Suppose that she has good evidence for this second belief. Should she not acquire the belief in her husband's faithfulness in hope of saving her marriage? Perhaps she also justifiably believes that undergoing this volitional process, of somehow acquiring a belief by willing to have it despite the evidence, will do no permanent damage to her noetic structure. After acquiring the belief and letting the belief direct her actions, the marriage will be saved; and after the marriage is saved, she will recall the process which she underwent in order to save the marriage. Now, however, she will be in a position to live with the unwelcome evidence and even speak openly with her husband about it. Given these factors, is not the wife morally obligated to take steps to obtain the belief in her husband's faithfulness?

Unlike the usual volitionalist strategy of advocating voluntary believing only in extreme cases, Meiland makes the rather daring claim that in every case of believing where there is insufficient evidence or sufficient evidence for an unwelcome proposition, extra-factual considerations are relevant considerations (p. 21).

While Meiland believes that believing is within the direct control of our will (except where there is conclusive evidence), he is content to let his case rest on the possibility that we may indirectly cause ourselves to believe against the evidence.

I want to outline four objections to Meiland's position on the ethics of belief: (1) his notion of evidentialism is overly rigid and ignores a broader form of evidentialism which obviates the need for a volitional alternative in most cases of believing; (2) a minor criticism is that Meiland fails to make clear why we may have an obligation to believe against the evidence when it is sufficient but may not have an obligation to believe against the evidence when it is conclusive; (3) his position undervalues the importance of having reliable belief-forming mechanisms and misconstrues the nature of belief acquisitions; and (4) if Meiland's position is interpreted by the principle of charity into making merely the weak claim that sometimes we have a moral duty to override our duty of seeking to have true, justified beliefs, then there is nothing new in his position. Let us look briefly at each of these criticisms.

(1) Meiland is correct in criticizing the Clifford-Chisholm line of evidentialism which focuses on a non-perspectival relationship between evidence and justification. This position seems to neglect or underemphasize the point that evidence is person-relative, so that each person views the data with a different noetic endowment. The Aristotelian and the Nominalist who hear the argument from contingency for the existence of God will each view its soundness differently. But, given their different world-views, each may well be justified in coming to the belief he does. While there may be such a thing as *propositional warrant* which provides objective evidence for a given proposition, justification has mainly to do with what is reasonable for a given person to believe, given his noetic structure, background beliefs, ability to pay attention, ability to weight evidence impartially, ability to interpret the evidence according to certain rules and the like. A person living in the Middle Ages may well have been warranted in believing that the earth is flat, even though there may have been objective evidence to support the proposition that it is round and which anyone in an ideal situation would have.

Meiland posits an unnecessary dichotomy between objective (sufficient) evidence and subjective factors where the will determines the belief. The only alternatives are not rigid evidentialism and volitionalism. Simply because objective evidence is not the only necessary factor in belief acquisition does not mean that the will can or should decide the matter. One must take into account such subjective factors as unconscious wants and past learning which have been internalized so that we are not aware of the information processing which our subconscious self is undertaking. For example, the chicken sexer, while failing the strong evidentialist's test of being able to give an account of his evidence, nevertheless probably has evidence for the reliable judgments he consistently makes. Given his high success rate in identifying the sex of chicks, it is more reasonable to say that he knows but cannot tell us or even himself how he knows the chick's sex than to attribute his success to acts of the will (or simply luck).

I am suggesting that a more moderate version of evidentialism includes a recognition of subjective factors in belief acquisition without admitting that the will directly causes belief or that it should cause it indirectly. We don't need to bring in volitions to account for the subjective element in belief formation. An alternative interpretation of one of Meiland's examples will illustrate what I mean. Imagine a defense attorney who agrees with the prosecution and the jury that there is sufficient evidence against his client but, who, nevertheless, continues to believe in his client's innocence despite the evidence. His belief is vindicated years later. This is supposed to show that the attorney has a right to believe that his client is innocent in spite of the evidence where there are pragmatic grounds for doing so. I doubt that the will is directly involved here at all, and I believe that the attorney's belief can be accounted for through my modified version of evidentialism. The attorney, Smith, hears and sees all the evidence E against his client, Brown. He concludes on the basis of E that Brown is probably guilty. But he pauses, introspects, and senses some resistance from within to that conclusion. He finds himself with a tendency to reject the first conclusion in favor of a belief that Brown is innocent. Perhaps, for a time, he vacillates between two belief tendencies or he experiences undulating alternate belief states. When he is in court or looking at the evidence in private, he feels a subtle certainty that Brown is guilty, but when he faces Brown, looks him in the eye, and speaks to him, he senses that he must be wrong in with the evidence that points to Brown's guilt. Perhaps we can say (following Price) that Smith half-believes that Brown is innocent and half-believes that he is guilty, the belief-states alternating so frequently that he cannot fully make up his mind. Perhaps the feeling that Brown is innocent finally wins out in the battle of Smith's mind. Meiland would explain this alternation and conclusion by means of a decision to believe. I doubt whether this is the correct description of what is going on and suggest that it is more likely that Smith's previous experience with people, especially defendants, both innocent and guilty, has caused him to form reliable beliefs about characteristic features and behaviors of the guilty and innocent, including the 'seemingly innocent' and the 'seemingly guilty'. He is unaware of this large repository of internalized evidence and cannot formulate it. Here, we want to say that Smith's reliability at judging character and legal evidence warrants our saying that he has internalized skills and sets of inductive generalizations (e.g., judging from certain characteristic looks on innocent faces to a conclusion of particular innocence) that cause individual belief occurrences. Smith has data and skills that the jury does not, which a less competent attorney does not, and which the judge may not have.

One can generalize from this case and say with regard to any proposition, p, and for any person, S, that if S finds himself believing p, the belief that p is prima facie evidence for p itself relative to S, that is, S is prima facie justified in believing p. It may not be very strong justification, and S may be forced to weaken his hold on p when he cannot defend p, but it is some evidence, enough to start with. Furthermore, to the extent that S finds himself a reliable judge in a given area, to exactly that extent is he justified in holding on to a belief tenaciously in the light of evidence to the contrary. Modified evidentialism accepts intuitive judgments as playing an evidential role in believing. If my account of evidentialism is correct, then the motivation for much of Meiland's volitionalism is dissipated. Simply saying that subjective factors enter into our belief acquisitions is not sufficient to justify volitionalism, for in a sense all believing involves subjective factors which are causative in belief formations.

(2) This leads to the second criticism of Meiland's position. This focuses on his distinction between insufficient evidence, sufficient evidence and conclusive evidence in relation to the ability to volit. According to Meiland, it is only possible to volit (or indirectly get ourselves into a belief state through volitional means) when the evidence is not conclusive. Hence, it can only be morally required that we volit in those cases. But unless we reduce 'conclusive

evidence' to the trivially true definiens 'that which we cannot will ourselves not to believe', we seem to have a problem; for if I have a moral obligation to believe (through volitional means) against sufficient evidence, why can I not have an obligation to believe (via those same means) against conclusive evidence? The answer cannot be simply that it is easier to do this in the first case. It may be that we must spend more time and effort getting ourselves to believe against conclusive evidence, going to a better hypnotist or whatever, but if our utilitarian cost-benefit analysis specifies that the psychic price is worth paying (e.g., we may be able to save our children's sanity or lives by keeping our marriage together by believing that our spouses are faithful even though we catch them in bed committing adultery), then, on Meiland's analysis, we should pay that price. I see no criterion to distinguish between believing against evidence where it is only sufficient and believing against the evidence where it is conclusive. If Meiland responds that there is a likelihood that such manipulations would mess up the subject's mind, we should respond, 'What makes you so confident that this isn't what happens in every case of purposefully getting ourselves to believe against or in the absence of sufficient evidence?' This leads to the most serious criticism of volitional positions on the ethics of belief.

(3) My main criticism of positions like Meiland's (including William James's) has to do with the importance of having well-justified beliefs and truth-seeking in general. We generally believe that these two concepts are closely related, so that the best way to assure ourselves of having true beliefs is to seek to develop one's belief forming mechanisms in such ways as to become good judges of various types of evidence, attaining the best justification of our beliefs that is possible. The value of having the best justified beliefs possible can be defended on both deontological grounds with regard to the individual and teleological or utilitarian grounds regarding the society as a whole. The deontological argument (Kantian in tone and receiving its best treatment in Richard Gale's article on this subject, discussed in chapter 11) is connected with our notion of autonomy. To be an autonomous person is to have a high degree of warranted beliefs at one's disposal upon which to base one's actions. There is a tendency to lower one's freedom of choice as one lowers the repertoire of well-justified beliefs regarding a plan of action, and since it is a generally accepted moral principle that it is wrong to lessen one's autonomy or personhood, it is wrong to

lessen the degree of justification of one's beliefs on important matters. Hence, there is a general presumption against beliefs by willing to have them. Cognitive-voliting is a sort of lying or cheating in that it enjoins believing against what has the best guarantee of being the truth. When a friend or doctor lies to a terminally ill patient about her condition, the patient is deprived of the best evidence available for making decisions about her limited future. She is being treated less than fully autonomously. While a form of paternalism may sometimes be justified, there is always a presumption against it and in favor of truth telling. We even say that the patient has a right to know what the evidence points to. Cognitive voliting is a sort of lying to oneself, which, as such, decreases one's own freedom and personhood. It is a type of doxastic suicide which may only be justified in extreme circumstances. If there is something intrinsically wrong about lying (making it prima facie wrong), there is something intrinsically wrong with cognitive voliting, either directly or indirectly. Whether it be Pascal, James, Meiland, Newman or Kierkegaard, all prescriptive volitionalists (consciously or not) seem to undervalue the principle of truthfulness and its relationship to personal autonomy.

The utilitarian, or teleological, argument against cognitive voliting is fairly straightforward. General truthfulness is a desideratum without which society cannot function. Without it language itself would not be possible, since it depends on faithful use of words and sentences to stand for appropriately similar objects and states of affairs. Communication depends on a general adherence to accurate reporting. More specifically, it is very important that a society have true beliefs with regard to important issues, so that actions which are based on beliefs have a firm basis.

The doctor who cheated her way through medical school and who, as a consequence, lacks appropriate beliefs about certain symptoms, may endanger a patient's health. A politician who fails to take into consideration the amount of pollution being given off by large corporations which support his candidacy, may endanger the lives and health of his constituents. Even the passer-by who gives wrong information to a stranger who asks directions may seriously inconvenience the stranger. Here Clifford's point about believing against the evidence is well taken, despite its all-too-robustious tone. The shipowner who failed to make necessary repairs on his vessel and 'chose' to believe that she was sea-worthy, is guilty of the deaths of the passengers. 'He had no right to believe on such evidence as was before him.'[4] It is because beliefs are action guiding, maps by which we steer, and, as such, tend to cause actions, that society has a keen interest in our having the best justified beliefs possible regarding important matters.

Nevertheless, Meiland might reply, while there may be a general duty to seek to have well-justified beliefs, there may be many cases where other considerations override our duty to believe according to the evidence. In fact, these cases may be so numerous that one is tempted to conclude (as Meiland does) that 'extra-factual considerations' are relevant to every case of belief-acquisition (and, following this logic, relevant to every case of maintaining each of our beliefs). The trouble with this response is that it ignores the sort of intention-skill that truth-seeking is. It is dispositional, a habit. If it is to be effective at all, it must be deeply engrained within us, so that it is not at all easy to dispense with. The wife, if she has been properly brought up as a truth seeker, may simply not be able to believe against the evidence without going through elaborate conditioning processes which might seriously affect her personality and even her personal identity.

Furthermore, our beliefs do not exist in isolation from each other, so that to overthrow one belief may have reverberations throughout our entire noetic structure, affecting many of our beliefs. Getting oneself to believe against the evidence which supports a belief that p may upset our other justified beliefs q, r, and s, which in turn may affect still other beliefs. Cognitive-voliting, as Bernard Williams has pointed out 'is like a revolutionary movement trying to extirpate the last remains of the *ancien regime*. The man gets rid of this belief that his son is dead, and then there is some belief which strongly implies that his son is dead, and that has to be got rid of. It might be that a project of this kind tends in the end to involve total destruction of the world of reality, to lead to paranoia.'[5] After the wife succeeds in believing that her husband is innocent, what is the effect of this on her noetic structure? What happens every time she looks at the suit on which the strand of hair was found or sees a handkerchief? What happens every time she sees a strand of blond hair? every time she sees her husband talking to a blond? every time she sees a telephone number? Does she have to repress memories and deny that this is important evidence against her spouse's faithfulness? Do we have enough control over our knowledge about our unconscious selves to be able to predict the final result of volitional believing on our personality and character?

The utilitarian argument against volitional manipulation of our belief mechanisms might be stated this way.

1 Voliting is morally justified only if we have adequate evidence (acquired nonvolitionally) that it will result in better consequences than if we abstain from voliting.
2 But our noetic structure is such that we almost never do have adequate evidence that it will produce better consequences.
3 Therefore, voliting is almost never morally justified.

We almost never know how we will be affected by frustrating and manipulating our normal belief forming mechanisms. Our subconscious realm, where normal beliefs are formed, seems very complex, so that in attempting to influence it over one matter, we may cause unpredictable chain reactions within our noetic structure.

Of course, Meiland might well reply that if, on reflection, the cost is going to be this great, we ought not believe against sufficient evidence in most cases. Perhaps this is a satisfactory reply, and perhaps our main difference is merely one of emphasis: Meiland arguing against rigid evidentialism which makes objective justification an absolute duty and I arguing for a presumption of truth-seeking, making it a very high moral duty. These are not incompatible views. However, I think that there is more to our difference than this. The difference is rooted in two different views on how evidence is processed and of the possibility of consciously willing to have certain beliefs against what is taken to be good evidence, Meiland simply believes that we have more control over our beliefs than I do, and this difference results in a difference about the relevancy of volitional strategies.

Meiland has a pragmatic justification of belief that goes like this.

1 A has sufficient evidence for p (i.e., there is a strong inclination on A's part to believe that p or A does believe that p), but A also has non-evidential reasons for believing not p.
2 A decides, after reflection, that it is morally permissible or obligatory to get herself into a position where she believes not-p.
3 A takes whatever steps are necessary in order to get into that position, and presumably, A comes to believe not-p.

There is something odd about this argument, for it raises the fundamental question, which we looked at in the last chapter, of whether a rational person can consciously carry out a cognitive volit or sustain a belief while knowing that one has obtained the belief solely through a fiat of the will. For example, what happens when the wife, in Meiland's example, reflects on her belief that her husband is innocent? She looks at her belief and looks at the way that it was brought about. Can she go on believing that her husband is innocent despite the sufficient evidence to the contrary? There seems to be something incoherent about the phenomena of consciously acquiring or sustaining a belief regardless of the perceived evidence against the belief. This brings us to our final criticism of Meiland's position.

(4) Meiland may escape all of my objections by arguing that while it is always relevant in principle to take pragmatic considerations into account in acquiring (and sustaining) beliefs, it may hardly ever be our actual duty. He may defend his flank by saying that he merely wants to show that truth-seeking (as the rigid evidentialist conceives of it) is not an absolute moral duty, but that it is overridable in some instances. But if this is all that he is saying, his position surely loses much of its brashness and excitement. It may be true, but it is hardly new. Most moral systems since William Ross and including such unlikely bedfellows as Richard Brandt, William Frankena, R.M. Hare, and J.L. Mackie would agree that there are few, if any, moral absolutes, and that truth-seeking is not a moral absolute (i.e., nonoverridable) but a strong prima facie duty. Meiland's position must be stronger than this in order to be interesting, but if it is stronger than this, it seems implausible.

Criteria for Morally Prescriptive Indirect Volitionalism

Let me conclude this chapter by offering a set of criteria by which to decide when it is morally permissible to indirectly volit. I agree with Meiland against Clifford, Gale and others who contend that we ought never under any circumstances to get ourselves to believe anything where the evidence alone doesn't warrant it but simply because we have a need to believe it. Although I think that instances of justified voliting (indirectly) are probably exceedingly rare, there may be some. Meiland's example of the neurotic wife concerned with saving her marriage may indeed be such a case. Another may be the following. Suppose that I gain some information about you which causes me to act in a way which you perceive as harmful to your interests and suppose that I have obtained this information in a morally unacceptable way, say, by reading your diary or private correspondence, and that I would not have had this information had I not read this material. Suppose, further, that there is a competent psychiatrist who can bring it about, at minimum risk, that I totally forget the information that I possess about your private life. Or suppose that there is a psychologically harmless pill that will do this same thing. Is it obvious that you would not have a right to demand that I take the necessary steps to forget the memory belief that I have? Perhaps a certain type of forgiveness involves getting ourselves, through auto-suggestion, to forget in part the seriousness of the acts against us. Of course, self-creating beliefs seem the best examples of what may be morally permissible in this area. Suppose that you must swim two miles to shore in order to save your life. You have never swum that far and have good evidence that you can't do it. However, you reason that if you can get yourself to believe that you can swim the distance, the confidence will somehow produce a physiological state giving you a better chance of swimming that distance (though not quite a 50% chance). Would you not be justified in getting yourself into that place?

If there are times when it is morally permissible or even obligatory to volit a belief against sufficient evidence, what are the conditions which must be met? I suggest the following: a prudential condition and two utilitarian conditions (a general and a specific).

(1) A Prudential Requirement: the justified volit would have to involve a nonvolitional cost-benefit analysis which might be undermined if the agent was not a dispositional evidentialist. The act must be seen as possible and worth doing on the evidence available. There must be some morally acceptable benefit which outweighs the cost involved in getting the new belief by voliting.

(2) A General Utility Requirement: others must not be significantly harmed by this act, or their harm must not outweigh the benefits which would accrue to the agent, and the benefits must be morally acceptable. Again, the leap is parasictical on evidentialism, for a mistake may be dangerous. For example, if I get myself to believe that the world will end shortly (for religious reasons) and then become Secretary of Interior, I may treat the environment so

poorly as to hasten the end of the world.

(3) The Chain of Deception Requirement: this is a special inst-ance of the Utility Requirement. In getting yourself into a state S where you will believe that *p*, which you presently do not believe on the evidence, you will be responsible for a chain of unnecessary false reports. That is, if you were to tell others that *p* was the case, you would be lying. While the self which actually reports *p* will not be lying, that self is spreading a falsehood (or reporting falsely), becoming an unreliable witness and starting a possible chain of false reports. In essence, in willing to deceive your future self, who will sincerely report to others, you are taking on the responsibility for deceiving others. As the beginning of a chain of misinformation, only the most extreme grounds would seem to justify the volit.

If, however, you can make a cost-benefit analysis in the most rigorously evidentialist fashion and can determine that the volit is both psychologically possible and worth the cost of deceiving yourself and possibly others, then perhaps the volit is justified. If you are sure that you are not going to bring harm to others or lessen their autonomy significantly, and that you will not harm your children by being an unreliable witness, then you might well be justified in acquiring a belief by willing to have it and doing what is necessary to bring it about. But who can be so certain, given the uncertainty of how all these factors will work out in life? James's stranded mountain climber at the edge of the gorge certainly seems to be, for his options are limited. The person who read your diary may also be justified in trying to forget his belief. Perhaps the hermit who lives alone on an island is justified, though perhaps he has some obligation to put a sign on the dock, warning people who approach that they trespass at their own risk, for the inhabitant has engaged regularly in voliting and may seriously misinform them on certain matters. For the rest of us, almost all of the time, indirect voliting will not be a relevant consideration, but will be an impru-dent and immoral act.

Having seen that there is an ethics of belief and that it is important to have the best justified beliefs possible, we turn to the subject of rationality and religious believing.

CHAPTER XV

Rationality and Religious Belief

In the debate on faith and reason two opposing positions have dominated the field. The first position asserts that faith and reason are commensurable and the second denies that assertion. Those holding to the first position differ among themselves as to the extent of the compatibility between faith and reason, most adherents relegating the compatibility to the 'preambles of faith' (e.g., the existence of God and his nature) over against the 'articles of faith' (e.g., the doctrine of the incarnation). Few have gone as far as Kant and Swinburne in maintaining a complete harmony between reason and faith, i.e., a religious belief within the realm of reason alone. The second position divides into two sub-positions: (1) that which asserts that faith is opposed to reason (which includes such unlikely bedfellows as Hume and Kierkegaard), placing faith in the area of irrationality; and (2) that which asserts that faith is higher than reason, is transrational. Calvin, Barth, and Plantinga assert that a natural theology is inappropriate because it seeks to meet unbelief on its own grounds (ordinary human reason). Revelation, however, is 'self-authenticating', 'carrying with it its own evidence'.[1] We may call this position the 'transrationalist' view of faith. Faith is not so much against reason as above it and beyond its proper domain. Actually, Kierkegaard and Shestov show that the two sub-positions are compatible. They hold both that faith is above reason (superior to it) and against reason (because reason has been affected by sin). The irrationalist and the transrationalist positions are sometimes hard to separate in the incommensurabilist's arguments. At least, it seems that faith gets such a high value that reason comes off looking not simply inadequate but culpable. To use reason where faith claims the field is not only inappropriate but irreverent or unfaithful.

195

In this chapter I would like to defend a strong commensurabilist position on faith and reason. My primary thesis is that a religion such as Christianity or Judaism is (among other things) an explanatory theory or hypothesis about the world, which as such is as much in need of rational justification as any other explanatory theory or hypothesis. That is, while a religion is also a form of life, a set of practices, it contains a cognitive aspect which claims to make sense out of one's experience. It answers questions as to why we are here, why we suffer, and why the world is the way it is. These answers form a coherent network which call for reasons why they (or the network as a whole) are to be preferred to other answers (or no answers at all). Here I will defend this thesis indirectly. I will try to clear some conceptual ground in order to bring support to a rationalist religious epistemology. If I can clear some of the major obstacles and arguments against the commensurabilist position, showing by the way the force of that position, I shall have succeeded in my task. My assumption is that unless there is good reason to have a different method for evaluating religious claims, there is a presumption in favor of using the rational methods employed elsewhere here as well. This may be called the 'no distinction without a difference' principle, which puts the burden of proof on anyone who would object to uniform treatment of subject matters.

After a few words on conceptual frameworks and how they affect rationality. I shall discuss four obstacles to the commensurabilist position: (1) that my thesis implies a neutrality towards religion which is inconsistent with the attitude of faith; (2) that the thesis subjects religious belief to totally inappropriate norms of formal (deductive and inductive) proofs; (3) that the thesis ignores the fact that a necessary condition for faith is its very lack of justification; and (4) that the thesis is itself incompatible with the biblical notion of faith and so cannot be applied to Judaism or Christianity.

Rationality and Conceptual Frameworks

Sometimes it is claimed that there is a clear cut decision making process in arriving at justified belief or truth similar to that in mathematics and empirical science. A person has a duty to believe exactly according to the available evidence. Hence there is no excuse for anyone to believe anything on insufficient evidence.

196

Such is the case of Descartes and Logical Positivism which is echoed in Clifford's classical formula, 'It is wrong always, everywhere, and for anyone to believe anything on insufficient evidence.' Laying aside the criticism that the statement itself is self-referentially incoherent (it doesn't give us sufficient evidence for believing itself), the problem is that different data will count as evidence to different degrees according to the background beliefs a person has. The contribution of Polanyi, Popper and Wittgenstein has been to demonstrate the power of perspectivism, the thesis that the way we evaluate or even pick out evidence is determined by our prior picture of the world, which itself is made up of a loosely connected and mutually supporting network of propositions, the non-perspectivist position, seen in Plato, Aquinas, Descartes, Locke, Clifford, Chisholm, and others in the first part of this work, seems impaired beyond repair. However, the reaction has been to claim that since what is basic is the conceptual (fiduciary) framework, no interchange between world views is possible. As Karl Barth says, 'Belief can only preach to unbelief.' No argument is possible. We may call this reaction to the post-critical critique of rationalism 'hard perspectivism'.[2]

While the nonperspectivist writes as though arriving at the truth were a matter of impartial evaluation of the evidence, the hard-perspectivist writes as though no meaningful communication were possible. The world views (*Weltanschauungen*) are discontinuous. As Plantinga says, 'The believer and unbeliever live in different worlds.'[3] There is an infinite qualitative distinction existing between various forms of life which no amount of argument or discussion can bridge. For hard-perspectivists, which include Wittgensteinian fideists studied in chapter 12 of Part I, reason can only have intramural significance. There are no bridges between world views.

However, hard-perspectivism is not the only possible reaction to the post-critical revolution. One may accept the insight that our manner of evaluating evidence is strongly affected by our conceptual frameworks without opting for a view which precludes communication across world views. One may recognize the depth of a conceptual framework and still maintain that communication between frameworks is possible and that reason may have an intermural as well as intramural significance in the process. Such a view has been called soft-perspectivist. The soft-perspectivist is under no illusion as to the difficulty of effecting a massive shift in the total evaluation of an immense range of data, of producing new patterns of feeling and acting in persons, but he or she is confident that the program is viable. One of the reasons given in support of this is that there is something like a core rationality common to every human culture, especially with regard to practical life. Certain rules of inference (deductive and inductive) have virtually universal application. Certain assumptions (basic beliefs) seem common to every culture (e.g., that there are other minds, that there is time, that things move, that perceptions are generally to be trusted, etc.). Through sympathetic imagination one can attain some understanding of another's conceptual system, through disappointment one can begin to suspect weakness in one's own world view and thus seek for a more adequate explanation. It is not my purpose here to produce a full defense of a soft-perspective position, only to indicate its plausibility. The assumption on which this work is written is that the case for soft-perspectivism can be made. And if it is true, then it is possible for reason to play a significant role examining, revising, and rejecting one's current beliefs and in attaining new beliefs. I turn now to the four objections against such an epistemology.

The Objection that Rationality implies a Neutrality which is Incompatible with Religious Faith

We may say that a post-critical rationalist of the soft-perspectivist variety is one who seeks to support all his beliefs (especially his convictions)[4] with good reasons. He attempts to evaluate the evidence as impartially as possible, to accept the challenge of answering criticisms, and to remain open to the possibility that he might be wrong and may need to revise, reexamine or reject any one of his beliefs (at least those not involving broadly logical necessity). This character description of the rationalist is often interpreted to mean that the rationalist must be neutral and detached with regard to his beliefs.[5] This is a mistake. It is a confusion between *impartiality* and *neutrality*. Both concepts imply conflict situations (e.g., war, competitive sport, a legal trial, argument), but to be neutral signifies not taking sides, doing nothing to influence the outcome, remaining passive in the fray; whereas impartiality *involves* one in the conflict in that it calls for a judgment in favor of the party which is right. To the extent that one party is right or wrong (measured by objective criteria) neutrality and impartiality are incompatible concepts. To be neutral is to detach oneself from the struggle; to be impartial (rational) means to commit oneself to a position – though not partially (i.e. unfairly or arbitrarily) but in accordance with an objective standard. The model of the neutral person is an atheist who is indifferent about football, watching a Notre Dame versus Southern Methodist football game. The model for the partial or prejudiced person is either coach, who, on any given dispute, predictably judges that his team is in the right and the other is in the wrong, and for whom it is an axiom that any judgment by a referee against his team is, at best, of dubious merit. The model of the impartial person is the referee in the game, who although knowing that his wife has just bet their life-savings on the underdog, Southern Methodist, still manages to call what any reasonable spectator would judge to be a fair game. He does not let his wants or self-interest enter into the judgment he makes.

To be rational does not lessen the passion involved with regard to religious beliefs. The rational believer, who believes that he has good grounds for believing that a perfect being exists, is not less likely to trust absolutely that being than the believer who does not think that he has reasons. Likewise, the person who lives in hope of God's existence may be as passionate about his commitment as the person who entertains no doubts. In fact the rational hoper or believer will probably judge it to be irrational not to be absolutely committed to such a being. Hence the charge levelled against the rationalist by Kierkegaard and others that rational inquiry cools the passions seems unfounded.

However, the non-rationalist has a slightly different but related argument at hand. He may argue that granted that if there were sufficient evidence available, it might be the case that one might be both religious and rational. But there is not sufficient evidence, hence the very search for evidence simply detracts the believer from worship and passionate service, leading him on a wild-goose chase for evidence which does not exist. Instead of passionate commitment, the believer spends his time in cool calculation, questioning instead of obeying.

There are at least two responses to this charge. First of all, how does the non-rationalist know that there is not sufficient evidence for a religious claim? How does he know that not merely a demonstrative proof but even a cumulative case with some force is impossible? It would seem reasonable to expect that a good God would not leave his creatures wholly in the dark about so important a matter. The non-rationalist's answers (e.g., that sin has destroyed the use of reason) seem unduly ad hoc and inadequate. Second, why cannot the search for truth itself be a way of worshipping God? a passionate act of service? Again one would expect the having of well-founded beliefs to be God's will for us. Is the person who in his doubt prays, 'God, if you exist, please show me better evidence', any less passionate a worshipper than the person who worships without doubts?

A word is in order about the relation of the emotions and passions to religious belief. The claims of a religion cannot but move a person. Anyone who does not see the importance of its claims either does not have a sense of selfhood or does not understand what is being said, for a religion claims to explain who and why he is and what he expects to become. It claims to make sense out of the world. For example, to entertain the proposition that a personal, loving Creator exists is to entertain a proposition whose implications affect every part of a person's understanding of himself and the world. If the proposition is true, the world is personal rather than mechanistic, friendly rather than strange, purposeful rather than simply a vortex of chance and necessity. If it is not true, a different set of entailments follow which are likely to lead to different patterns of feeling and action. If Judeo-Christian theism is accepted, the believer has an additional reason for being a moral person, for treating fellow humans with equal respect. It is because God has created all persons in his image, as infinitely precious, destined to enjoy his fellowship forever. Theism can provide a more adequate metaphysical basis for morality. Hence it can be both descriptively and prescriptively significant.

Towards a Theory of Rationality

It is often said that the rational person tailors the strength of his beliefs to the strength of the evidence. The trouble with this remark is that it is notoriously difficult to give sense to any discussion of discovering objective criteria for what is to count as evidence and to what extent it is to count. We saw this in Peirce and Hick's criticism of philosophies (like Swinburne's) that try to apply the concept of probabilities to world views.

Deciding *what* is to count as evidence for something else in part depends on a whole network of other considerations and deciding to *what extent* something is to count as evidence involves weighing procedures which are subjective. Two judges may have the same evidence before them and come to different verdicts. Two equally rational persons may have the same evidence about the claims of a religion and still arrive at different conclusions in the matter. It would seem that the prescription to tailor one's beliefs according to the evidence is either empty or a shorthand for something more complex. I think that it is the latter. Let me illustrate what I think it signifies.

Consider any situation where our self-interest may conflict with the truth. Take the case of three German wives who are suddenly confronted with evidence that their husbands have been unfaithful. Their surnames are Uberglaubig, Misstrauisch and Wahrnehmen. Each is disturbed about the evidence and makes further inquiries. Mrs. Uberglaubig is soon finished and finds herself rejecting all the evidence, maintaining resolutely her husband's fidelity. Others, even relatives of Mr. Uberglaubig, are surprised by her credulity, for the evidence against Mr. Uberglaubig is the sort that would lead most people to conclude that he was unfaithful. No matter how much evidence is adduced, Mrs. Uberglaubig is unchanged in her judgment. She seems to have a fixation about her husband's fidelity. Mrs. Misstrauisch seems to suffer from an opposite weakness. If Mrs. Uberglaubig overbelieves, she seems to underbelieve. She suspects the worst and even though others who know Mr. Misstrauisch deem the evidence against him weak (especially in comparison to the evidence presented against Mr. Uberglaubig), she is convinced that her husband is unfaithful. No evidence seems to be sufficient to reassure her. It is as though the very suggestion of infidelity were enough to stir up doubts and disbelief. Mrs. Wahrnehmen also considers the evidence, which is considerable, comes to a judgment, though with some reservations. Suppose she finds herself believing that her husband is faithful. Others may differ in their assessment of the situation, but Mrs. Wahrnehmen is willing and able to discuss the matter, gives her grounds and considers the objections of others. Perhaps we can say that she is more self-aware, more self-controlled, and more self-secure than the other women.

She seems to have the capacity to separate her judgment from her hopes, wants, and fears in a way the other two women do not.

This should provide some clue to what it means to be rational. It does not necessarily mean having true beliefs (though we would say that rationality tends towards truth), for it might just turn out that by luck Mr. Wahrnehmen is indeed an adulterer and Mr. Uberglaubig innocent. Still we would want to say that Mrs. Wahrnehmen was but Mrs. Uberglaubig was not justified in their respective beliefs.

What does characterize rational judgment are two properties, one being *intentional* and the other being *capacity-behavioral*. First, rationality involves an intention to seek the truth or having a high regard for truth especially when there may be a conflict between it and one's wishes. It involves a healthy abhorrence of being deceived combined with a parallel desire to have knowledge in matters vital to one's life. Mrs. Wahrnehmen and Mrs. Misstrauisch care about the truth in a way that Mrs. Uberglaubig does not. But secondly, it involves a skill or behavioral capacity to judge impartially, to examine the evidence objectively, to know what sort of things count in coming to a considered judgment. It is as though Mrs. Wahrnehmen alone were able to see clearly through the fog of emotion and self-interest, focusing on some ideal standard of evidence. Of course, there is no such simple standard of evidence, no more than there is for the art critic in making a judgment on the authenticity of a work of art. Still the metaphor of the ideal standard may be useful. It draws attention to the objective feature in rational judgment, a feature which is internalized in the person of the expert. Like learning to discriminate between works of art or with regard to criminal evidence, rationality is a learned trait which calls for a long apprenticeship (a lifetime?) under the cooperative tutelage of other rational persons. Some people with little formal education seem to learn this better than some 'well educated' people, but despite this uncomfortable observation, I would like to believe that it is the job of education to train people to judge impartially over a broad range of human experience.

As a skill combined with an intention, rationality may seem to be in a shaky situation. How do we decide who has the skill or who has the right combination of traits? There is no certain way, but judge we must in this life, and the basis of our judgment will be manifestations of behavior which we classify as truth directed, noticing that the person seeks out evidence and pays attention to criticism and counter claims, that he usually supports his judgment with recognizable good reasons, that he revises and rejects his beliefs in the light of new information. These are not foolproof and it seems impossible to give an exact account of the process involved in rational decision or belief, but this seems to be the case with any skill. In the end rationality seems more like a set of trained intuitions than anything else.

Let us carry our story a little further. Suppose now Mrs. Wahrnehmen receives some new information to the effect that her husband has been unfaithful. Suppose it becomes known to others who were previously convinced by her arguments acquitting her husband, and suppose that the new evidence infirms many of those arguments, so that the third parties now come to believe that Mr. Wahrnehmen is an adulterer. Should Mrs. Wahrnehmen give up her belief? Perhaps not. At least, it may not be a good thing to give it up at once. If she has worked out a theory to account for a great many of her husband's actions, she might better cling to her theory and work out some ad hoc hypotheses to account for this evidence. This principle of clinging to one's theory in spite of adverse evidence is what Peirce debunkingly and what Lakatos and Mitchell approvingly call the principle of tenacity.[6] It receives special attention in Lakatos' treatment of a progressive research program. In science, theoretical change often comes as a result of persevering with a rather vaguely formulated hypothesis (a core hypothesis) which the researcher will hold onto in spite of a good many setbacks. The scientist must be ready to persevere (at least for a time) even in the face of his own doubts and his recognition of the validity of his opponents' objections. If maximum fruitfulness of the experiment is to be attained, it must endure through many modifications as new evidence comes in. As Mitchell has pointed out, his thesis is like a growing infant, which 'could be killed by premature antisepsis'. The biographers of eminent scientists and scholars are replete with instances of going it alone in the face of massive intellectual opposition, and finally overturning a general verdict. Hence the researcher cushions the core hypothesis against the blows and shocks that might otherwise force him to give it up. He invents ad hoc explanations in hopes of saving the core hypothesis. He surrounds the core hypothesis with a battery of such hypotheses, and as the ad hoc hypotheses fall, he invents new ones. Mitchell compares this process to a criminal network in which the master mind (core hypothesis) always manages to escape detection and punishment 'by sacrificing some of his less essential underlings, unless or until the final day of reckoning comes and his entire empire collapses'.[7]

Admittedly, each ad hoc hypothesis weakens the system, but the core hypothesis may nevertheless turn out to approximate a true or adequate theory. But the more ad hoc hypotheses it is necessary to invent, the less plausibility attaches to the core hypothesis until the time comes that we are forced to give up the core hypothesis and conclude that the whole project has outlived its usefulness. In Lakatos' words, it has become a 'degenerative research project'.[8] No one can say exactly when that time comes for him, but every experimenting scientist fears it and, meanwhile, lives in hope that his project will bear fruit.

Let us apply this to the rational religious believer. Once he finds himself with a deep conviction, he has a precedent or model in science for clinging to it tenaciously, experimenting with it, drawing out all its implications, surrounding it with tentative ad hoc or auxiliary explanations in order to cushion it from premature anti-sepsis. Nevertheless, if the analogy with the scientist holds, he must recognize that the time may come when he is forced to abandon his conviction because of the enormous accumulation of counter evidence. The rational person probably cannot say exactly when and how this could happen, and he does not expect it to happen; but he acknowledges the possibility of this happening. There is no clear decision procedure which tells us when we have crossed over the fine line between plausibility and implausibility, but suddenly the realization hits us that we now disbelieve theory A and believe in B whereas up to this point the relation was the reverse. Conversions or paradigm switches occur every day in both the minds of the highly rational and the less rational, and there is a middle zone where the person can see two explanatory theories which seem incompatible, but each seems to have something to be said in its favor, so that the individual cannot be said to believe either one. Still he may hope in one, live by his theory in an experimental faith, and keep himself open to new evidence, main-taining the dialogue with those who differ in order not to slip into a state of self-deception. The whole matter of double vision and experimental faith is quite complicated, and I shall have more to say about it in the next chapter. Here I want to emphasize that more important than *what* a person believes is the manner in which he believes, the *how* of believing, the openness of mind, the willingness to discuss the reasons for his belief, the carefulness of his examination of new and conflicting evidence, his commitment to follow the argument and not simply his emotions, his training as a rational person which enables him to recognize what is to count as a good argument.

This leads me to say a few things about the role and mode of argument in rationality. One of the problems which has plagued discussion in philosophy of religion through the ages is that philosophers have written as though unless one had a deductive proof for a religious thesis, one had no justification for it. The result of this narrow view of argument in religious matters has pushed those who believe in religion to the point of conceding too much, i.e., that religion is not rational. This is one of the main reasons for the incommensurabilist position. I think that this is a mistake. Our concept of argument must be broadened from mere deductive and strict inductive argument to include non-ruled governed judgments. What I have in mind is the sort of intuitive judgment referred to earlier in this work with regard to such judgments as those of the art critic in assessing an authentic work of art, those of the chicken sexer who reliably identifies the sex of the baby chicks but who cannot tell us or himself how he knows the chick's sexual identity, and those of the water diviner who discovers underground springs without knowing how he does so. Another example of non-rule governed reasoning is a child's making up new sentences. The child follows rules, which seem to be programed into her, but she does not consciously do so and cannot tell us what the rules are. Later, however, she may be able to do so.

Perhaps even more typical of everyday non-rule governed reasoning is that of a judge or jury making judgments where the evidence is ambiguous or where there is considerable evidence on both sides of an issue. The judge or jury in weighing pros and cons, in assessing conflicting evidence, does not normally go through standard logical procedures in arriving at a verdict. They rely on intangible and intuitive weighing procedures. It is hard to see how the deductive and strict inductive schemes of argument can account for our judgments when we have good reasons for and against a conclusion. Nor is it easy to see how deductive and strict inductive reasoning account for the decisions which the expert makes in distinguishing the valuable from the mediocre. He cannot formalize his judgment, and we may not be able to offer an account of it, but we would still recognize it as valid and importantly rational. Perhaps we ought generally to aim at formalizing our judgments as carefully as possible, using the traditional forms of reasoning, but it is not always necessary or possible to do this. We can be said to be rational because we typically arrive at decisions and judgments which other rational creatures would regard as a fair estimation of the evidence (this excuses the occasional idiosyncratic judgments), because we attempt to face the challenge of our opponent with the grounds of our beliefs, and because we are honest about the deficiencies of our positions. It is a whole family of considerations which lead us to an overall conclusion about whether another person is rational and not simply whether or not he is able to provide sound deductive or inductive arguments. Of course, induction plays a strong role in our relying on another's judgments. It is because we have generally found that people of this sort usually make reliable judgments in such-and-such type cases, that we are ready to take their intuitions as credible.

A great deal more needs to be said about non-rule governed judgments, but, at least, this shows that something broader than the standard moves is needed in an account of rational argument. There is a need to recognize the important role that intuition plays in reasoning itself, or, at least, in the reasoning of the trained person. This is what the Greeks called *phronesis* (wise insight), and it should be given greater emphasis in modern philosophy.

The Objection that the Commensurabilist Program is Misconceived because a Lack of Rational Justification is Essential to Religious Faith

One of the objections that has often been brought against the commensurabilist position by the incommensurabilist is that the attempt to reconcile faith and reason is misconceived because religious faith is by definition the sort of thing which cannot be reasoned about. Religious belief is in no sense an 'hypothesis', for it cannot be and ought not be justified rationally. We examined this position in chapter 12 of Part I when considering Wittgensteinian fideism, especially the work of Norman Malcolm who classifies religious beliefs with other 'groundless beliefs' such as the belief that things don't just vanish and our belief in the uniformity of nature and inductive reasoning. These basic beliefs belong to the framework of our thinking about the world, and there is no way that we can really get behind them or try to justify them, for they provide the very structure of our justification. 'We grow into a framework. We do not question it. We accept it trustingly.' Malcolm treats all such groundless beliefs as 'religious'.

As I pointed out in chapter 12 this sort of fideism has been attacked for neglecting the strong apologetic strain in traditional Western religion and for making an unwarranted categorization of religious beliefs with groundless beliefs. E.g., religious beliefs do not seem to enjoy the universality and necessity of the belief in the laws of induction or the uniformity of nature. We also noted Gary Gutting's criticism that it fails to show that religious language is *sui generis* from our normal first order language.

My own criticism of fideism is that it tends towards irrationalism. If a religious belief is religious to the extent that it lacks justification, then it would seem that the less justification I have for believing something, the more religious is my believing. It would follow that the religion that has more rational support for itself is less religious than the religion that has less rational support. The more a religion can divest itself of rational support, the more religious it is, until the most religious religion is the one that is the most counter intuitive, the most implausible, the one that erects the highest epistemological obstacle for rationality to hurdle. On this criterion Charles Manson's views would be more religious than Roman Catholicism, and if a religion were to commence, stating that God was a bionic rat, that religion would surpass most other religions in genuine religiosity. In fact, on these premises it is difficult to separate religion from insanity. Little wonder then that Malcolm states that, 'by and large religion is to university people an alien form of life'.[9] Perhaps neither Malcolm nor many other fideists would care to own these conclusions, which Shestov and Kierkegaard seem to espouse, but there is a tendency in that direction. The question is, how do the fideists distinguish irrationality from groundlessness?

The hard perspectivist or fideist has a valid point when he stresses the difficulty of using reason to persuade or convert others engaging in other forms of life, who see the world as a different world than himself, but when he says it is impossible, he seems to have prejudged the matter with less than convincing reasons. Some people have been convinced by argument, and we are able to communicate intermurally between forms of life. The liberal democrat can via sympathetic imagination get to know what it feels like to be a Marxist. The Jew can put himself into the shoes of a Christian. Sometimes even the Christian can perform the thought experiment of being an atheist. Literature's task in part is to be a bridge builder to other forms of life. All this presupposes a core rationality in humanity, a common experience which all persons share. It is true that we cannot will ourselves to see the world *as actual* simply through the imagination. The liberal democrat is not likely to be changed into a Marxist, nor the Marxist into a liberal democrat simply by sympathetic imagination, but through imagination and argument and counter argument, there is the possibility of change, of both parties recognizing validity in the other's position, and perhaps of one or both parties modifying their positions.

The Objection that the Commensurabilist Position is Incompatible with the Biblical Picture of Faith

Let me turn finally to an objection related to the above but a bit more tempting. This objection is that the position that I have outlined distorts the biblical notion of faith. Biblical faith is, the critic affirms, believing against or without sufficient evidence. As Hick points out there is little deductive reasoning in the Scriptures, but the Holy of Holies is taken as the starting point of all thinking (cf. chapter 12).

But the claim that this is the sole meaning of faith in the Bible seems an unwarranted generalization. Actually, the Bible seems to exhibit several different but related concepts of faith, as we noted in Part I, chapter 1, including loyalty, trust, fear, obedience as well as propositional belief. What we have called rational faith seems duly accounted for in the miracles and prophecy of the Bible, especially the Old Testament, which in part are to serve as evidence for the Hebrew faith. When Elijah, in I Kings 18, competes with the priests of Baal on Mt. Carmel to determine which god is more powerful, we have a concrete scientific testing of competing hypotheses. When John the Baptist's disciples come to ask Jesus if he is the Messiah, Jesus does not rebuke them for seeking grounds for their beliefs but immediately 'cures many diseases and plagues and evil spirits' and opens the eyes of the blind and only after this answers them, 'Go and tell John what you have seen and heard: the blind receive their sight, the lame walk, lepers are cleansed, and the deaf hear, the dead are raised up, the poor have the good news preached to them' (Luke 7:20–22). When Jesus does chide his disciples for unbelief it seems to be for good reasons. 'Don't you remember what the Scriptures demand? Don't you trust me in spite of my being with you so long and having proved my reliability over and over?' What the Scriptures deny is *sight*. We cannot see God directly and live, for there is another dimension to his reality, but we can see him *indirectly* through his works (Rom 1:20f). When Thomas doubts good evidence (viz., the witness of his fellow disciples and the words of Jesus' prophecy), he is given evidence, the point being not that evidence is contrary to faith but that dependence on too much outward evidence may get in the way of inward discernment. There is just enough evidence for a person passionately concerned but not enough to produce a comfortable proof.

Usually, the non-rationalist makes his point about the antipathy between faith and reason in the Bible by pointing to Abraham's reliance on God even to the point of being willing to kill his son, Isaac. Abraham, the father of faith, is put forth as the paradigm of believing against all evidence. As Kierkegaard puts it, 'Abraham believed by virtue of the absurd', despite the impossibility of the promise to give him a son when he was old or to bring him back after Abraham would sacrifice him. He believed God would somehow bring it about that Isaac would live in spite of the fact that he was intending to kill him. The reader will recall the story. God told Abraham to go to Mt. Moriah and sacrifice Isaac in order to prove his love for God. Abraham proceeds to carry out the command, but at the last moment an angel stops him, showing him a lamb in the thicket to be used for the offering. This has usually been taken as the height of religious faith, believing God where it really affects one's deepest earthly commitments. This is taken to prove that faith is irrational, believing against all standards of rationality.

Of course, many Old Testament scholars dismiss the literalness of the story and interpret it without the context of mid-east child sacrifice. The story, according to these scholars, provides the pictorial grounds for breaking with the custom. But even leaving this plausible explanation to the side, we might contend that Abraham's action can be seen as rational given his noetic

209

framework. One can imagine him replying to a friendly skeptic years after the incident in the following manner.

> I heard a voice. It was the same voice (or so I believed) that commanded me years before to leave my country, my kindred and my father's house and venture forth into the unknown. It was the same voice that promised me that I would prosper. I hearkened and though the evidence seemed weak, the promise was fulfilled. It was the same voice that promised me a son in my old age and Sarah's old age, when childbearing was thought to be impossible. Yet it happened. My trust was vindicated. My whole existence has been predicated on the reality of that voice. I already became an exception by hearkening unto it the first time. I have never regretted it. This last call was in a tone similar to the other calls. The voice was unmistakable. To deny its authenticity would be to deny the authenticity of the others. In doing so, I should be admitting that my whole life has been founded on an illusion. But I don't believe that it has, and I prefer to take the risk of obeying what I take to be the voice of God and disobey certain norms than to obey the norms and miss the possibility of any absolute relation to the Absolute. And what's more, I'm ready to recommend that all people who feel so called by a higher power should do exactly as I have done.

It seems to me that even if we accept the story of Abraham offering his son as a sacrifice at face value, we can give it an interpretation not inconsistent with the commensurabilist's position. Abraham has had inductive evidence that following the voice is the best way to live. We can generalize the principle on which Abraham acted to be:

> If one acts on a type of intuition, I, in an area of experience, E, over a period of time, t, and with remarkable success, and no other information is relevant or overriding, one can be said to have good reason for following that intuition (I_n, an instance of type I) the next time it presents itself in an E type situation.

Given the cultural context of Abraham's life, his actions seem amenable to a rationalist account. Of course, what this shows is that given enough background data, almost any proposition could be considered *rational* for an individual believer. Irrationality would occur if Abraham was neglecting counter fully evidence at his disposal.

My point has not been to prove that the Bible contains a developed philosophy of faith and reason but simply to indicate that it seems far closer to the commensurabilist's position than the fideist might imagine. My impression is that Scriptures pay a great deal of attention to evidence, acts of deliverance and the testimony of the saints and prophets, who hear God's voice and sometimes even get a vision of his splendor.

Let me end this chapter on a conciliatory note. I can appreciate the criticism of someone who feels that my approach overemphasizes the rational and intellectual aspects of believing at the expense of the emotional and volitional aspects, the feelings of divine presence and inner certainty and devotion. I do not want to deny the importance of these feelings and will say more about them in the next chapter. My point has been simply that they are compatible with a rationalist perspective. Further thought on the matter may reveal that my approach to religion as an experimental faith in a viable hypothesis fails to get at the heart of religious commitment. But, even so, the general quest for justification may not be inappropriate. Complex as religious phenomena are, profound as the feelings are, at some point religious experience needs to be scrutinized honestly and carefully by the believer himself. When Barth and Bultmann protest that God does not need to justify himself before man, the proper response is to re-echo Karl Jasper's reply to Bultmann, 'I do not say that God has to justify himself, but that everything that appears in the world and claims to be God's word, God's act, God's revelation, has to justify itself.'[10] This outline of a commensurabilist position with regard to religious belief is intended as a small step in doing just that.

211

CHAPTER XVI

Faith, Doubt and Hope

It is worth noting, by way of conclusion, that the mature
believer, the mature theist, does not typically accept belief in
God tentatively, or hypothetically, or until something better
comes along. Nor, I think, does he accept it as a conclusion
from other things he believes; he accepts it as basic, as a part of
the foundations of his noetic structure. The mature theist
commits himself to belief in God; this means that he accepts
belief in God as basic (Alvin Plantinga, 'Is Belief in God
Rational?').[1]

Entombed in a secure prison, thinking our situation quite
hopeless, we may find unutterable joy in the information that
there is, after all, the slimmest possibility of escape. Hope
provides comfort, and hope does not always require
probability. But we must believe that what we hope for is at
least possible (Gretchen Weirob in John Perry's imaginative *A
Dialogue on Personal Identity and Immortality*).[2]

For many religious people there is a problem of doubting various
credal statements contained in their religions. Often propositional
beliefs are looked upon as a necessary, though not sufficient
condition, for salvation. This causes great anxiety in doubters and
raises the question of the importance of belief in religion and in life
in general. It is a question that has been neglected in philosophy of
religion and Christian theology. In this chapter I shall explore the
question of the importance of belief as a religious attitude and
suggest that there is at least one other attitude which may be
adequate for religious faith even in the absence of belief, that
attitude being hope. I shall develop a concept of faith as hope as an

212

alternative to the usual notion that makes propositional belief that God exists a necessary condition for faith, as Plantinga implies in the quotation above. Finally, I shall deal with objections to this position as set forth by Gary Gutting in his recent book, *Religious Belief and Religious Skepticism*. For simplicity's sake I shall concentrate on the most important proposition in Western religious creeds, that which states that God exists (defined broadly as a benevolent, supreme Being, who is responsible for the creation of the universe), but the analysis could be applied *mutatis mutandis* to many other important propositions in religion (e.g., the Incarnation and the doctrine of the Trinity).

Many reflective religious people find themselves at one time or another doubting God's existence. If they have studied the alleged proofs for God's existence, they may become convinced that these 'proofs' do not work as probative but, at best, simply point to the possibility of an intelligent force that influences the universe. For many of these people God's existence is not self-evident, nor is it properly basic for them. They are troubled by the lack of evidence for God's existence and believe that the move made by some philosophers to set it into the foundations of one's noetic structure is not acceptable for them. Their prayer is, 'God, if you exist, show me better evidence.' Although they would like to believe with confidence that God exists and are tempted to take the Pascalian-Jamesian line of acquiring this belief by getting themselves into a context where viewing selective evidence will cause belief, they resist this temptation as unethical. They adhere to an ethics of belief that prevents them from manipulating their noetic structure in such ways as to cause a belief that the evidence alone does not warrant. Such a maneuver would constitute a breach in their concern for having the best justified beliefs, a concern that puts a high premium on impartial regard for evidence. They also have the prudential concern of worrying about the possible bad effect such belief manipulations might have on their belief-forming mechanisms. It may even be that some of these doubters have tried but failed to get oneself to believe by using auto-suggestion or getting oneself into a favorable context as Pascal suggests.

The Importance of Belief

Being unable to believe either because of the lack of evidence or because of moral compunctions against acquiring beliefs through volitional means, these people have the unwelcome prospect of being denied the benefits of religious faith altogether or, at least, of being designated 'immature theists', since faith with belief is generally regarded by orthodoxy as the sole manner of being a genuine believer with the benefits of salvation. The question immediately arises, What is so important about believing anyway? May there not be other propositional attitudes that are equally as effective as believing or, at least, adequate for the essential benefits of religion?

The traditional virtues of the attitude of belief have been (1) its ability to give intellectual and emotional surcease to the pain and insecurity of doubt and (2) its action-guiding function. Both of these virtues are ably discussed in C.S. Peirce's essay 'The Fixation of Belief'. According to Peirce, doubt is a type of pain, which, as such, is necessary as a warning mechanism to make us aware of the need for evidence. It is, like all pain, undesirable in itself, and a state from which we seek release. 'Doubt is an uneasy and dissatisfied state from which we struggle to free ourselves and pass into the state of belief; while the latter is a calm and satisfying state which we do not wish to avoid, or to change to a belief in anything else. On the contrary, we cling tenaciously, not merely to believing, but to believing just what we [already] believe.'[3]

Furthermore, argues Peirce, beliefs are action guides, directing our desires and shaping our actions. It is important to arrive at beliefs, because unless we do so, we cannot act. Beliefs are necessary conditions for actions. Let us look a little closer at these two theses.

Turning to the first thesis, why is belief restful or relief-ful, whereas doubt is anxiety ridden and stressful? Perhaps it is because in many cases, unless we have a conviction, we cannot act with abandon and singlemindedness. If we doubt our course, the doubt may deflect us from our goal. The runner who believes the prize to be uncertain may flag in his zeal. Furthermore, there may seem to be something unstable and unreliable about a doubter. The doubter, who wavers in his beliefs, 'is like a wave of the sea driven with the wind and tossed . . . A double minded man is unstable in all his

214

ways' (Epistle of James 1:6,8). One cannot imagine, the objection continues, a lover who doubts the beloved, a guerrilla fighter who doubts his cause, a successful businessman who doubts the free enterprise system, a skillful gambler who doubts his luck or a successful musician who wonders about her talent while performing. Doubt is the hobgoblin against every successful venture.

Contrast the doubter with the 'mature believer', who confidently asserts, 'I know whom I have believeth', or 'The testimony of the Spirit is superior to all reason. . . . [It] is an undeniable truth, that they who have been inwardly taught by the Spirit feel an entire acquiescence in the Scripture, and that it is self-authenticating, carrying with it its own evidence, and ought not to be made the subject of demonstration and argument from reason. . . . We feel the firmest conviction that we hold an invincible truth.'[4] Such absolute confidence certainly does offer a pleasant feeling of security, as well as a sense of rest from the further search for truth on this issue.

But, while doubt may be painful, it may be a wholesome suffering that causes us to recheck our propositional states, which may lead to greater accuracy and approximation of the truth. It is true that the runner who doubts may flag in zeal, but it is equally true that doubt may deflect him from the wrong course. In any case, we can learn to live gracefully with necessary pain, and it may be necessary for many religious people to learn to live gracefully with doubt, using it to probe deeper into ultimate questions. The suffering of doubt may be a cross that a disciple must learn to bear.

Turning to Peirce's second reason for having beliefs, i.e., that they are action-guiding; we can agree that this is an important aspect of fixing a belief. However, we need not agree with him that a belief is a necessary condition for action; at least it is not necessary to believe that a proposition is true in order to act on it. For many actions belief that the state of affairs in question will occur is not a necessary condition. I may act on the mere possibility of something being the case without actually believing that it will be the case. I can believe that a hypothesis is the best among a series of weak hypotheses and worth following through without believing that it is true. I can believe that it is worthwhile to bet on a horse that is underrated at 10 to 1 odds, when I have only $10 and need $100 soon and have no other way of getting it. I can bet on the horse, risk everything on it and still not believe that it will win. I only need to believe that it is a worthwhile action to bet in this way, given my overall set of goals and beliefs about reaching these goals. Likewise, I can attempt to swim five miles to shore after my ship has sunk, in hope of reaching the shore, without believing that I can or will reach the shore safely. Finally, Columbus' sailors need not have believed that the earth was round in order to have embarked from Spain to sail to the New World. They simply had to believe that the risk was worth taking.

When the evidence is perceived as weak, too weak to produce belief in the veracious person, and where the ethics of belief forbids mind manipulations of acquiring beliefs volitionally, but where the consequences are great, the best a person can do is live belief-lessly according to the hypothesis in question. That is, we may be justified in doing a cost-benefit analysis in order to determine whether the proposition is worth following for the possible consequences. For example, I may have two incompatible goals at some moment and need to decide which one to aim at. Suppose that I determine that goal A has a probability index of 0.4, whereas goal B has one of 0.6, making it positively probable. Although B has a better chance of being reached than A, I might still be justified in aiming at goal A rather than B. I would be justified in doing so just in case I desired A sufficiently more than B – if, for example, I give A a preference value of 0.7 and B only a value of 0.4. Of course, we usually do not give exact quantified indices and preference values to possible courses of action, but we do make rough approximations of this type very often. When a graduate student accepts a challenging job with a questionable future over a more secure job with less challenge, a decision process has often gone on which has weighed subjective probabilities and strengths of desires. If I believe that there is only a slight chance that there is a bomb in the briefcase on the other side of the room, I do not need to make a formal cost-benefit assessment of the matter in order to act swiftly. I leave the room because the stakes are very high, even though I may not be convinced that there really is a bomb in the briefcase. It seems that our sub-conscious is constantly making rough cost-benefit assessments in the various situations which we find ourselves, maximizing expected utility.[5]

If my analysis is correct, positively believing in the existence of objects in question may not be as important as we have sometimes been led to suppose. We may be guided by weak probabilities, and the distressing doubt that we feel may often be redemptive, causing us to check our evidence, justify our beliefs, and obtain more accurate beliefs.

Faith as Hope

We have argued that it is not necessary to believe that a proposition is positively probable in order to act on it. The perception of its possibility is often sufficient to incite activity. One such alternative propositional attitude to belief is hope (or, negatively, fear). In the next section (A) I shall examine the concept of hope. In Section B I shall compare it with its close relatives: 'belief-in', 'trust', 'living-as-if' and 'optimism'. Then, in Section C I shall apply the analysis of hope to religious faith, showing that faith need not be belief-ful, but may be an expression of hope.[6]

A   An Analysis of Hope

Let us begin with some examples of expressions of hope.

1 Mary hopes to get an A in her History course.
2 John hopes that Mary will marry him.
3 Mary hopes that Happy Dancer will win the Kentucky Derby next week.
4 John hopes that the Yankees won their game yesterday.
5 Mary hopes that the sun is shining in Dallas today for her sister's wedding.
6 Although John desires a cigarette, he hopes that he will not give in to his desire.

If we look closely at these examples of hoping, we can pick out certain necessary features of the concept of hope. First of all, hope involves belief in the possibility of a state of affairs obtaining. We cannot hope for what we believe to be impossible. If Mary hopes to get an A in History, she must believe that it is possible that she get one in that course, and if she hopes that Happy Dancer will win the Kentucky Derby, she must believe that it is possible that he will win. The Oxford English Dictionary defines 'hope' as an 'expectation of something desired', but this seems too strong. Expectation implies belief that something will occur, but we may hope even when we do

217

not expect the object of desire to obtain, as when John hopes that Mary will marry him but realizes that the odds are greatly against it or when Mary hopes that Happy Dancer will win the Kentucky Derby although she accepts the official odds against it. I may likewise hope to win a lottery but not expect to do so. Belief that the object of desire will obtain is not necessary for hope. It is enough that the hoper believe that the proposition in question is not impossible. What separates hope from belief is that in believing one necessarily believes that the proposition is true (has a subjective probability index of greater than .5), whereas in hoping this is not necessary.[7]

Secondly, hope precludes certainty. John will not be certain that Mary will marry him or that the Yankees won the game yesterday. There must be an apparent possibility of the states of affairs not obtaining. We would think it odd to say, 'John knows that the Yankees won the game yesterday, for he was at the game, but he still hopes that the Yankees won the game yesterday.' 'For hope that is seen is not hope: for what a man seeth, why doth he yet hope for' (Epistle to the Romans 8:24). Hope entails uncertainty, a subjective probability index greater than 0 but less than 1.

Thirdly, hope entails desire for the state of affairs in question to obtain or the proposition to be true. In all of the above cases a propositional content can be seen as the object of desire. The state of affairs envisaged evokes a pro-attitude. The subject wants some proposition p to be true. It matters not whether the state of affairs is past (case 4), present (cases 5 and 6) or future (cases 1–3), though it generally turns out – because of the role hope plays in goal orientation – that the state of affairs will be a future situation.

Hope is to be distinguished from its near relatives, other pro-attitudes, especially from wishing. In wishing for something one need not even believe that it is possible. Mary can wish that she had never been born but she cannot hope this. I may wish I were smarter than I am, but I cannot now hope that. After John discovers that the Yankees lost the game yesterday, he may wish that his favorite team had won, but he can no longer hope for it. Furthermore, we can wish for possible things which we are not ready to do anything about because the cost-benefit analysis shows that the possible benefit is not worth the risk involved. I might wish to make an extra $100 this week, but I may conclude that the loss of my free time in working overtime is not worth the extra money. Here I cannot be said to hope to make the extra $100, though I might wish that it were somehow possible to have the requisite extra time to do so.

This brings us to our fourth characteristic of hope. If one hopes for p, one will be disposed to do what one can to bring p about, if there is anything that one can do to bring it about. In hoping, unlike wishing, there will be a tendency to try to bring about the state of affairs if there is anything that can be done to bring it about. In the examples above cases 1, 2 and 6 are situations where the hoper can make a difference, whereas there is nothing he or she can do to bring about the desired result in cases 3 through 5. In this, hoping seems more reflective than wishing or merely having a desire. It is closer to having a want-on-balance, having considered the alternatives, as in case 6, where John has three desires but only one hope. (1) He wants to smoke. (2) He wants to stop smoking, and (3) he has a second order desire, in that he wants his second desire to win out over his first. He will try to bring it about that he will be successful in this. In this case it would be odd for John to speak of two hopes, that of having a cigarette and that of not smoking. John's full-blooded hope is to lick the habit, beginning by refraining from taking the cigarette.

In this sense hoping (where something can be done to bring about the state of affairs) is similar to intending where the agent desires that some state of affairs obtain and will try to bring it about. The difference between this dimension of hope and intending is that in intending to do action A one must believe that one will succeed, whereas no such requirement is necessary in hoping. If I intend to get an A in History, I must believe that I will, but I may hope to get an A without believing that I will be successful.[8] Hope stands midway between wishing and intending. In the former category, I may not believe that p is possible and in the latter, I must believe that I will probably bring it about. I hope I must believe that it is possible, but I need not believe that I will be able to bring in about.

A more difficult question is whether one can have incompatible hopes. Muyskens, in his important study *The Sufficiency of Hope*, follows Aquinas in denying that we can have conflicting preferences on balance. We may have conflicting wishes but not hopes.

If S hopes for p, either S prefers p on balance or S believes that he does not prefer anything that opposes his desire for p. The following formulation of this necessary condition is most perspicuous: It is not the case that *p* is not preferred by S on balance, or that S believes that *q*, which he prefers on balance, is incompatible with *p* (p. 18).

But why can't we have incompatible hopes, even as we have incompatible desires? It may not be rational to have them, but we are not talking about justified hopes, simply about having hopes. Can I not hope to travel to Greece this summer and also hope to finish my manuscript, which I can only do if I stay home from Greece? Perhaps the full analysis of this state is something like the following. I desire both to go to Greece and to finish my manuscript, but since there are many other contingencies that may prevent either of these from happening (e.g., I may have to teach summer school in order to earn some money or go in for an operation, either of which will prevent me from realizing either of my desires about going to Greece or finishing my manuscript) or prevent one of these from happening (e.g., I may not have enough money to go to Greece, or I may have my contract cancelled and so lose my motivation for writing my manuscript), I may be said to have a disjunctive hope: I hope either to go to Greece this summer or write my manuscript. It would be odd to say, under these circumstances, 'I hope both to write the manuscript and go to Greece this summer, but I know that I cannot do both.'

There may be a tendency to emphasize the desiderative aspect of hope and maintain that incompatible hopes are possible, as incompatible desires are. Hoping does not entail belief, but a mere pro-attitude. I cannot believe that *p* and *q* where they are incompatible (and I realize it), but I can desire both. Because hope does not necessitate belief, it may seem that we cannot rule out the possibility of incompatible hopes. However, the key phrase here is 'desiring on balance', which connotes a more reflective or intentional stance. If hope is closely allied to intention, as I have argued, it would seem to rule out incompatible hopes in the sense that if someone realizes that he hopes for two separate states of affairs, he must give up one in order to try to bring about the other. It seems to me that this attitude carries over to situations where one is powerless to affect the outcome. Mary may unreflectively hope that Happy Dancer wins the race and that Slippery Heels wins the same race, but when she realizes that these horses are running in the same race, she must give up one of her hopes or at least hope something like the following: that either Happy Dancer or Slippery Heels will win, or, if Happy Dancer does not win, that Slippery Heels will.

It may be objected that we can have incompatible hopes but that they are vain, ill-advised, foolish or whatever. This seems to call for a normative notion of hoping, separating rational hopes from irrational ones, incompatible hopes, being a version where at least one hope is irrational. Mary may believe that she hopes to get an A in History but also hopes to go to a party on the two nights preceding the exam. We want to say that such hope is irrational or imprudent. Mary should realize that it is virtually impossible for her to get an A in History without studying the two nights before the exam. If Mary were more rational, she would reflect on her incompatible hopes and decide on one of these hopes to the exclusion of the other. If hope is made up of a desiderative and an estimative factor, we may call hope unjustified or irrational just in case we can call either of its components unjustified or irrational. If John hopes to square the circle, we want to say that since the belief in question is irrational, the hope is also. If Mary hopes to party instead of studying, but has long-term goals which entail getting good grades, which in turn entail studying instead of partying, then we can speak of Mary having irrational hopes.

It may be countered that what is irrational about Mary is not her hoping but her believing that there is a chance of getting an A without studying. Or we may say that Mary really doesn't hope to get an A. She is self-deceived about her attitude and really only wishes to get the A. If hope has the intentional dimension that I have argued for, either of these redescriptions of Mary's state seem preferable to saying that Mary has consciously incompatible, though irrational, hopes. The issue is difficult, but I am inclined to hold to the irrational/rational distinction regarding hoping. Since hoping has an estimative (doxastic) and desiderative component, if one of these is irrational, the whole (i.e., the hope itself) may be irrational. At the very least we can say that a hope is irrational if the agent should know that the object in question is either certain or impossible. If John hopes he is God or Mary hopes to be forgiven by John after John has made it clear that he has freely forgiven her, their hopes are irrational. There is also the phenomenon of something being so close to impossible or certain that hoping may be irrational, as when an average person hopes to live to 200 or an average high school football player with no great promise hopes to make the pros and gives up all else in order to do this.[9]

If we can apply the rational-irrational distinction of hopes, can we also speak of morally unjustified and justified hopes? Are there moral constraints to hoping? Day denies, but Muyskens affirms, that there are such.[10] We may have morally unacceptable hopes in a way that we cannot have immoral beliefs. This is because hope statements involve desire in a way that beliefs do not. Consider the difference between:

1 I believe that the US and the USSR will annihilate the world in a nuclear war.

and

2 I hope that the US and the USSR will annihilate the world in a nuclear war.

Beliefs may be formed through a culpable lack of attention and thus have a moral dimension, but the belief itself cannot be judged moral or immoral. Hopes can. Having certain hopes, like having certain desires, shows bad character in a more fundamental way than belief acquisition does. But the most important difference is that the belief may be evidential and justified while the affective state of hoping is still inappropriate. We ought not allow ourselves to give in to such malicious desires.

B Hope and Other Propositional Attitudes

We have argued that hoping need not involve a subject's actually believing a proposition, but only that the proposition could be or could become true. In believing a proposition, the doxastic state has a subjective probability index of greater than 0.5, but in hoping that p is true, one need not believe that the proposition has that high an index.[11] John need not believe that Mary will marry him in order to hope that she will, nor need he believe that the Yankees have won the baseball game in order to hope that they have.

But if hoping does not entail belief-that so-and-so is the case, does it, at least, entail belief-in, a relationship of trust? Believing-in or trusting is a relational attitude. 'S trusts X' or 'S trusts in X' or 'S believes in X' indicates a sense of dependency and willingness to run a risk (however small) because of the positive valuation on the object in question. Some instances of hope do entail believing-in the object of hope. Consider case 3 (Mary hopes that Happy Dancer will win the Kentucky Derby next week). What would it mean to say that Mary believed-in Happy Dancer in this context? She must act or be disposed to act in some way as to manifest trust in Happy Dancer. She may bet on Happy Dancer without believing that he will win the race, but she cannot hope that Happy Dancer will win the race without being inclined to take some action in appropriate circumstances. The most likely action would be to bet on Happy Dancer, if she is able to do so, and the degree to which she hopes in Happy Dancer may be to some degree measured by how much she would bet on Happy Dancer. Of course, she may not bet on Happy Dancer, just in case her desire is sufficiently weak, or she has compunctions against gambling, or her estimation of Happy Dancer's chances are too low to warrant a risk. We can weakly hope (all things considered) without acting when there are countervailing desires (e.g., the desire not to risk one's hard earned money on a long shot). There is a fine line where our desire for something ceases to be a weak hope (with some inclination to act) and becomes a mere wish.

Although because of the desiderative nature of hope, there will be some inclination or tendency for the subject to believe-in or trust the object of hope, but there are cases where there is nothing one can do (e.g., when I hope that the Yankees won their game yesterday or that the sun will shine in Dallas today for my sister's wedding) or where the hope is so weak that it is easily overridden by other considerations (e.g., when I hedge my bet, when I hope the sun will shine but take an umbrella or hope to live a long life but take out an expensive life insurance policy or hope that the enemy will not attack but keep my powder dry).

Here we need to make a distinction between ordinary hope or weak hope and a deep hope. Consider Mary's situation as she hopes in Happy Dancer. She may only believe that Happy Dancer has a 1 in 10 chance of winning the Kentucky Derby, but she may judge this to be significantly better than the official odds of 100 to 1 against him. Suppose that she has only $10 but wants desperately to enter a special professional training program next week which will cost $1000. She has no hope of getting the money elsewhere but sees that if she wins on Happy Dancer, she will get the required amount.

Since she believes that the real odds are better than the official odds and that winning will enable her to get into the training program, she bets her $10 on the horse. She both hopes and trusts in Happy Dancer, though she never really believes that he will win. We might call these cases where one is disposed to risk something significant on the possibility of the proposition's being or becoming true 'deep' or 'profound hope' and cases where the person hopes against belief, against the available evidence and is even ready to risk something significant 'desperate hope'. Desperate hope is a species of deep or profound hope. In all cases of profound hope hoping entails trusting in the object of hope. There are rational and irrational, moral and immoral profound hopes. A morally acceptable, rational, profound, desperate hope is exemplified by a version of William James's classical mountain climber, who cannot believe but only hopes that he will be successful in jumping across the gorge.[12]

Sometimes it is thought that belief-in statements entail existential belief-that statements. That is, belief-in some object x presupposes that one believe-that x exists or will exist.[13] But this seems to be incorrect. The object need not be realizable, nor need the subject believe that he will realize it. All that is necessary is that the individual believe that there is some possibility of realizing it. A scientist may risk his reputation and spend enormous time and energy on a hypothesis that involves the possible existence of an entity which may not exist or which is far different from his tentative description of it.

If belief-in, or trusting, can be analyzed in terms of commitment to a course of action or a disposition to act, then it seems that we do not need to believe-that x exists in order to believe-in or deeply hope in the existence of x. We can live in profound hope, trusting in the object of hope. In ordinary hope we may not act according to the proposition in question, but may hedge our bet, as I have indicated above. But in profound hope (and especially in desperate hope) the desire for the object is so great that the subject is ready to act even in the light of very little evidence or subjective probability that the object in question will be realized. In such hope enormous risk is warranted by the strength of the desire and the felt need. The person lives *as if* the proposition were true or would become so. Columbus' sailors live on the hypothesis that the world is round, even though they doubt it. The explorer hopes to find the Fountain of Youth, even though he has doubts that such a fountain exists. A seriously sick woman can act in desperation, writing to an unknown person (who may not exist) for a wonder drug which in fact does not exist, but which she has heard about from misinformed friends.

We can imagine a situation where Mary has merely heard a rumor about some horse running in the Kentucky Derby at ridiculously low odds. She isn't sure that she has the name right, but in despair she goes to the local bookmaker in order to place her bet on Happy Dancer. She may doubt whether Happy Dancer exists and doubts the ill-reputed bookmaker who assures her that there is such a horse (suppose that she has good grounds for her suspicions). We may, nevertheless, say that she trusts that there is, that she lives *as if* there is such a horse. She lives in profound, desperate hope.

Genuinely living *as if* must be distinguished from pretending. You can pretend and act as though you love your neighbors, for you may believe that it is good policy to give this impression; but in genuinely profound hope the intentional state is different from that of pretending.

Finally, we should examine the relationship between hoping and optimism. If John hopes to marry Mary, must he be optimistic about his possibility? Can we imagine John hopeful with regard to marrying her and still pessimistic about its occurrence? We can imagine him hoping desperately, against hope, as it were, and we can imagine an alternating between hope and despair (distinguishing desperation from despair by the fact that despair tends to paralyze or cause inaction, whereas desperation tends to cause action). If we mean by pessimistic 'a low estimation of the chances of realizing the state of affairs', then we certainly can be hopeful and pessimistic at the same time, but if we mean 'a psychological state of resigning or despairing of realizing the state of affairs', then we cannot be hopeful and pessimistic. Resignation, despairing and fearing, as Day has shown, are all contraries to hope. I think, in fact, the terms 'optimistic' and 'pessimistic' are ambiguous in this way, so that we may be able to conjoin pessimistic with hopeful if we are emphasizing the estimative aspect of pessimism or optimism. It is possible, then, to be a hopeful pessimist, while living *as if* a proposition were true. Indeed, one can live *as if* a proposition were true without hope, in a desperate way, trusting, but not deeming the outcome significantly possible. Profound hope, then, is a species of faith, but it is not identical with it. Normally, however, the profound hoper will tend to envision the best outcome, even while realizing the objective factors that count against it. He won't be dominated by the objectively low probabilities of success.

We conclude, then, that hoping is distinguished from believing in that it involves a strong volitional or affective aspect in a way believing does not and that, as such, it is subject to moral assessment in a way that believing is not. Hoping is desiderative, but is more inclined to action than mere wishing. Profound hope is distinguished from ordinary hope by the intensity of the desire and willingness to take great risk towards obtaining one's goal, and desperate hope is a type of profound hope where the estimative aspect is low. Hope is not identical with optimism, if optimism is defined as estimatively, looking on the brighter side. A hoper may see that the odds are objectively against him and yet profoundly try to realize a state of affairs. Nevertheless, in spite of the intensity of desire, the moral hoper will continue to keep his mind open to fresh argument and evidence which could either incline him towards belieful hope or abandoning one hope for another.

C Profound Hope and Religious Faith

Can we apply this analysis of profound hope to religious faith without loss? Can we have religious faith in a religion like Christianity without believing that the object of faith exists? Let me tell a story in order to have some data for our analysis. Suppose Aaron and Moses both have an obligation to defend Israel from the Canaanites, who are seen as a present danger. The question is whether or not Israel should launch a preemptive strike against the neighboring tribe or whether there is still room for negotiations. One morning Moses sincerely reports that he has been appeared to by God, who has commanded him to annihilate the Canaanites because of their wickedness and idolatry. He has no doubts about the reality of the revelation, claims that it was self-authenticating, and tries to convince Aaron to help him prepare for war. Aaron must make a decision whether or not to support Moses, for he doubts whether God exists, let alone whether he has revealed himself to his brother. However, he doubts these things only weakly, deeming it possible that Yahweh exists and has so revealed himself to Moses. He wonders at the clouds by day and the fire in the distance by night which Moses claims are God's means of leading his people to their destination. Aaron is agnostic about both the existence of Yahweh and the revelation to Moses. Since he would like it to be the case that a benevolent guide for Israel exists, he might be tempted to take William James's advice and get himself to believe the requisite propositions by willing to believe them; but we may suppose that he does not believe that volitional believing is possible for him or morally acceptable. His only option is to live *as if* the proposition in question were true. He assists Moses in every way in carrying out the campaign against the Canaanites. He proclaims the need for his people to fight against the enemy, and if he sounds more convinced than he really is, he judges this deception to be justified. True, he may not act out of spontaneous abandon as Moses does. On the other hand, his scrupulous doubt may help him to notice problems and evidence which might otherwise be neglected, to which the true believer is impervious. This awareness may signal danger which may be avoided, thus saving the tribe from disaster. Doubt may have as many virtues as belief, though they may be different ones.

Moses and Aaron do not act out of entirely different noetic structures. Moses entirely believes what Aaron only hopes for. Moses acts because he believes that p and that it is a good thing that p. Aaron acts because he believes that it would be a good thing if p, that p is possible and that it is rational and morally permissible to hope that p. He exemplifies what we have called living *as if* God exists and has revealed himself to Israel. He lives in profound hope (and if he estimates the chances of God's existing to be very low, he also lives in desperate hope). He identifies an ideal state of affairs, believes it to be possible, though not probable, and being a hopeful person, plumps for the better scenario, rather than the worse. He lives experimentally with theism, in an experimental faith in which he continues to keep his mind open to, and to search for, new evidence which would either confirm or disconfirm the hypothesis on which his hopeful faith is based. While the hoper may live in a deep or even desperate hope, his eye, if he holds to an ethics of hope, is always on the evidence, so that there may come a time when the available evidence (or his subjective probability estimate) becomes too low to sustain faith.

My analysis suggests that the difference between faith and belief is more radical than has usually been supposed. Usually, it is assumed that faith is a special type of belief, one in which, in addition to belief in the existence of the religious object, one trusts in it and allows its influence to dominate one's life. To have faith in God is to believe that he exists and to commit one's life to him. This seems to have New Testament backing, especially in the Epistle to the Hebrews (chapter 11), where we read that unless we believe that God exists, we can neither come to God nor please him. However, as prominent as this view has been in Western thought (note its presence in the quotation by Plantinga at the beginning of this chapter), I suggest that it is an illicit entailment and that the writer of the letter to the Hebrews either had an overly behavioral interpretation of belief or was engaging in religious rhetoric, for I see no good reason to exclude the possibility of coming to God in hope rather than belief. On my analysis one may alter the passage 'Lord, I believe, help Thou my unbelief' to read: 'Lord, I hope in you; if you exist, please give me better evidence.' To believe that God exists is to believe that there is a being with certain necessary properties such as omnipotence, omniscience, omnibenevolence and being the maker of heaven and earth. But to believe-in God implies only that one regards such a being as possibly existing and that one is committed to live *as if* such a being does exist. Whether it is rational to commit oneself in this way depends on doing an analysis of how one sees comparative values in relationship to probable outcomes. It is the sort of assessment that goes on in any cost-benefit analysis.

It may usually be the case that those who believe *in* God also believe *that* God exists, but there is no entailment between the two states. One might believe that God exists without believing in God, and one might believe in God without believing that God exists, either as an atheist (who finds the proposition 'God exists' as genuinely possible and decides to live by it) or as an agnostic (who finds the God-hypothesis worth living in accordance with). Often, it has been supposed that there can be no hypothetical element in religious commitment and that to treat God's existence as such is to violate the very essence of religious faith.[14] Supposedly, the hypothetical stance is inadequate to produce the requisite commitment and unreserved worship which religion demands. But if this is true of traditional religious beliefs, I see no need to accept it as the only valid type of faith. An *experimental faith* that is open to new evidence is also an option. In this regard, my analysis has in common with William James the notion of theism being a live option (an hypothesis that is momentous and which the subject sees as calling for a decision). It agrees with James that it would be a good thing if theism and Christianity were true and can accept James's own rejection of the necessity of sufficient evidence for the proposition that Christianity is true before we can have faith. 'If religion be true and the evidence for it be still insufficient, I do not wish, by putting [the rationalist's] extinguisher upon my nature . . . to forfeit my sole chance in life of getting upon the winning side.'[15] I would also agree with James against Pascal that there is a psychological aspect to the decision of choosing religion which must supplement the merely calculative. While an atheist (who does not rule out the possibility of God's existence) may be persuaded of the logic of Pascal's Wager, he might not be moved by it. James is right when he says that the hypothesis in question must be a psychologically 'live hypothesis'. My analysis differs from James's in that I don't think it is necessary to get oneself to believe that the hypothesis is true in order to choose it in a profound way. One can have faith in God and Christianity without belief. Aaron is just as much in faith as Moses. There are different types of faith.

Belief-that may be overrated in regard to explanatory hypotheses that involve world views such as religions, political theories, and metaphysical systems. It is important to come as close as possible to a fit between the best objective evidence and the degree with which one believes propositions, but, admittedly, this is a person-relative experience. My analysis presupposes that it makes sense to speak of proportioning the strength of one's belief (which I separate from the value of one's belief to the individual, the depth of ingress of the belief) to the evidence, but it accepts intuitive beliefs as themselves prima facie evidence for themselves and their entailments. Ultimately, if someone counts her intuitions as evidence more than we do, all we can do is try to get her to see that she really has counter-evidence or intuitions which should lessen the strength of her apparent intuitive beliefs. There may be a more objective notion of proportioning one's beliefs to the evidence, but my analysis is content with this weaker thesis. It is possible that the belief that God exists is properly basic for some people, but, by the same standard, it may be that the belief that the Devil is really God is properly basic for others, given their noetic structure. For many of us neither are properly basic.

If my analysis is correct, agnosticism and even an interested type of atheism are possible religious positions. Doubt about God's existence, immortality, the Incarnation, or the Trinity, though agonizing in the extreme at times, may be necessary for some intellectually honest people. If there is an obligation to seek to have true or justified beliefs, then what God desires is not sycophantic struggling to get oneself to manipulate one's mind to believe what seems implausible on a clear look at the evidence, but a doxastic morality that allows the mind to be impartially shaped by the evidence.

If this is the case, then an interesting implication follows. Sometimes, as in the Athanasian Creed or Evangelical theologies and sermons, religious people have asserted that a belief that certain propositions are true is a necessary condition for eternal salvation. We will be judged by whether or not we have believed these propositions (e.g., those contained in the doctrine of the Trinity, the Incarnation, and so forth). Pascal and others believed this so strongly that they advocated that you should 'pretend you believe' in order to get yourself to believe what you don't believe by an impartial look at the evidence. But if we have ethical duties to have the best justified beliefs possible in important matters, and if those duties include a duty to acquire beliefs through impartial investigation of the evidence, then it would seem that we cannot be judged unrighteous for not believing in these propositions, if we justifiably find the evidence inadequate. It would follow that there is a moral basis even to religious believing, so that a moral God could not judge us merely on the basis of the beliefs we have. What we can be judged for is how well we have responded to criticism of our beliefs, including our religious beliefs, how faithful we have been to the truth as we have seen it. On this basis it might well be the case that in heaven (or purgatory) Calvin, Barth, Billy Graham and Jerry Falwell may have to be rehabilitated by taking catechism lessons in the ethics of belief from such archangels as David Hume and Bertrand Russell.

Is Experimental Faith Adequate for Religious Belief?

In philosophical literature I know of only one serious set of objections to the position that I have set forth. It has to do with the alleged inadequacy of any sort of tentativeness or non-tenacity in religious believing. Experimental faith lacks the ultimate commitment that is necessary for an adequate religious faith. This objection is given its best expression by Gary Gutting in his incisive work *Religious Belief and Religious Skepticism*, in which he distinguishes between 'interim assent' and 'decisive assent'. Decisive assent terminates the process of inquiry into the truth of the core propositions, whereas interim assent keeps the inquiry going.[16] In decisive assent one ends the search for justifying reasons and becomes wholly concerned with understanding the implications of what one believes. In interim assent one accepts the propositions in question without terminating the search for their truth. While there may be a difference between Gutting's notion of interim assent and what I have been calling experimental faith or hopeful commitment – the former but not the latter presupposing, at least, weak belief – much of his attack on interim assent is applicable to my account. On Gutting's account such faith is inadequate for religious life.

Essentially, interim assent is inadequate for genuine religious belief because of the way religious belief functions in the life of the believer. Gutting gives three reasons for thinking that religious faith demands decisive assent and prohibits interim assent. (1) Religious belief is a (relative) end of a quest for 'emotional and intellectual satisfaction'. 'Any religious belief worthy of the name must surely call for and legitimate a longing for God as the all-dominating longing of the believer's life, the believer's "master passion". By contrast, the life of a believer who gave only interim assent to God's reality . . . could be rightly dominated not by the longing for God but, at best, only by the longing to know whether or not God exists.'[17] (2) Religious belief requires total commitment to the implications of what is believed and this is incompatible with continuing reflection on its truth. Believers must often make fundamental sacrifices, which only decisive assent would allow. (3) Merely interim assent is inconsistent with the typically religious attitude towards nonbelief, which sees nonbelief as intrinsically bad. Interim assent has not the single-mindedness of decisive assent and cannot 'proclaim the ideal of its belief as "the one thing needful".'[18]

My first reaction to Gutting's insistence that decisive faith is a necessary condition for adequate religious belief is to say that perhaps there is something morally repugnant about 'adequate'

231

religious belief, since it seems to demand a premature closure of inquiry. If there were good objective grounds for theism, the mandate might be understandable. Since there doesn't seem to be that kind of requisite evidence, the closure seems unwarranted. Even if experimental faith failed to give what Gutting deems the necessary conditions for adequate religious belief, this doesn't mean that experimental faith is a less valid position. It might mean that traditional religious belief is not the only meaningful possibility for intelligent persons. Perhaps traditionally necessary conditions are not the necessary conditions that we would want to use to define an adequate faith for today. It might be the case, for example, that traditional religions have under-emphasized the role of an ethics of belief and assumed that a rigid set of beliefs was necessary for genuine faith. If my analysis is correct, too much emphasis may have been placed on credal affirmation in the past.

Gutting's analysis of the inferiority of interim assent has other problems. Regarding his first point that 'any religious belief worthy of the name must surely call for and legitimate a longing for God as the all dominating longing of the believer's life' and that interim assent fails here, we may demur at two points. (a) Not every religion makes this longing the dominant passion. Buddhism doesn't. Neither does Sikhism or Quakerism. On what independent grounds does Gutting exclude these religions as 'worthy religious beliefs', except by begging the question? (b) Even if Gutting is right, however, I see no reason for concluding that the person who hopes in God cannot be dominated by this passion, even while questing for truth. To have faith in God, in the sense I have described, is to long for God passionately, to live *as if* God exists. But why is this incompatible with seeking the best evidence on the matter, of admitting that one only weakly believes this (or is agnostic on the matter)? Doesn't the believing biblical scholar have to inquire impartiality into the evidence for important events upon which faith is based? I think that it is a rather narrow notion of 'passionate longing' which rules out impartial inquiry. The hoper in God worships with passion and commitment; only he or she acknowledges and is committed to doxastic integrity, to continuing the dialogue with those who differ, and regards engaging in the dialogue as one aspect of worship. Otherwise, how is it possible for the person of faith to find honest 'intellectual satisfaction', which Gutting acknowledges as a necessary condition for adequate religion?

Gutting's second criticism of interim assent is that it precludes the sort of unconditional commitment necessary for decisive action and fundamental sacrifices. It is true, as our discussion of Peirce and our parable of Aaron and Moses show, that the doubter's steps are tripped by obstacles over which the true believer hurdles with the greatest of ease. The question is whether this sort of commitment is of the essence of genuine religion. This same imperviousness to difficulty has led to some of the greatest intolerance and fanaticism the world has known. We can rightly spot it as evil in fanatical Nazis or Shiite Moslems following the Ayatolah Khoumeni, but we sometimes miss it in ourselves. Gutting may have in mind the martyrs who are willing to die for belief in the Incarnation or the existence of God, and perhaps the hoper in God will not be as willing to die as the believer. But the hoper in God may, nevertheless, be willing to live and die for the moral principles which he sees tied up with the essence of the religious faith and which express much of the importance of believing in God in the first place. The hoper in God may question whether we have any reason to believe that a morally adequate religion or God's will demands that people give their lives for the proposition that God exists. If God is all-powerful and benevolent, surely, he could insure that the witness to his existence is not lost.

The third criticism that Gutting makes of interim assent is that it does not allow for the deep conviction that belief in God is the 'one thing needful', that it is an unspeakably sad thing not to believe that God exists. Gutting is saying that it is the relationship with God, trust in Him, that is needful, but he implies that this entails believing that God exists. 'For the believer, the world would be a better place if everyone could see his way to accepting the believer's faith', but interim assent must allow 'equal value' to opposing beliefs, an essential element in continuing discussion. But this objection misses the point that the *manner* of holding a belief may be as important as the belief itself. If everyone in the world came to believe that god existed by manipulating their minds, it might well turn out that these belief states were disconnected from the rest of their noetic structure and represented a deep character flaw. It is not clear that honest doubt is less a state of reverence for God than fearful prohibition of doubt.

Gutting and I agree that belief in God can make a profound difference in the way we live and that theism, which is at the basis of

Judaism and Christianity, is greatly inspiring and can motivate to high moral action. My point is that one need not be a full-fledged believer *that* God exists in order to draw inspiration from this insight. One can live imaginatively in hope, letting the thought of the possibility of a benevolent Being motivate one to a more dedicated and worshipful moral life.[19]

Conclusion

In the second part of this work I have tried to outline the various relations between the will and belief, showing on the one hand that it is unlikely that we use the will directly to obtain beliefs and that it is morally wrong in general to do so indirectly and, on the other hand, that the will's proper role is centered in loyalty to the truth as we see it, that which I have called 'faith'. Rather than a long summary of the way we have come, perhaps a parable will best sum up this project and lead to further thought on the nature of belief, will and faith.

A Parable

Suppose that the proposition that there is extra-terrestrial rational life in the universe becomes a consuming issue for scientists. A significant part of the scientific community wants to know whether there are other intelligent beings living on other planets and wants to divert large sums of money from other research to explore this hypothesis. The scientists divide into warring parties, something like this. (a) There are those who believe strongly in extra-terrestrial life and who want the research to confirm their convictions. They are called the 'Galacticans', for their faith in the hypothesis that there is rational life on other planets. (b) There are those who positively disbelieve that there is such life – perhaps some for religious reasons. They believe that man is unique in the universe, the apple of God's eye, and see such research as a waste of time and worse – a diversion from other important activities that science should be about. These are called 'anti-Galacticans'. Finally, (c) there are those who are agnostic on the matter but agree that it is an interesting question and worthy of some investigation and research funds, though not nearly enough to satisfy the Galacticans. Their policy is one of bet-hedging – do the most amount of research possible on the project compatible with our major humanistic research. That is, they advocate little costly research in the area for its own sake but wherever there is a project that is worth funding (e.g., space travel or communication), try to work into it the low cost additional research regarding extra-terrestrial life.

The parties argue with each other and before the appropriate research funding panels. The Galacticans argue that it could be vital to our survival to know if there are other intelligent beings in the universe. We could learn much about life from them, have data with which to compare our human history, and possibly find allies in the universe. The opponents argue that the research is too costly and that there is no evidence of other life in the universe. The money will just be wasted. The agnostics divide on the issue, but few take extreme positions on either side. They generally agree that given the paucity of positive evidence a cost-benefit analysis would seem to favor making this a low priority item, but not one to be entirely dismissed. A few agnostics, however, see the project as highly worth doing and are willing to give a good bit of their time, talents and money to this project.

Eventually, funds for the project begin to become available, and an interesting thing happens. A cleavage appears within the ranks of the Galacticans, some of whom argue that the agnostics should not be given these valuable funds and opportunities because their commitment isn't deep or complete. Doubters cannot be trusted to work with complete devotion on a project that demands so much of one. Either one must be completely committed to this project or one should stay out. Some within this group contend that it is not enough to believe in the project. One must also believe that such life actually exists. Only by being absolutely convinced in the reality of the object of the search would the research be likely to be success-ful. Of course, the agnostics deny this, saying that their interests and talents are sufficient for the job and besides, their very lack of bias in the matter would help insure that the no cheating takes place in assembling the findings. This would actually help in finding extra-terrestrial life (if, indeed, it exists) for it would tend to abort false leads and subtle traps which the true believers were likely to fall into.

Conclusion

An interesting debate transpires between the Galacticans and the sympathetic agnostics. The issue is whether it really matters whether one believes in the existence of the extra-terrestrial beings or not. Some of those who do argue that, although there is scarce evidence for them, they couldn't help believing that they exist and that what's more it is properly basic for them to do so. Their belief is like the belief in other minds or memory beliefs which can't be checked. The other side see this as strange, for the scope of properly basic beliefs should be restricted to beliefs that are either self-evident, incorrigible or, at least, enjoying almost universal consensus. But this belief is not like other beliefs, the advocates argue. It is a *sui generis* belief. Perhaps, they suggest, evil lust prevents others from believing that such a belief is natural. The extra-terrestrial creatures, who now take on creative powers in the minds of these scientists, have made us all with an inclination to believe that they exist, but darkness has clouded the hearts of humans so that now only an elect still believe in them.

But, argue the sympathetic agnostics, why is it important to believe that they exist in the first place? If we live moral lives isn't that sufficient to legitimate our life styles? Wouldn't it even be immoral to try to get ourselves to believe against the evidence available to us? If the extra-terrestrialians are moral, they will no doubt appreciate our intellectual honesty – and perhaps value it more highly than the sycophant-like devotion of some of the believers who are more worried about losing their belief than helping their fellow humans?

Is there not an ethics of believing, so that we ought to be suspicious of beliefs which are not supported by evidence or clearly seen to be self-evident, evident to the senses (or memory) or universally accepted? And does it, after all, really matter whether we believe in extra-terrestrial life? What *difference* does it make?

Notes

Chapter I Belief and Faith in the Bible and the Early Christian Movement

1 Arthur Weiser, 'The Old Testament Concept [of Faith]', in *Bible Key Words* (vol. III), from Gerhard Kittel's *Theologisches Wortenbuch zum Neuen Testament*, tr. Dorothea M. Barton, P.R. Ackroyd, and A.E. Harvey, New York: Harper, 1960, p. 10.
2 Ibid., p. 46.
3 Ibid., p. 13.
4 Rudolf Bultmann, 'The Group of Concepts Associated with *pistis* in the New Testament' in *Bible Key Words*, op. cit., p. 57ff.
5 Ibid., p. 68.
6 Ibid., p. 109.
7 Wilfred C. Smith, *Belief and History*, University of Virginia Press, 1977.
8 Cf. Theodotus in the *Anti-Nicene Fathers* vol. VIII, p. 43. 'He who has believed has obtained forgiveness of sins from the Lord; but he who has attained knowledge, inasmuch as he no longer sins, obtains from himself the forgiveness of the rest.' Cf. Origen, *On First Principles*, p. 186f.
9 Harry Wolfson, *The Philosophy of the Church Fathers*, pp. 115–17; cf. Clement of Alexandria, *Stromateis* II, 12; II, 2; V, 13, 86).
10 Henry Chadwick, *The Early Church*, London, 1967, pp. 84ff.

Chapter II Plato on Knowledge and Belief

1 Cf. Michael Morgan, 'Belief, Knowledge and Learning in Plato's Middle Dialogue' for a discussion of the problem of the relation of belief to knowledge in the *Meno* and *Republic*. The clearest analysis of Plato's concepts of 'knowledge' and 'belief' in the *Republic* is Cross and Woozley's *Plato's Republic* (chapter 8). I have profited greatly from these works.
2 For a discussion of this point see Gwynneth Matthes, *Plato's Epistemology*, pp. 18ff.

Chapter III   Augustine on Faith

1 Origen, *Contra Celsum* III. 45, 46. In I, 9 he writes, 'If every man could abandon the business of life and devote his time to philosophy, no other course ought to be followed but this alone. For in Christianity . . . there will be found no less profound study of the writings that are believed; we explain the obscure utterances of the prophets, the parables. . . . However, if this is impossible, since, partly owing to the necessities of life and partly owing to human weakness, very few people are enthusiastic about rational thought, what better way of helping the multitude could be found other than that given to the nations by Jesus?' Cf. also VI. 10.

2 *Contra Celsum* IV.9; Clement of Alexandria, *Stromateis*, Bk II, ch. VI.31; Bk V, ch. IV–IX.

3 *On the Usefulness of Believing*, ch. 25.

4 *Retractions* I, xiv in *Augustine: Early Writings*, p. 284.

5 *Enchiridion*, ch. v.

6 Romans 1:18.

7 *Luther's Table Talk*, cited in Anders Nygren, *Agape and Eros*, tr. Philip Watson, p. 561.

8 However, later Augustine reprimands the Platonists for not following Socrates' example in this. 'The Platonists do not perceive that man does not know God because he does not love God. These best philosophers do not comprehend the plight of man' (Confessions VII.21, 27).

9 There is in Augustine a primacy of belief over doubt, similar to principles found in William James and Roderick Chisholm. We are enjoined to believe a proposition until the proposition is proven guilty. 'What is doubtful believe until either reason teaches or authority lays down that it is to be rejected that it is true or that it has to be believed always' (*On Religion*, p. 19).

10 *In Joannis Evangelium tractatus* XXVI, in *Library of Nicene Letters*, ed. E.B. Pusey. Many of the Church fathers held to a form of volitionalism. Clement of Alexandria taught that our obedience to God involved voluntary assent to authority (*Stromata*, p. 349f). Irenaeus wrote, 'And not only in works but also in faith God has kept the will of man free and subject to man's control, saying "according to thy faith be it unto thee," thus showing that man's faith is his own because his will is his own' (*Against Heresy* 4: 37,5). And in Origen we read, 'If a man only believes that he must entrust himself to God and do everything in order to please him, he will be transformed. But even if it be exceedingly difficult to effect a change in some persons, the cause must be held to lie in their own will, which is reluctant to accept the belief that God over all things is a just judge of all the deeds done during life' (*Contra Celsum*, p. 491).

Chapter IV   Aquinas on Faith

1 My discussion is heavily indebted to two works: Terence Penelhum's 'The Analysis of Faith in St. Thomas Aquinas', in *Religious Studies* vol. 13, 1977; and Michael McLean's Ph.D. dissertation, *An Exposition and Defense of St. Thomas Aquinas' Account of the Rational Justification of Religious Belief*, University of Notre Dame, 1981.

2 ST 2a2ae. 2 & 3.

3 DV 14.1. The psychology of the inter-relatedness of mind and will integrates the volitional cause of assent with the position that it remains essentially an act of intellect. The will is the one power in which the radical inclination of the person to the human good is concentrated. Because the truth proposed for belief and the act of belief itself are from God, inviting man to share in his own life, the mind's responsive assent to God stands as a good which can and does engage the will. Conviction of the reality of God's grace-address to man is what ultimately guides the explanation of the volitional element in belief (T.C. O'Brien in his commentary to the section on Faith in *Summa Theologiae*, p. 211).

4 John Hick, *Faith and Knowledge*, p. 20f; Terence Penelhum, 'The Analysis of Faith in St. Thomas Aquinas', p. 150ff; Timothy Potts, 'Aquinas on Belief and Faith', in *Inquiries into Medieval Philosophy*, ed. James Ross. In his book, *The Basis of Belief*, (vol. 13 in *The Twentieth Century Encyclopedia of Catholicism*, the Thomist Illtyd Trethowan decries a form of volitionalism as an alternative to faith in reasonable authority. 'From what then can [the claims of the Church] be derived save from a supernatural apprehension of God as Revealer, as acting in, and so guaranteeing, his Church? The alternative is to adopt a theory according to which the will becomes a source of certainty instead of the intellect – an obscurantist position', p. 135). Yet, the question may be seriously raised whether the condemnation fits the very Thomistic view of faith which he is appealing to.

5 McLean, op. cit., p. 134f.

6 Martin Luther, *The Reformation Writings of Martin Luther*, tr. B.L. Woolf, vol. 1, London, 1952. For a good summary of Luther's position, cf. Philip Watson, *Let God be God*, London: Epworth Press, 1947. Luther does make and emphasize the distinction between belief-that and belief-in as few before him. 'We should note that there are two ways of believing. One way is to believe *about* God, as I do when I believe that what is said of God is true; just as I do when I believe what is said about the Turk, the devil, or hell. This faith is knowledge or observation rather than faith. The other way is to believe *in* God, as I do when I not only believe that what is said about Him is true, but put my trust in Him, surrender myself to Him and make bold to deal with Him, believing without doubt that He will be to me and do to me just what is said of Him' (cited in *A Compend of Luther's Theology*, ed. H.T. Kerr, Philadelphia: Westminster Press, 1953, p. 33).

7 Kenneth Konyndyk, 'Faith and Evidentialism', an unpublished paper

delivered at the Conference on Philosophy of Religion at the University of Nebraska/Lincoln, April 14, 1984; Paul Helm, *The Varieties of Belief*, London: George Allen & Unwin, 1973, ch. 6.

8 John Calvin, *Institutes of the Christian Religion*, tr. F.L. Battles, Philadelphia: Westminster Press, 1960, III. 2. 14.

Chapter V   The Rationalists on Belief and Will: Descartes and Spinoza

1 Descartes' *Meditations on First Philosophy*, tr. L. Lafleur. New York, 1951, p. 57. Cf. *Rules* II. The interpretation that I have adopted here is the standard one, set forth or consistent with that of E.M. Curley, *Descartes Against the Skeptics* (Cambridge, 1978) and 'Descartes, Spinoza and the Ethics of Belief', in *Spinoza: Essays in Interpretation*, eds. M. Mandelbaum and E. Freeman (La Salle, IL., 1975); J.L. Evans, 'Error and the Will', *Philosophy* (April, 1963); Bernard Williams, *Descartes: The Project of Pure Inquiry* (London, 1978); and Peter Markie, 'Descartes's Theory of Judgment', *Southern Journal of Philosophy* (Supplemental Volume, 1983). This view has been attacked by Anthony O'Hear, 'Belief and Will', (*Philosophy* (April, 1972) and Jeffrey Tlumak, 'Judgment and Understanding in Descartes's Philosophy', *Southern Journal of Philosophy* (Supplemental Volume, 1983). While the latter writers have pointed out problems with the standard interpretation, I don't find their reconstructions compelling. For a lucid exchange on this matter see the debate between Jeffrey Tlumak and Peter Markie (cited above).

2 *Descartes Philosophical Writings*, eds and trs Elizabeth Anscombe and Peter Geach (Indianapolis, 1971), p. 286, abbreviated 'A & G' in the text. My translations of the *Principles* are those of Elizabeth Haldane and G.R.T. Ross in *Philosophical Works of Descartes* (New York, 1911), abbreviated 'HR' in the text.

3 E.M. Curley, 'Descartes, Spinoza and the Ethics of Belief', in *Spinoza: Essays in Interpretation*, ed., M. Mandelbaum and Eugene Freeman. LaSalle, I1: Open Court, 1975.

Chapter VII The Empiricists' Notion of Belief: Locke and Hume

1 E.M. Curley, 'Descartes, Spinoza and the Ethics of Belief', in *Spinoza: Essays in Interpretation*; J.A. Passmore, 'Hume and the Ethics of Belief' in *David Hume: Bicentenary Papers*, ed. G.P. Morice. Austin, TX: University Texas, 1977; W.J. Kinnamann, *The Ethics of Belief: an Examination of the View that Belief is Subject to Voluntary Controls*, Ph.D. dissertation, The University of Connecticut, 1978, ch. I.

2 Curley, *op. cit.*, p. 180; Kinnamann, *op. cit.*, pp. 19–26.

3 Locke corroborates this interpretation in his *Letter Concerning Tolera-*

tion where he writes 'To believe this or that to be true does not depend on our will.'

4 Hume noticed this in his *Dialogue Concerning Natural Religion*, pt II, p.185. Cf. Hick's disucssion in *Faith and Knowledge*, p.136.
5 Charles Peirce, 'The Probabilities of Induction', in *Essays in the Philosophy of Science*.
6 *David Hume, A Treatise of Human Nature*, ed. L.A. Selby-Bigge, Oxford: Oxford University Press, 1958 (abbrev. 'T' in text). David Hume, *Enquiries Concerning the Human Understanding and Concerning the Principles of Morals*, ed. L.A. Selby-Bigge, Oxford: Oxford University Press, 1962 (abbrev. 'E' in text).
7 Passmore, op. cit., p. 89f.

Chapter VIII   Kant and Kierkegaard on the Nature and Place of Faith

1 James Collins, *The Emergence of Philosophy of Religion*, p. 129.
2 *Opus Postumum*, p. 823, quoted in Clement Webb, *Kant's Philosophy of Religion*, p. 197.
3 From Kant's *Opus Postumum*, p. 778, quoted in Clement Webb, *op. cit.*, p.193).
4 Allen Wood, *Kant's Moral Religion*, and Stephen Evans, *Subjectivity and Religious Belief.*
5 See Kierkegaard, *Concluding Unscientific Postscript*, p. 25ff.
6 For a discussion of this point see my *Logic of Subjectivity*, p. 69f.
7 Ibid., pp. 35ff; 118ff; 131ff.

Chapter IX   Clifford and James on the Ethics of Belief

1 George Mavrodes, 'Intellectual Morality in Clifford and James,' forthcoming in a series in the ethics of belief.
2 William James, *The Will to Believe and other essays in popular philosophy* (abbrev. WB), New York: Dover, 1957 (reprint of the 1897 edition). 'The Sentiment of Rationality' is also found in this collection of essays.
3 Peter Kauber and Peter Hare, 'The Right and Duty to Believe'. *Canadian Journal of Philosophy*, vol IV.2, 1975. In a diary entry James shows that he sees the difference between believing and acting and that action is not the measure of belief. The entry is also important because it shows a possible source for his idea of a 'will to believe'. 'I think that yesterday was a crisis in my life. I finished the first part of Renouvier's second "Essais" and see no reason why his definition of Free Will – "the sustaining of a thought *because I choose to* when I might have other thoughts" – need be the definition of an illusion. At any rate, I will assume for the present – until next year – that it is no illusion. My first

act of free will shall be to believe in free will. For the remainder of the year, I will . . . voluntarily cultivate the feeling of moral freedom, by reading books favorable to it, as well as by acting . . . and consequently accumulate grain on grain of willful choice like a very miser . . . I will go a step further with my will, not only act with it, but believe as well.'

4 George Mavrodes, 'Intellectual Morality in Clifford and James,' unpublished manuscript.
5 *Pragmatism*, p. 145.
6 *Either/Or II*, p. 356. Cf. *Fear and Trembling*, p. 30.

Chapter X Modern Catholic Volitionalists: Newman, Pieper and Lonergan

1 Jamie Ferreira, 'Newman and the "Ethics of Belief" ', *Religious Studies*, 1983.

Chapter XI The Contemporary Debate on Belief and Will

1 H.H. Price, 'Some Considerations on Belief' (1934), reprinted in *Knowledge and Belief*, A. Phillips Griffiths, Oxford: Oxford University Press, 1967; p. 42.
2 Ibid., p. 52.
3 Frank Ramsey, *The Foundations of Mathematics*. London: Routledge & Kegan Paul, 1931.
4 Ibid., p. 170.
5 R.B. Braithewaite, 'The Nature of Belief', first appeared in *Proceedings of the Aristotelian Society*, vol. 33 (1932–33). Reprinted in *Knowledge and Belief*, ed. A. Phillips Griffiths. Oxford University Press, 1967. I have used the latter source.
6 Price, 'Some Considerations about Belief' (1933), *op. cit.*, p.45.
7 Price, 'Belief and Will' in *Belief, Knowledge and Truth*, eds Robert Ammerman and Marcus Singer. NY: Scribner's Sons, 1970.
8 Roderick Chisholm, 'Lewis' Ethics of Belief' in *The Philosophy of C.I. Lewis*, ed. P.A. Schilpp. Open Court, 1968, p. 223.
9 Roderick Chisholm, *Perception*. Cornell University Press, 1957, p. 9.
10 Roderick Chisholm, 'Lewis' Ethics of Belief' in *The Philosophy of C.I. Lewis*, ed. P.A. Schilpp. Open Court, 1968, p. 226.
11 Roderick Firth, 'Chisholm and the Ethics of Belief' in *Philosophical Review*, LXVIII 1959.
12 Jack Meiland, 'What Ought We to Believe? or The Ethics of Belief Revisted' in *American Philosophical Quarterly*, vol. 17, no. 1 January, 1980.
13 Richard M. Gale, 'William James and the Ethics of Belief' in *APQ*, vol. 17:1, January, 1980; pp. 1–14.
14 J.T. Stevenson, 'On Doxastic Responsibility' in *Analysis and Metaphysics*, ed., Keith Lehrer. Dordrecht: Reidel, 1975.

15 Louis Pojman, 'A Critique of Holyer's Volitionalism', *Dialogue* (forth-coming).

Chapter XII   The Contemporary Debate on Faith and Reason: Fideism and Rationalism

1 D.Z. Phillips, *Faith and Philosophical Inquiry*, London: Routledge & Kegan Paul, 1970 and 'Belief, Change and Forms of Life: The Confusions of Internalism and Externalism' in F. Crosson, ed., *The Autonomy of Religious Belief*. University of Notre Dame, 1981; Peter Winch, 'Understanding a Primitive Society' in *Philosophy of Religion*, S.M. Cahn, ed. New York: Harper & Row, 1970; G.E. Hughes, 'Martin's *Religious Belief* in *Australasian Journal of Philosophy*, 1962; and Norman Malcolm, 'The Groundlessness of Religious Belief' in *Reason and Religion*, ed. S.C. Brown. Ithaca: Cornell University Press, 1977.
2 John Hick, *Philosophy of Religion*. Englewood, NJ: Prentice Hall, 1963, p. 63.
3 Terrence W. Tilley, 'Norman Malcolm on Religious Belief and Evidence', a paper delivered at the American Academy of Religion, December 1978; Louis Pojman, 'Rationality and Religious Belief', *Religious Studies*, 1979.
4 Gary Gutting, *Religious Belief and Religious Skepticism*.
5 Kai Nielsen, 'Wittgensteinian Fideism', *Philosophy*, 1967.
6 *Op. cit.*, p. 41.
7 *Op. cit.*, p. 48.
8 John Hick, *Faith and Knowledge*, Ithaca: Cornell University Press, 1957, chapter 7.
9 Cf. Alvin Plantinga, 'Is Belief in God Rational' in *Rationality and Religious Belief*, ed. C.F. Delaney, Notre Dame, 1979; 'Is Belief in God Properly Basic' in *Nous*, XV, 1 (1981); and 'Reason and Belief in God' in *Faith and Rationality*, eds Alvin Plantinga and Nicholas Wolterstorff. Notre Dame, 1983. Since the last of these is the latest and more complete statement of Plantinga's position, we shall focus on it in our discussion. All references are to this article unless otherwise specified.
10 Gary Gutting, *Religious Belief and Religious Skepticism*, chapter 3.
11 Robert Audi, 'Direct Justification and Theistic Belief' (unpublished manuscript which has been read at various philosophical conferences).

Chapter XIII   Direct Descriptive Volitionalism

1 Cf. E.M. Curley, 'Descartes, Spinoza and the Ethics of Belief', in *Spinoza: Essays in Interpretation*, eds M. Mandelbaum and E. Freeman (LaSalle, Illinois, 1975).
2 Cf. John Hick, *Faith and Knowledge* (Cornell University, 1957), p. 46.

See also the section on the Church fathers and Augustine in the first part of this work.

3 Descartes, *Meditations* (Penguin Edition), IV, p. 137; *Replies* (Haldane and Ross), vol. I, p. 175.

4 John Henry Newman, *The Grammar of Assent* (Westminster, 1870), p. 232.

5 Bernard Lonergan, *Insight, A Study of Human Understanding* (New York, 1960), p. 709.

6 Joseph Pieper, *Belief and Faith* (New York, 1961), pp. 25–7.

7 Cf. Part One of this work where I discuss the concept of faith in the New Testament. Note especially such passages as Matthew 17:20; 21:21; Mark 9:23; Romans 10:9f; and Hebrews 11:6.

8 Pascal's *Pensees*, tr. H.F. Stewart (New York, 1953), p. 125.

9 Roderick Chisholm, 'Lewis' Ethics of Belief' in *The Philosophy of C.I. Lewis*, ed. Paul Arthur Schilpp (LaSalle, 1968).

10 Jack Meiland, 'What Ought We to Believe? or the Ethics of Belief Revisited' *American Philosophical Quarterly*, vol. 17 (January 1980). Cf. also George Naknikian, *An Introduction to Philosophy* (New York, 1967) pp. 257, 275, for a similar view.

11 Stuart Hampshire, *Thought and Actions* (London, 1966), p. 155f.

12 Alexander Bain, *The Emotions and the Will* (1959); R.B. Braitewaite, 'The Nature of Believing' *Proceedings of the Aristotelian Society* 33 (1932–33); Gilbert Ryle, *The Concept of Mind* (1949) and Robert Audi, 'The Concept of Believing' in *The Personalist* (1972).

13 Bain, *op.cit.*

14 D.M. Armstrong, *Belief, Truth and Knowledge* (Cambridge, 1973), pp. 3–5.

15 William James, *op. cit.*, p. 88f. Cf. Kierkegaard, *Concluding Unscientific Postscript*, p. 109.

16 Gary Gutting, 'A Critique of Pojman's "Volitionalism and the Nature of Belief" ', read at the University of Notre Dame, February 2, 1979.

17 Wayne Davis's comments on my paper 'Volitionalism and the Acquisition of Belief', delivered at the American Philosophical Association in Chicago, April 30, 1983.

Chapter XIV Indirect Volitionalism, Prescriptive Volitionalism and the Ethics of Belief

1 John Stuart Mill, *On Liberty*. Mill continues, 'the appropriate region of human liberty . . . comprises liberty of conscience in the most comprehensive sense: Liberty of thought and feeling, absolute freedom of opinion on all subjects practical and speculative, scientific, moral or theological'. The statement is ambiguous, seeming to conflate the right to be protected from doxastic coercion and the right to manipulate our minds as we see fit.

2 Jack Meiland, 'What Ought We to Believe? or the Ethics of Belief

Revisited'. *American Philosophical Quarterly*, vol. 17, January, 1980.
3 Chisholm, *op. cit.*, Stephen Nathanson, 'The Ethics of Belief' in *Philosophy and Phenomenological Research*, 1982.
4 W.K. Clifford, 'The Ethics of Belief', p. 39. Cf. ch 9 of this work.
5 Bernard Williams, 'Deciding to Believe' in *Problems of the Self*. Cambridge University Press, 1972.

Chapter XV   Rationality and Religious Belief

1 John Calvin, *Institutes of the Christian Religion*, book I, chapter 7.
2 Hard perspectivists include Kierkegaard, Wittgenstein, D.Z. Phillips, Peter Winch, Karl Barth, Rudolf Bultmann, as well as Reinhold Niebuhr. Soft perspectivists include Basil Mitchell, John Lucas and John King-Farlow, all of whom have influenced my views on these matters. This position has an analogue in philosophy of science where philosophers such as W.F. Sellars and Mary Hesse recognize that all science emerges within conceptual frameworks but that there is still the possibility of communication between frameworks.
3 Alvin Plantinga, 'Reason and Belief in God' in *Faith and Rationality*, eds. Alvin Plantinga and Nicholas Woterstorff. University of Notre Dame, 1983.
4 I follow McClendon and Smith's definition of 'conviction' here as 'a persistent belief such that if X has a conviction, it will not be easily relinquished without making X a significantly different person than before'. *Understanding Religious Convictions*. University of Notre Dame Press, 1975; p. 7.
5 Even McClendon and Smith make this mistake in their usually reliable work. Ibid., p. 108.
6 Basil Mitchell, 'Faith and Reason: A False Antithesis?' *Religious Studies*, vol. 16, June, 1980; I. Lakatos, 'Falsification and Methodology of Scientific Research Programs' in *Criticism and the Growth of Knowledge* eds, Lakatos and Musgrave. Cambridge, 1970; pp. 91–196.
7 Mitchell, ibid.
8 Lakatos, op. cit., p. 118. Norman Malcom, 'The Groundlessness of Belief' *op. cit.* Quoted in John Macquarrie. *Twentieth Century Religious Thought*, p. 334.
9 John Hick, *Arguments for the Existence of God*, ch. 7.
10 Quoted by John Macquarrie, *Twentieth Century Religious Thought*, p. 334.

Chapter XVI   Faith, Doubt and Hope

1 Alvin Plantinga, 'Is Belief in God Rational?' in *Rationality and Religious Belief*, ed. C.F. Delaney, Notre Dame: University of Notre Dame Press, 1979, p. 27.

2 John Perry, *A Dialogue on Personal Identity and Immortality*, Indianapolis: Hackett Publishing Company, 1978, p. 2.

3 C.S. Peirce, 'The Fixation of Belief' in *Collected Papers of Charles Sanders Peirce*, volume V, eds. Charles Hartshorne and Paul Weiss, Cambridge: Belnap Press of Harvard University, 1962.

4 John Calvin, *Institutes of the Christian Religion*, Philadelphia: Westminster Press, 1960, Book I, ch. 7, pp. 79, 80.

5 Jon Elster, *Ulysses and the Sirens*, Cambridge: Cambridge University Press, 1982, chapters 1 and 2, contains a vigorous defense of this point.

6 Much of the analysis of hope in this and the following part of my paper has been influenced by James Muyskens' excellent study, *The Sufficiency of Hope*. Philadelphia: Temple Universty Press, 1979.

7 Cf. J. P. Day, 'The Anatomy of Hope and Fear', in *Mind*, vol. LXXIX (July 1970).

8 Cf. Robert Audi, 'Intending' in the *Journal of Philosophy* (LXX, 13, 1973) for a good discussion of this point.

9 The comments by William Alston and an anonymous reader of an earlier version of this chapter caused me to rethink and alter my position on this point.

10 J.P. Day, *op. cit.* and James Muyskens, *op. cit.*, p. 44f.

11 While it is controversial whether 'belief that' statements involve probability estimates, I think a plausible case for this can be made based on the fact that we believe propositions to various degrees. If we can set numbers from 0 to 1, indicating absolute disbelief and absolute conviction, with 0.5 as withholding belief or suspending judgment, we can roughly fix the degree of other belief-states on a continuum between these points. All that is needed is an arbitrary measure and the notion of 'believing that p to a greater degree than that q'. Muyskens' counterexample that a gambler can believe that the odds are 100:1 against his winning and yet believe that he will win can be accommodated by making a distinction between objective inductive evidence and subjective probability, which is simply a function of a belief-state. Cf. Muyskens, *op. cit.*, p. 38.

12 William James, 'The Sentiment of Rationality', in *Essays in Pragmatism*, ed., Alburey Castell. New York: Hafner Publishing Company, 1948.

13 Cf. for example, Swinburne, *Faith and Reason*, Oxford: Clarendon Press, 1979, p. 105. Nicholas Wolterstorff in the Introduction to *Faith and Rationality*, Notre Dame: University of Notre Dame Press, 1983, p. 14, writes: 'One *cannot*, for example, trust God if one does not even believe that God exists.' Plantinga in his article, 'Reason and Belief in God' in the same book, p. 18, writes, 'Nor can one trust in God and commit oneself to him without believing that he exists; as the author of Hebrews says, "He who would come to God must believe that he is and that he is rewarder of those who seek him." (Heb. 11:6).'

14 Cf. Wittgenstein, *Lectures and Conversations*, Berkeley: University of California, 1966, for an example of this point of view.

15 William James, *The Will to Believe*, New York: Dover, 1897; p. 19.

16 Gary Gutting, *Religious Belief and Religious Skepticism*, Notre Dame: University of Notre Dame Press, 1982, p. 105. In correspondence Gutting says that he has sympathy for my approach and that 'I am merely pointing out the incompatibility of interim assent with faith as it has been traditionally regarded.' Letter dated October 6, 1983.
17 Ibid., p. 106.
18 Ibid., p. 108.
19 Work for this chapter was begun during the National Endowment for the Humanities' Summer Seminar for College Teachers in Philosophy ('Reasons, Justification, and Knowledge') at the University of Nebraska/Lincoln under the direction of Robert Audi, July 1981. Comments on a previous draft by William Alston and an anonymous reader were very helpful in writing this chapter.

Bibliography

Ammerman, Robert, 'Ethics and Belief,' *Proceedings of the Aristotelian Society*, 1965.

Aquinas, St Thomas, *Summa Theologiae,* New York: McGraw-Hill, 1974.

Armstrong, D.M., *Belief, Truth and Knowledge*, Cambridge: Cambridge University Press, 1973.

Audi, Robert, 'The Concept of Believing,' *The Personalist*, vol. 53 (1972).

Augustine: Earlier Writings, ed. and tr. John Burleigh, Philadelphia: Westminster Press, 1953.

Braitewaite, R.B., 'The Nature of Belief,' in *Knowledge and Belief*, ed. Phillips Griffiths, Oxford University Press, 1967.

Brett, F., 'Doubt and Descartes' Will,' *Dialogue*, vol. XIX (1980).

Chisholm, Roderick, *Perceiving: A Philosophical Study*, Ithaca: Cornell University Press.

Chisholm, Roderick, 'Lewis' Ethics of Belief,' in *The Philosophy of C.I. Lewis*, ed. P.A. Schilpp. Open Court, 1968.

Clifford, W.K., 'The Ethics of Belief,' in *Belief, Knowledge and Truth*, eds. R.R. Ammerman and M.G. Singer, NY: Scribners, 1970.

Cross, R.C., and Woozley, A.D., *Plato's Republic: A Philosophical Commentary*, London: Macmillan, 1964.

Curley, E.M., *Descartes Against the Skeptics*, Cambridge: Cambridge University Press, 1978.

Curley, E.M., 'Descartes, Spinoza and the Ethics of Belief,' in *Spinoza: Essays in Interpretation*, ed. M. Mandelbaum and E. Freeman. LaSalle, Illinois: Open Court, 1979.

Day, J., 'Hope,' *American Philosophical Quarterly*. vol. 6, no. 2, April, 1969.

Evans, J.L., 'Error and the Will,' *Philosophy*, April 1972.

Evans, Stephen, *Subjectivity and Religious Belief*, University of America Press, 1978.

Ferreira, Jamie, 'Newman and the "Ethics of Belief",' *Religious Studies*, 19, 1984.

Firth, Roderick, 'Chisholm and the Ethics of Belief,' *Philosophical Review*, 1959.

Gale, Richard, 'William James and the Ethics of Belief,' *American Philosophical Quarterly*, vol. 17, 1980.

Govier, Trudy, 'Belief, Values and the Will,' *Dialogue*, vol. XV, 1976.

Grant, C.K., 'Belief and Action,' Durham: University of Durham, 1960.

Griffiths, A. Phillips, ed., *Knowledge and Belief*, Oxford: Oxford University Press, 1967.

Gutting, Gary, *Religious Belief and Religious Skepticism*, University of Notre Dame Press, 1982.

Harvey, Van, 'Is There an Ethics of Belief?', *Journal of Religion*, 1969.

Harvey, Van, 'The Ethics of Belief Revisited,' unpublished paper, 1978.

Hick, John, *Faith and Knowledge*, Ithaca: Cornell University Press, 1957.

Hume, David, *Treatise of Human Nature*, ed. Selby-Bigge, Oxford: Clarendon Press, 1967.

James, William, *The Will to Believe*, NY: Dover Publications, 1956.

Kant, Immanuel, *The Critique of Pure Reason*, tr. R.G. Smith, London: Macmillan, 1950.

Kant, Immanuel, *The Critique of Practical Reason*, tr. Lewis Beck, Indianapolis: Bobbs-Merrill, 1956.

Kauber, Peter and Hare, Peter, 'The Right and Duty to Will to Believe,' *Canadian Journal of Philosophy*, 1974.

Kierkegaard, Sören, *Concluding Unscientific Postscript*, tr. David Swenson and Walter Lowry, Princeton: Princeton University Press, 1941.

Kinnamann, W.J., *The Ethics of Belief; An Examination of the View that Belief is Subject to Voluntary Controls*, Ph. D. dissertation, The University of Connecticut, 1978.

Kittel, Gerhard, *Theological Word Book of the New Testament*, tr. D. Barton P. Ackroyd and A.E. Harvey, New York: Harper, 1960.

Livingston, James C., *The Ethics of Belief; An Essay on the Victorian Religious Consciousness,* Tallahasee, FLA: American Academy of Religion, 1974.

Lonergan, Bernard, *Insight: A Study of Human Understanding*, New York: Philosophical Library, 1961.

McClendon, James and Smith, James, *Understanding Religious Convictions*, University of Notre Dame, 1975.

McLean, Michael, *An Exposition and Defense of St. Thomas Aquinas' Account of the Rational Justification of Religious Belief*, Ph. D. dissertation, University of Notre Dame, 1981.

Malcolm, Norman, 'The Groundlessness of Belief,' in *Reason and Religion*, ed. Stuart Brown, Ithaca: Cornell University Press, 1977.

Markie, Peter, 'Descartes's Theory of Judgment,' *Southern Journal of Philosophy*, supplement volume, 1983.

Matthews, Gwenneth, *Plato's Epistemology*, New York: Humanities Press, 1972.

Mavrodes, George, 'Intellectual Morality in Clifford and James,' an unpublished paper.

Meiland, Jack, 'What Ought We to Believe? or the Ethics of Belief Revisited,' *American Philosophical Quarterly*, vol. 17, 1980.

Mitchell, Basil, 'Faith and Reason: A False Antithesis,' *Religious Studies*, 1980.

Morgan, Michael, 'Belief, Knowledge and Learning in Plato's Middle

Dialogues,' in *New Essays on Plato*, eds. F.J. Pelletier and John King-Arlow, Guelph, Ontario: Canadian Association for Publishing in Philosophy, 1983.

Musgrove, A. and Lakatos, I., eds, *Criticism and the Growth of Knowledge*, Cambridge: Cambridge University Press, 1970.

Muyskens, James, *The Sufficiency of Hope*, Philadelphia: Temple University Press, 1979.

Nathanson, James, 'Nonevidential Reasons for Belief: A Jamesian View,' *Philosophy and Phenomenological Research*, 1982.

Newman, John Henry, *The Grammar of Assent*, London: Westminster Press, 1980.

Nielsen, Kai, 'Wittgensteinian Fidesim,' *Philosophy*, 1967.

O'Hear, Anthony, 'Belief and Will,' *Philosophy*, April, 1972.

Palmer, Anthony, 'Belief,' *Philosophy*. vol. 56, 1981.

Passmore, J.A., *A Hundred Years of Philosophy*, New York: Macmillan, 1957.

Passmore, J.A., 'Hume and the Ethics of Belief,' *David Hume: Bicentenary Papers*, ed. G.P. Morice. Austin, TX: University of Texas Press, 1977.

Peirce, C.S., 'The Fixation of Belief,' in *The Problems of Philosophy*, eds Delaney, Loux, Gutting, and Moore, University of Notre Dame Press, 1976.

Penelhum, Terrance, 'The Analysis of Faith in St. Thomas Aquinas,' *Religious Studies*, vol. 13, 1977.

Pieper, Joseph, *Belief and Faith*, NY: Pantheon, 1953.

Plantinga, Alvin, 'Is Belief in God Rational?' in *Rationality and Religious Belief*, ed. C.F. Delaney, University of Notre Dame Press, 1979.

Plantinga, Alvin, 'Reason and Belief in God,' in *Faith and Rationality*, ed. Alvin Plantinga and Nicholas Wolterstorff, University of Notre Dame Press, 1983.

Pojman, Louis, 'Rationality and Religious Belief,' *Religious Studies,* 1979.

Pojman, Louis, *The Logic of Subjectivity*, University of Alabama Press, 1984.

Pojman, Louis, 'Believing and Willing,' *Canadian Journal of Philosophy*, September, 1985.

Price, H.H., *Belief*, London: Unwin & Allen, 1967.

Price, H.H., 'Some Considerations about Belief,' in *Knowledge and Belief*, ed. Phillips Griffiths.

Putnam, Hilary, *Reason, Truth and History*, Cambridge: Cambridge University Press, 1981.

Ramsey, Frank, *The Foundations of Mathematics,* London: Routledge & Kegan Paul, 1931.

Smith, William Cantwell, *Belief and History*, University of Virginia Press, 1979.

Stevenson, J.T., 'On Doxastic Responsibility,' *Analysis and Metaphysics*, ed. Keith Lehrer, Dordrecht: Reidel, 1975.

Swinburne, Richard, *Faith and Reason*, Oxford: Clarendon Press, 1981.

Tlumak, Jeffry, 'Judgement and Understanding in Descartes's Philosophy,' *Southern Journal of Philosophy*, Supplemental volume, 1983.

Williams, Bernard, 'Deciding to Believe,' in *Problems of the Self*, Cambridge: Cambridge University Press, 1972.

Winters, Barbara, 'Believing at Will,' *Journal of Philosophy*, vol. LXXVI, 1979.

Wood, Alan, *Kant's Moral Religion*, Ithaca: Cornell University Press, 1970.

Religious Belief and the Will

Index

253

Index